William T Wilson

The Ideal Humanity, and Other Parish Sermons

With some words commemorative by the Right Rev. Henry C. Potter, D.D.

William T Wilson

The Ideal Humanity, and Other Parish Sermons
With some words commemorative by the Right Rev. Henry C. Potter, D.D.

ISBN/EAN: 9783337114497

Printed in Europe, USA, Canada, Australia, Japan

Cover: Foto ©Lupo / pixelio.de

More available books at **www.hansebooks.com**

THE IDEAL HUMANITY

AND OTHER

PARISH SERMONS

BY

The Rev. WILLIAM T. WILSON
LATE RECTOR OF THE CHURCH OF THE MEDIATOR
KINGSBRIDGE, NEW YORK

Died June 19th, 1890
AGED 56 YEARS

WITH SOME WORDS COMMEMORATIVE
BY
The Right Rev. HENRY C. POTTER, D.D.

A MEMORIAL VOLUME

Edited by His Wife

NEW YORK
THOMAS WHITTAKER, PUBLISHER
1892

Press of J. J. Little & Co.
Astor Place, New York

SOME WORDS COMMEMORATIVE.

By the Bishop of New York.

In the year 1859 there graduated from the General Theological Seminary a young man whose singularly engaging presence made, upon those who encountered him on his entrance into Holy Orders, a very unusual impression. There was the aspect of extreme youth—a freshness and purity of expression almost womanly—but, combined with these, the intimations of a mind of singular vigor and insight, and of rare and beautiful courage and directness in the search for truth.

Those earlier prophecies were not disappointed. After spending his diaconate in New York, Mr. Wilson was called to the rectorship of St. Peter's Church, Albany, then, as now, the foremost parish in what is now the Diocese of Albany; and then, as now, one of the most important and conspicuous cures in our American Church. If there were any who doubted as to the capability of the young stripling to assume responsibilities so grave, their doubts were soon dispelled. Mr. Wilson was fortunate in having the help, as his associate, of the Rev. William Tatlock, who had been his classmate, and it would not have been easy to find two men who more admirably supplemented each other. The writer, then beginning his ministry in a neighboring town, was privileged to enjoy the friendship and to be stimulated by the example of these two men, one of whom survives, and of whom, therefore, he may not speak as he would.

But the other—who that ever knew him will forget the rare spell of his original and acute mind, and the still rarer charm of his transparent and really heroic nature? After a brief ministry in Albany, his frail health constrained him to retire to a less exacting charge, and for twenty-three years (with the exception of a single year's absence) he ministered to the people of the Church of the Mediator, South Yonkers. It was not a large cure, and the opportunities for extended work were wanting. Indeed, if it had been otherwise, he could not have undertaken such work ; for, before a great while, his sight became impaired, and during his latter years he was indebted to the beautiful devotion of another for almost everything that made his ministry effectual. But though he had to read with another's eyes, and write with another's hand, his great soul—for his, verily, was one of the few really great souls that are given to a generation —glowed within him, and as he mused once and again, " the fire burned and he spake." He preached like one who had seen a vision—as, indeed, he had ; and an exquisite command of speech " most apt and fit," was matched by an elevation and grasp of thought that made men know that there was a prophet among them—hidden away, it is true, from the eyes of the great multitude, but sensitive alike to all that was best and worst in his generation, and welcoming the one and rebuking the other with equal discernment and courage. His partial blindness made it, somehow, possible for him to see better when freed from the glare of daylight, and much of his parish visiting was done on dark and stormy nights, when the belated wayfarer would meet him feeling his way along the lonely highways with his cane, as he returned from some home of penury or sorrow. It was after such an almost midnight ministry to a bereaved household that he came home, well-nigh breathless and exhausted, to die.

Defenceless, thus, enfeebled, frail, and largely alone in the world, without powerful influence or support to shield him, he nevertheless did not know what it was to be afraid. When once his life was threatened because of his determined effort to close some vile resort which was ruining the youth of his neighborhood, he smiled in the quiet, half-wondering way that no one who ever saw it will forget, and said : " I think they can hardly know me if they think that I could be frightened. I have but one life to lose, and I could not lose it in a better cause." And he went on his way as before.

Yes, like another, " he went on his way, and God met him."

In an instant the end came—while he was on his feet, and never dreaming that it was so near—and then the white soul passed on to be forever with its Lord. But the rare and winning presence, the steadfast and uncomplaining ministry, the gifted mind and soul, made, as others believed, for great tasks and rightful preëminence, and yet tarrying patiently in the shadow till the end—these remain, a glorious and inspiring memory at once to cheer and rebuke less noble natures, and to make them forever grateful that so true a servant and saint of God has lived and wrought and suffered—steadfast and unspotted till the end.

> "Now let the Lord arise
>   And put thy foes to flight,
> Let all the immortal Panoplies
>   Array thee in their might!
> Fenced round about by holiest things,
> From Satan screened by angel wings,
> To God who made thee, God who bought,
> And God whose grace thy cleansing wrought,
> That hell no part in thee should claim—
> Go forth, sweet soul, in Jesus' name!"

H. C. P.

NEW YORK, *St. John Baptist's Day*, 1890.

INTRODUCTORY NOTES.

By a Sub-editor.

THIS volume of Sermons is set forth not to introduce the preacher to a public audience, but to recall him to a circle of loving friends in his parish ministry at Kingsbridge; in his one year's pastorate at York, Pa.; and in his earlier promise at St. Peter's, Albany.

It is true that, as a memorial, the volume is most incomplete. Indeed, it has been a matter of serious debate whether it were just to his memory to publish it. For the ripeness of the preacher's thought and speech came later than this record. Most of these Sermons were preached between the years of 1869 and 1877. One which gives its title to the book, and another at the close of it, bear the still earlier date of 1865. Whereas, notwithstanding his enfeebled health, the best utterances of the preacher's manhood were given during his very last years, say from 1885 to 1890. But, during these and many preceding years, he was struggling with the fatal malady which finally vanquished him. He became almost totally blind. He could use no manuscripts; wrote nothing; and of his extempore speech, too rapid, as it was found, for a stenographic report, no record was preserved.

We can therefore present to his friends, in this memorial, only the germ, as it were, and incomplete beginnings of Mr. Wilson's highest thought, and of his best work.

Not that the earlier treasures of this broken ministry need an apology. For those who remember the preacher in his later years will not miss out of his early sermons the fine quality of his thought; its directness and simplicity; its clearness and penetration; its masterly hold of a subject; its subtle analysis; its scope and beauty; its spiritual discernment and sympathy; its wide humanity; its reasonableness; its reverence; and, crowning all, its virility of faith.

This man of God—and yet who would believe it to read his restful words?—was buffeted by adversity. Innumerable troubles compassed him about. " Without were fightings, within were fears." His soul was swept by all the storms of doubt and questioning that during thirty years of his life tormented the minds of intellectual men. But how immovable and simple, how unworldly is his confidence! With what assurance of strength he gathers in his arms, like the Good Shepherd, the little flock committed to him, and carries them in his bosom; not permitting them to dream of the stormy wind and tempest which he was breasting and beating back for them. No wavering step or accent of uncertainty is discoverable in any ministration of this faithful pastor and priest. He has the calm and assured conviction of the Lord and Master of this faith, who in the days of His own distress and anguish and terror, when death confronted Him and darkness closed in upon Him, and enemies crowded about Him, thirsting for His blood, cried to " His own," with unwavering and inspiring courage: "Fear not, little flock, it is your Father's good pleasure to give you the kingdom."

It has proved a pleasant though pathetic task for one who brings to it the moving recollections of a long and intimate friendship, to read and re-read these pages as they return from the printer, and to receive from them, once more, as if from the living face of this departed friend, "the Benediction of Peace," and a renewed illumination of "the Light which lighteth every man."

With a great love we recall him, from the days when we sat by his side, a divinity student at Chelsea, and our heart was knitted to him as the heart of Jonathan to David, through all his self-forgetful ministry to its ripeness and close—this man, as we remember him, of exquisite mental gifts, of tender and passionate feeling, and of absolute integrity, mental and moral and spiritual—a child of the Truth and of the Light, whose faith was wrought into the fibre of his life, strong and sweet and simple, like the faith of the patriarchs and prophets of old time, and *to be accounted for righteousness* as truly in the nineteenth century as it was in the days of Abraham.

With our vivid memory of him, of which his written words are but an echo, we seal his book and send it forth to seek a welcome from those for whom it is prepared. Imperfect and broken memorial though it be of the priest and pastor whose gifts were so prematurely extinguished, it cannot fail, we think, to minister, to an open heart, a new sense of the love of righteousness and of the love of God; a higher assurance of immortal hope; a stronger confidence of renewed manhood; a wider fellowship in the great human, but divine brotherhood, of which Jesus Christ is the Eternal Head and the Gracious Redeemer.

A word concerning the choice and arrangement of these sermons.

They have been selected to represent as faithfully as possible the marked characteristics of Mr. Wilson's preaching, not only at a certain stage of it, but throughout. The first of the series, delivered at St. Peter's, Albany, has been given the leading place, partly for its significant title, "The Ideal Humanity," but especially for its clear expression of the preacher's fundamental faith in that essential relationship of the eternal Son of God to man, which lies behind all revelations of the Father, and is the deep occasion and reason of the coming of Christ to save the world. Here, laid down by the preacher in his early manhood, is the broad basis of all his afterthought and teaching.

Then follow sermons of various dates, early and late, touching (1) The historical fact of Christ's coming; (2) The opening of the Saviour's personal ministry by the Sermon on the Mount, with other personal teachings of the Lord by parable and miracle; (3) The catastrophe and sacrifice of Christ's death; (4) His resurrection from the dead; (5) The incident of His ascension into heaven; (6) The character of the Church which He has founded, as constituted (*a*) a family in God with (*b*) a mixture of good and evil in it, and (*c*) the wide charity enjoined upon it. After this are placed, in order, several sermons applying the doctrine of Christ to social life and public morals; and the series closes again with two early sermons, which bring back the burden of His work to the personal winning of souls to Jesus Christ, showing Him in His most intimate character, first and last, the pastor of Christ's flock, caring chiefly for the wandering sheep and for the little ones.

We cannot close these prefatory notes without laying stress upon a characteristic of Mr. Wilson's preaching, which distinguishes it from contemporaneous preaching with its modern modes of speech, and gives to it an air almost of the Church's primitive days.

Many who remember him, and knew his sympathy with modern research, his jealousy for the truth, his boldness in accepting the verified results of critical scholarship, his familiarity with all high thinking, will be surprised, perhaps, to discover in his sermons not so distinctively an intellectual, as a purely spiritual and evangelical savor.

There is intellect here—perhaps of the highest order. Several sermons in the book, notably II., V., XIII., XIV., XVI., will at once take their place in the front rank of sermons, for insight, strength, beauty, and inspiring thought. The last mentioned of these as an example simply of literary skill and power is surpassingly fine. The idea conveyed is penetrating and profound; and though it be in substance old and true, it is in form novel, original, and revolutionary of current and long-used modes of thought and to find it, as it is here, completely unfolded, within so short a compass, and in so clear, convincing, and cogent a speech, is an intellectual surprise and delight.

Nevertheless this preaching, as to its essence, its spirituality, its personal appeal, its experimental character, may be called distinctly evangelical. In many respects an "Evangelical" of the old school would recognize this quality, and, like enough, be ready to claim the preacher. But the "evangelical" theology, technically so-called, in certain peculiarities of it, is at the very antipodes of his thought. Let us enter at once into his secret.

With the writer of these sermons the spiritual life is very real. It is interwoven in his thought with the reality of nature, with reason, with the understanding. With him there are not two kinds of reality, but, in all things, one and the same kind. All things, in his conception of them, are bound up in God. In God—that is, *in Christ, who is "God manifest"*—"all things consist."

He starts forth with this conception of life and of the universe. Life to him is spiritual. The universe is spiritual. It is Divine. Spiritual intuition is his keenest sense. Running through the entire scheme and system of created things, as they presently appear, he perceives as the deepest truth of all, and as the very reason of all, the explanation of all, man's spiritual being, man's divinity, his constitution in the eternal Son of God, which gives him relationship to the eternal Father, and explains his relationship to "all things visible and invisible."

Out of this divine constitution of man, which is fundamental, springs Revelation. For an intuitive knowledge of God lies in man's spiritual being, back of all other knowledge, and, unless man's spiritual nature be dead, makes living intercourse between God and man inevitable. Sympathy with God and intercourse with God are at the source of all man's knowledge, natural and spiritual.

This vision of the preacher, keenly penetrating into the nature of things, gives fixity and substantiality to his creed. It is the substratum of it, its reasonable ground, standing upon which he is immovable. He opens his eyes to see, he reaches forth his hands to touch the things of the spirit; exercising this power not mystically, as lifted out of the sphere of nature and life, but practically, with his feet upon the earth, and in touch with all earthly interests and values.

In this mind he reads Holy Scripture, discerns its meaning, interprets it with all simplicity; and often, with perfect naturalness, uses its manner and speech.

His most Catholic Theology shapes itself upon this fundamental conception of the "state of things." His idea of the Church grows out of it—as a family constituted in God. His idea of the earthly family is sweetened and sanctified by it. All earthly relationships are made sacred in it, and draw their meaning from it. Humanity, with him—the wide humanity, in its true conception, its "ideal"—is *the fellowship of God's children in Jesus Christ.* In his clear, spiritual vision, the KINGDOM OF GOD upon earth is, to-day, the actual ruling power in life and history.

And now, with this conception of things spiritual and real, the evangelical manner of speech into which the preacher often falls, loses its strained and technical effect, its sometimes unreality, and becomes in his use of it, in the highest sense of the word, *natural*. Making the comparison with utmost reverence, we find in the use of the evangelical mode of speech by this preacher that *naturalness* which it assumes in the lips of the Master himself; who, with eyes open and lips unsealed, beholding all things as they are, says to those who hear: "We speak that we do know, and testify that we have seen." "No man hath ascended up to heaven but he that came down from heaven, even the Son of man who is in heaven." The realities of the universe are open to Him as He stands in the divine relationship, and, beholding them, He speaks, with calm conviction, "words of truth and soberness."

So, then, it is the manner of Christ, which we discern in this spiritually-minded, true, and human preacher of the Everlasting Gospel. And it is the Christ-manner which, to our thought, sets apart his preaching from other preaching, giving us confidence to commend it to the affectionate acceptance of those who knew him, and of those who may get their introduction to him by these pages, which seem to us most sacred, as they breathe the spirit of his self-devoted life.

U. T. T.

GARDEN CITY, *Christmas*, 1892.

CONTENTS.

SERMON		PAGE
I.	THE IDEAL HUMANITY	1
II.	CHRISTMAS	16
III.	THE BENEDICTION OF PEACE	27
IV.	HOME AND HOME'S TEACHINGS	38
V.	THE AUTHORITATIVE CHARACTER OF THE SERMON ON THE MOUNT	53
VI.	THE INCREDULITY OF GAIN	76
VII.	THE FEEDING OF THE FIVE THOUSAND	92
VIII.	THE UNJUST STEWARD	106
IX.	THE SINFULNESS OF LITTLE SINS, AND THE WORTH OF LITTLE VIRTUES	122
X.	THE WEDDING GARMENT	139
XI.	THE PENITENT THIEF	155
XII.	THE CRUCIFIXION	171
XIII.	THE CREDIBILITY OF THE RESURRECTION	188
XIV.	THE POWER OF THE RESURRECTION	200
XV.	THE ASCENSION	214
XVI.	THE CHURCH A UNIVERSAL AND IMMORTAL FAMILY	230
XVII.	THE SUFFERANCE OF THE TARES	245
XVIII.	ST. PETER'S DISCOVERY	261
XIX.	THE WIDOW WOMAN AND ELIJAH	275
XX.	SAMUEL'S CHALLENGE	289
XXI.	THE REBELLION OF KORAH	303
XXII.	THE INDICTMENT OF JUDAH	318
XXIII.	THE MURDER OF JOHN THE BAPTIST	335
XXIV.	THE JOY OF HEAVEN OVER EARTH'S REPENTANCE	349

I.

THE IDEAL HUMANITY.

[St. Peter's, Albany, 1865.]

"There is neither Jew nor Greek, there is neither bond nor free, there is neither male nor female: for ye are all one in Christ Jesus."
—Gal. iii. 28.

THE position of Christ in the world's history is best given, perhaps, in the statement that all history is incomprehensible without Him. Take Christ away, and the human race is without a ruling head, without a beating heart, without an animating soul, without a certain origin or end—an inexplicable enigma. The centuries before and since His coming have their interpretation either in their preparation for Christianity, or in the part they have acted in its development. And whatever may be thought of His nature and person, it would seem as if that must be a wilful blindness which can fail to refer the great changes that have passed over the world and society and human thought to the influence of His teaching. His advent forms the boundary between the old and the new; and of all history since that, the wisest and most earnest thinkers have confessed Christianity to be the pulse and heart-blood and central stream. And this has been only the growing fulfilment of the prophecy which He Himself had given. His mission was not temporary or local. In His own statement of it, He came to establish the kingdom of God, a kingdom that should have no end. His work on earth was to realize the reign of righteousness and truth and love; to lay the foundation of that universal society—His Church—which should become the embodiment of heavenly things, and into which all nations and characters and conditions should be built. He speaks of Himself as a sower going forth to sow; for His word was to be a living principle, working in the hearts and minds of men, until His ideal of the race should be realized in fact, and humanity reflect back upon Him the likeness of His own image. We read in the Book of the Acts how that kingdom was set up and its foundations laid. There is unfolded there the germ, imperfect, indeed, yet purer and better than any after age has seen, of that ultimate Christendom for which we look, and toward which we move. The first company of believers, in its harmony of many tongues, "Parthians and Medes and Elamites;" in its heavenly charity, "they had all things in common," and each ministered to each as each had need; in its actual, living brotherhood and sisterhood of men and women, realized a practical Christianity of which the world has not since seen the like. A fair picture; too fair, indeed, to last. Human society was not to be regenerated in a day. It would seem as if there was given us at first a glimpse, and only a glimpse, of what in the idea of God humanity is and will be; and then the colors faded, and the lights grew dim, and the traces of the kingdom upon earth became indistinct and uncertain. The after progress of Christianity has been sometimes through tortuous and rugged ways; sometimes through revolutions, as in the Reformation, which were almost as a new creation; sometimes through apparent defeats, when its course seemed to be baffled and turned back. And even now, after eighteen hundred years, the wisest feel that we stand but midway in the divine providences; that all this modern enlightenment and civilization of which we boast are but the beginnings of that which is to be; only the first-fruits of what may prove a still far distant harvest. Yet even in that there is hope; and if at any time the strifes and enmities and disorders which we still see in the world tempt us to be sceptical of human progress, we need only sit down and read faithfully the records of any preceding age to find in them abundant cause for comparative contentment. All things move toward the consummation which is appointed, even though the millennium be not yet.

The kingdom which Christ came to establish has its origin in two great truths; namely, the fatherhood of God, and the brotherhood of man. Yet these did not become facts for the first time at the advent; they had been so from all eternity; and the kingdom was to be only the manifestation of them upon earth. And in that the work of the Church is but the continuation of the work of Christ. He did not make God our Father, but He showed that He is such. He did not make men brethren, but He disclosed to them the eternal ground of their brotherhood. His whole life was a manifestation of realities, a revelation of things as they are. And in that aspect of it, the Church calls it an Epiphany, a manifestation; and in the season which commemorates it gathers into her services all those words and acts of our Lord by which He made Himself known to us as He really is—the One in whom we have our common relation to God, and our common relation to each other. He is the divine bond of society, the upholder of every human relation, the Head and Elder Brother of the race, in whom, and in whom alone, it is one. The Scriptures speak of Him as the corner-stone; and St. Paul says, "There is neither Jew nor Greek, there is neither bond nor free, there is neither male nor female: for ye are all one in Christ Jesus." Thus the true unity of the race consists not in our common descent from Adam, but in our common relation to Christ; not in the first man which is of the earth, earthy, but in the second man which is the Lord from Heaven. The natural relationship is not lost, but finds its fulfilment in a higher and spiritual one which is eternal. The tie of blood becomes the witness of that other deeper, unseen tie which is permanent, surviving circumstances and surviving death. "Ye are all one in Christ Jesus"—that is a mere gospel commonplace, yet it is a commonplace on which the Church is built. To the assertion of it must we look for that society of the future, which has been the dream of every age. It holds an ideal of humanity beyond any that the mere declaimer of equality and fraternity ever reached. And though at times forgotten or denied, we must believe, if we believe our

Bibles, that it is a truth which cannot pass. It alone holds the promise which is sure. We have little faith in any brotherhood which shall be realized through schemes of socialism or the regenerating power of self-interest. "Other foundation can no man lay than that is laid, which is Jesus Christ." Only as we build on Him can our work be worthy and abiding.

The Apostle makes our unity in Christ the ground of that Christian fellowship which shall gather to itself all ranks and classes, and nations and conditions. Standing on that truth, he sees in prophetic vision that universal family which is to be, in which all separations between man and man shall be swallowed up and lost. "There is neither Jew nor Greek," he says; "there is neither bond nor free, there is neither male nor female: for ye are all one in Christ Jesus." Let us consider these points now in the order of our text.

"There is neither Jew nor Greek." This was a declaration so new and strange to men, that the Apostle speaks of it as the mystery which had been hid in God for ages. We know something of the antipathy of races, and yet we can form but a faint conception of the animosity then existing between the Jewish and the Gentile world. The Jew looked upon all the nations round about him with bitter, intolerant contempt. Human love with him did not pass beyond the pale of the circumcision. He recognized no larger philanthropy than this: "Thou shalt love thy neighbor and hate thine enemy;" and with him every foreigner, as such, was an enemy.

The Gentile, too, had no sympathies beyond his own nationality. How little sense he had of any wider brotherhood may be seen in the fact, that one of the best and wisest men of Greece could thank God that he was born a man and not a brute, a Greek and not a barbarian, as if to be a barbarian were identical with being a brute. Yet to these races, so hostile and alien, the Apostle could proclaim a common unity in Christ, "who," he says, "hath made both one, and hath broken down the middle wall of partition; having abolished in His flesh the enmity, to make in Himself of twain one new man, so making peace." The Jew, with all his special training, knew nothing higher than patriotism. He had no equivalent for our word mankind. His great prophet never lifted a prayer for any other than his own people. But there came a time when the prayer of Moses for his nation should pass into the prayer of Christ for the universe; when the cry of the servant, "Yet they are thy people and thine inheritance," should pass into the cry of the Son, "That they all may be one; as Thou, Father, art in Me, and I in Thee, that they all may be one in us."

"There is neither Jew nor Greek." If we translate this expression now into the terms of modern speech, do we not learn from it the duty of a worldwide charity; that all men, far or near, of whatever race or clime, are our brethren; that in Christ all enmities and separations are abolished and done away? Yet philanthropy, in its widest application, is something that we do not quickly learn. It is only now and then that we can reach up to even a partial fulfilment of that great requirement—the love of all mankind. It is easy to extend our sympathies to our family, our friends, our country, but there they often seem to fail. Patriotism is indeed a virtue, but it may become only another form of selfishness, after all. Not infrequently we speak of the outside world as if its fate were a matter of indifference to us, as if we had no concern or interest in that. Yet Christ is the heritage of every people; they too have their place in the household of God, though Abraham be ignorant of them, and Israel acknowledge them not. "Other sheep" He has, "not of this fold;" and His world-wide charity, upon which we profess to pattern ours, is the same that said, "Go, and teach all nations." To the conquering power of a love like His, and only to that, can we look for the fulfilment of the prophecy, when the nations "shall beat their swords into ploughshares, and their spears into pruninghooks:" and "nation shall not lift up sword against nation, neither shall they learn war any more." *

But Christianity, in its effort to realize a universal family, does not depreciate the more immediate duties and relations which are about us. It does not denaturalize any affection, but deepens and sanctifies it. The wide philanthropy which it demands of us is not inconsistent with the intensest patriotism; it does not weaken in any way those special bonds which bind us to the land and nation

---

* Isaiah, ii. 4.

into which we are born. He who died for all mankind could yet feel a peculiar tenderness of affection, as He wept over His own city of Jerusalem, and pronounced her doom.

Nor does Christianity reverse the natural order, and begin with the greater rather than the less. It does not call us to realize the love of man as man, until our affections have been trained in the schools of the family and the state. It does not even require of us a divine, until we have known something of a human love; for "how," asks St. John in a kind of astonishment, "if we love not our brother whom we have seen, how can we love God whom we have not seen?" Love is a living principle, and must pass, therefore, through successive processes of growth. The child begins to learn it at his mother's knee; and then, as his relations widen, it grows with his growth and strengthens with his strength, until his heart is filled with a world-wide charity. It is through little offices of love that we enter into the fulness of love. In all life, loyal affection to the relation that precedes is made the condition of loyal affection to the relation that follows. It is the good son, brother, husband, father, friend, that makes the good citizen; and he, again, is alone capable of sympathy with all men. There are those, indeed, who call themselves cosmopolites—citizens of the world— who boast that they have no patriotism, that they care for all nations alike; which means that they care for none. For you can no more expect true philanthropy from the man who owns no country than you can expect devotion to the commonwealth from the man who repudiates the sanctities of his own hearth.

"There is neither bond nor free." This, too, was a startling declaration, startling alike to oppressor and oppressed. A strange message, that, in an age when slavery had reached perhaps its most fearful form, and captives were forced to fight in the amphitheatre with wild beasts, or with each other, to pleasure a Roman audience upon a Roman holiday! Yet the apostle could proclaim an equality in the sight of God, a common unity in Christ, both to the amused spectator of such a scene, and the victim who knew but too well the sad tragedy of it. The proud Roman in his purple, and the vile serf with his heart naked to the cold, stood upon the same ground after all. There was no inner or inherent inequality to correspond to the outward difference of condition. To both the apostle says, "There is neither bond nor free: for ye are all one in Christ Jesus." That was his central truth; "the mystery that had been hid;" and, therefore, he could bid the Christian master regard his servant "not as a servant, but as a brother;" and to the other he could say, "Art thou called, being a servant, care not for it." In the vision thus opened to the bondman, of things spiritual, invisible, eternal, outward conditions became only secondary. Nothing could take from him his spiritual liberty. Amid all the hardships of his lot, his consolation was to be in that Gospel which could make him truly free, even with the fetters on his feet and the shackle on his arm.

The interference of Christianity with existing institutions, as such, is indirect. It does not wage open war with them, however unjust they may be, while yet it silently undermines them, and quietly sows the seeds which bear fruit in their gradual extinction. The Gospel works from within outwards, from the internal to the external. Nowhere do we read of any encouragement given the slave of the empire to forcibly assert his freedom; but a revolution in human thought had begun when he came to realize his spiritual equality with his master, and when the latter was led to take a new and Christian view of his relation to him. And though in this respect the work of Christianity was indirect, none the less surely in the lapse of centuries did the Gospel mould the institutions of mankind. It was the leaven hid in three measures of meal until the whole was leavened. Christ did not promise political liberty, yet He gave it. It could not but be a consequence of regarding bond and free as one and alike in the presence of God, that their spiritual freedom became in time also an actual and external one.

But it would be only a partial interpretation of the expression of St. Paul were we to limit his meaning to the mere literalism of these two words. With him they stand for all possible inequalities of social condition. Perhaps the terms rich and poor come nearer home to us, and have a reference more direct. In our own immediate community, at least, there is no formal servitude. But the separations between man and man may be none the less for that. The civilization before which some evils disappear seems to bear in itself the seeds of others; and in the modern world the words wealth and poverty represent distinctions as great as the words bond and free. Is there not a great gulf, impassable almost, between those who have and those who have not? Who of us feels, and acts as if he felt, that the mendicant on the streets is one with him in Christ, his equal in the sight of God? "There is neither rich nor poor: for ye are one in Christ Jesus." Would not that be a declaration quite as startling to the avenue and the alley as was that of the Apostle to the Roman master and his serf? What a message that would be! How revolutionary! What a contradiction of all our thought, if we could only coin some words or invent some way to get it believed! But it would seem sometimes as if no one really did believe it, as if wealth thought itself of an altogether different kind of clay from that of labor, and claimed a heaven and redemption and salvation of its own. And even we who have no wealth, are we not conscious of a miserable servitude to it—a base and abject homage, which courts the bad rich man, and turns coldly from lowly worth and probity? This is the growing evil of a commercial age, when even religion bears the taint, and is thought of chiefly as a salutary check upon the poor, and its ministers are regarded as a kind of spiritual police. But for one passage in the Bible which speaks to the poor of contentment and endurance and submission, there are a hundred which proclaim woes against the rich for their neglect or oppression of the poor, for their pride or their indifference. That, both in the Old Testament and in the New, is repeated with tremendous reiteration.

Our Gospel is, indeed, unto the poor; but not because they need to be preached to more than others, but because in every beggar there is a man whom God is speaking to as his child. "There is neither bond nor free, there is neither high nor low, there is neither rich nor poor: for ye are all one in Christ Jesus." If we believed that, would the practical denial of Christian fellowship so often find an expression even in Christian temples? Have we not need in this reference to apply to ourselves some words written in an ancient Book very long ago? "My brethren, have not the faith of our Lord Jesus Christ, the Lord of glory, with respect of persons: for if there come into your assembly a man with a gold ring, in goodly apparel, and there come in also a poor man in vile raiment; and ye have respect to him that weareth the gay clothing, and say unto him, Sit thou here in a good place; and say to the poor, Stand thou there, or, Sit here under my footstool: are ye not then partial in yourselves and are become judges of evil thoughts? If ye fulfil the royal law according to the Scripture, thou shalt love thy neighbour as thyself, ye do well: but if ye have respect to persons, ye commit sin, and are convinced of the law as transgressors." *

"There is neither male nor female." When we seek the causes of the changed condition of woman, we find them almost exclusively in Christianity, since that has invested with the highest sanctity the name of mother, and made the family the type of

---

* St. James, ii. 1-4, 8, 9.

that union in which the heavens and the earth are joined. To realize how great that change has been, we need only recall the long period of degradation which, with scarcely an exception, had fallen to her lot; for even the condition of the Hebrew woman, though higher than any other, was not high. To Christianity, and almost to that alone, she owes all that she is and all that she has yet to gain. No other influence could have so ennobled and exalted her position, or conferred such honor and dignity upon her. The Gospel asserts her equality with man, and, though that may not now seem a very startling truth, yet it could have found expression in none but a Christian century. Since then her place has been a new one in the world, and has met with a larger recognition in every succeeding age. We are not unmindful of the wild extravagances to which the assertion of this equality has sometimes led—extravagances from which one turns away with weariness and disgust—but it is none the less a truth for that. St. Paul declares her subordination to man, but not her inferiority, and has set aside forever the assumption of one sex to be greater and better than the other, by declaring that both are great and good and worthy of equal honor in being respectively what God intended them to be.

The expression of the Apostle, however, seems to have a still further significance. He says in Christ "there is neither male nor female;" that is, there is no predominance in His Gospel of either the masculine or feminine types of character to the exclusion or depreciation of the other. It has fit place and equal honor for all qualities; for all that is manly and all that is womanly; for truth, courage, and endurance; but also for meekness, pity, and submission. No human virtue is excluded. The more imposing qualities of man, which were honored from the earliest times, it does not honor less; but it has brought to others, and they the more feminine, which were formerly despised, the recognition of their true worth. It has given an ideal of character, which rose far above the earth in its solemn and transfigured beauty. It has declared the strength of gentleness and the divineness of compassion. It has shown that it is godlike to forgive. It has written among its chiefest words, mercy, humility, obedience, and, enthroned over all, love. It has honor for the waiting patience of Mary and the quiet service of Dorcas, no less than for the indomitable energy of St. Peter and the fiery enthusiasm of St. Paul. If it leans at all, it leans rather to the feminine than to the masculine type of character; for it does not say, " Blessed are the true and the brave," but " Blessed are the meek," " Blessed are the pure in heart," " Blessed are the poor in spirit."

" There is neither male nor female: for ye are one in Christ Jesus." We may learn again from these words, that while Christianity honors and has a place for the distinctive qualities of each sex, it yet seeks to blend in each the qualities of both; that while it makes man more manly, and woman more womanly, it would also have "man become more of woman, and she of man." For it is thus, and only thus, that we can grow more and more into the divine likeness.

The Scriptures tell us that God created man in His own image, the words being added, "male and female created He them." It is not, therefore, the individual man who is the image of God, but humankind—the humanity whose opposite sides are manhood and womanhood. And so in every noble character, just in proportion to its nobleness, just in proportion as it approaches its ideal, will you find blended the distinctive graces of both sexes. That was eminently so in the character of St. Paul. I need not recall to you the manliness of one who has filled the world with his fame, who compassed sea and land with his heroic deeds; nor yet can you read the record of that life without being struck by its more than womanly tenderness and sympathy and compassion. And in the application of this truth, we have need to insist most upon the cultivation in ourselves of what have been called the more feminine, or passive virtues. For, notwithstanding their marked commendation in the Gospel, we learn of them but reluctantly and slowly. It is comparatively easy to be true and steadfast and brave; but it is not so easy to be meek, patient, gentle, and submissive. It is always hard to suffer. It is always hard to forbear. It is always hard to forgive. Every man admires heroism; but scarcely have we learned that charity is still the "more excellent way."

II.

CHRISTMAS.

[KINGSBRIDGE, 1876.]

"Unto us a child is born, unto us a son is given."—ISA. ix. 6.

EVER and anon in the progress of the Bible story there breaks forth a strong, exultant cry. That note of victory which is sounded at the very outset never wholly dies away, but runs like an undertone through each succeeding age, and is lifted up from time to time in those shouts of joyful assurance and far-reaching triumph which have made the Scriptures our comfort and our hope. The different voices, however deeply laden with the burden of their several woes, yet take up and continue, each in its own way and turn, the same victorious strain, which goes sounding on from generation to generation, in lofty psalms and noble prophecies, and glad, exultant cries.

Upon one of these great utterances we have come to-day. Isaiah, in turn, takes up his prophecy of deliverance and victory. "The people that walked in darkness," he says, "have seen a great light; they dwell in the land of the shadow of death, upon them hath the light shined: for unto us a child is born, unto us a son is given." His heart is uplifted in the presence of a great nativity; it is a kind of birthday ode which gives the solemn gladness to his voice. The assurance of his joy is in the child that is born; the inspiration of his hope is in the son that is given. That oft-repeated miracle, the entrance of a new life into the world, the birth of a son and heir, this is the occasion of Isaiah's thanksgiving. It is an occasion which took on a more solemn import as the years went by, and gathered to itself new meaning as each succeeding generation came. For whatever may have been the immediate reference of the prophet's words, we feel and know that they are completed only in that divine event, that transcendent Nativity, which we have come together once again, to-day, to honour and commemorate.

But let us begin at the beginning of this glad strain, and move on by successive steps in the interpretation of the great joy that is in it.

"Unto us a child is born, unto us a son is given." The words simply in and by themselves might stand for man's natural, instinctive feeling in the presence of his common, every-day experience. They might be applied to any ordinary birth, to any lowly, undistinguished nativity. Nor would they thereby be emptied of their meaning, as though the congratulation which they suggest were an exaggerated or unreal thing. We may be tempted, indeed, to think the common, the ordinary, unworthy of reverential consideration. But however common nativities may be, no nativity is or can be common place. Birthdays are indeed innumerable, yet every one of them is sacred. Whenever a new, fresh life enters into our world, the spontaneous impulse of man's heart is to rejoice. He stands in the presence of mystery and wonder—a miracle oft repeated, yet none the less strange and wonderful for that. All life is clothed with mystery in his eyes, and he looks upon it with instinctive awe and reverence. He commemorates its coming into the world as a glad event, and celebrates as a household festival each anniversary of its coming. That, at least, is the unbidden impulse of his heart when his feelings are most genuine and true—when he has neither fallen below nor risen above the broad current of human sympathies. For the reversal of that we must go to a low barbarism on the one hand, or to a sophisticated civilization on the other, both of which regard the child that is born and the son that is given as an incumbrance, and not a blessing, and meet the birthday not with welcomes, but with regrets. But the true witness of human nature is to be found not in its immaturity, nor yet in its decrepitude. It is to be found in those common impulses and sympathies which characterize our common humanity. And these are the feelings which consecrate the birthday, which make every nativity sacred, which testify that it is an occasion for joy, for exultation, for praise. The Scripture, too, as might be expected, confirms and deepens the witness of our own hearts. When the Lord said of one who should betray him, "It were better for that man if he had never been born," he gave the strongest possible testimony, in an indirect way, to the worth of every human life. For if the worst that can be said of any one is this, "It were better that he had never been born," what an unspeakable blessing must the gift of life be! A blessing, too, not only to its possessor, but to others also; for the same divine voice, interpreting the consolation of every true motherhood, has said, "She remembereth no more the anguish, for joy that a man is born into the world." A man born into the world is, therefore, in the recognition of Christ, an occasion of thanksgiving to the man himself, and to that world also into which the man is born. Often and often, indeed, we may be tempted not to think so. There are facts and aspects of life which seem to contradict this high, exultant faith. We think of the millions who toil and die in misery, and ask doubtfully, were it not better if they had never been born? But when we say that of them or of ourselves, let us remember that we are using the very same words which Christ applies, and applies only to the son of perdition. Life and the worth of life cannot be truly estimated in any surface external view of it. Its roots go deeper than we see. There is an invisible whence we came; there is another invisible whither we are going. We move here amid the shadows and symbols of eternal things. Only when the veil is taken away shall we know ourselves, and in the knowing find the justification of our own hearts and the vindication of the Scripture. But meanwhile we shall not enter into the joy of our Lord's nativity unless we have faith enough to enter into the joy of our own. His nativity, indeed, transcends all others; but the first step in any human appreciation of it begins and must begin in those common, natural sympathies which find an occasion for rejoicing whenever a man is born into the world.

"Unto us a child is born, unto us a son is given." As you listen to the words you feel that the utterer of them is appropriating to himself in some special sense the congratulation which fills them. That is, his heart is not simply uplifted before the mystery of all life, but swells and exults in the assurance which has come to him of the continued identity and perpetuation of his own. It is the cry of fatherhood —the exultation of a man who, in "the child" that "is born" and "the son" that "is given" him, has won his victory over decay and time and the inexorable years. Now, indeed, he feels and knows himself to be immortal—immortal even with an earthly immortality. For he shall not fail and pass away when he is numbered with the dead, and the places which knew him once know him again no more. He shall live again in his children, and his life shall deepen and enlarge itself in theirs. This is the assurance to which consciously or unconsciously he has been always reaching out. For life is not a distinct, separate, isolated thing. Man lives only in his relationships, and apart from them he may be said to have no true life at all. His life does not begin in himself, nor is it in himself that it is completed. It begins in the ancestry which preceded him, it is continued in the posterity which shall follow. He stands between the fathers and the children, looking back to the one and onward to the other. Yet the law of his nature is that the forward-looking gaze is the stronger, the more earnest, the more intense. For it is there that the life which he has received, and which he in turn transmits, shall be continued and completed; there that it shall take on higher and higher forms, advancing always in a continuous process of development. His own fragmentary, fleeting individual life may be weak and vain, but it shall gather to itself volume, power, dignity, worth, in his descendants. Thus he looks back to the fathers with reverence, but he looks on to the children with hope. His yearnings, his aspirations, his prophetic dreams are all garnered there. For this he will toil and strive, content to sacrifice himself, and build in that future which yet his own eyes shall never see. The necessity of his heart is his son and heir—the heir of his name, of his place, of his calling in the world. How strongly does this necessity assert itself in all the Scripture! What mystic meanings are gathered into it! The consolation of Adam was in his promised seed. The blessing of Abraham was that he should be the father of the faithful; ennobled, as has been said of him, in his posterity, as other men are by their ancestors, bearing in his body the persons of Moses and David and Christ. The true dignity of the royal David himself was in the son who should be greater than he. No Hebrew household that did not rejoice when a nativity had assured it of eternal years. No Hebrew mother that did not lift with Mary her lowly *Magnificat* when her reproach was taken away among men. The most awful doom that could come upon an apostate was in the words, "Write this man childless." We must understand what fatherhood is—we must realize and appreciate how man's hopes are garnered in his children, how in them his own life is to be ennobled and completed—before we can understand even the human joy of that great exultant cry, "Unto us a child is born, unto us a son is given!"

The aspiration of one man's heart is great, but the aspiration of a nation's heart is greater; the on-looking of a single household is inspiring, but it must yield in inspiration to the on-looking of a whole people. And this necessity of the individual of which I spoke just now, had come in time to be the conscious necessity of all Israel. Onward and ever onward their forward-looking gaze was bent. The nation lived in expectation of its son and heir. The whole people were travailing, as it were, with child; waiting and longing for the nativity which should make them glad. There was in them the promised seed, and as the years went on, they might have appropriated the expression of the apostle, and said with him, "Now is our salvation nearer than when we believed." The birthday drew ever nigher and more nigh at hand. It was the one event on which all their hearts were set. For their identity, their calling, their destiny, their very name and place among the nations, were all staked upon it. For their golden age was not in the past, but in the future. Their greatest name was not one who had been, but one who was to be. Kingly as were the traditions of the House of David, there was to come forth out of that royal line one mightier and more kingly than ever David was. All their glories as a people were to centre about him; he was to embody their loftiest ideals; in him all their hopes and dreams were to be realized. And at last how feverish, painful, agonizing almost, this mighty expectation grew to be! We see them running to one and another, questioning earnestly if he be the Christ. We see them led away at times by the passionate delusion of their own hearts that they have found the Messias. We hear them asking of their prophets from generation to generation, "Watchman! what of the night?" What a moving, pathetic spectacle is this—a whole nation waiting breathlessly for tidings of a birth! And the tidings came. That wondrous nativity was realized. Unto Israel a child was born, unto Israel a son was given. And though Israel knew him not, but rejected and denied him, yet in a deeper sense Israel's joy was fulfilled, and Isaiah's words came true: "Of the increase of his government and peace there shall be no end, upon the throne of David, and upon his kingdom, to order it, and to establish it, with judgment and with justice, from henceforth even for ever."

Yes! Israel's expectation was realized, but not in the way for which he looked. Had it been so, the birthday would have been only a national festival, not the commemoration of a world. The child would have been only a Jewish child, not the child of humanity; the son would have been only the son of Israel, not the Son of man. But humanity, too, had shared in Israel's great expectation. The promise was for all nations. In Him all the families of the earth were to be blessed. The wide world was to be his inheritance. In the distant East wise men were already on the way to greet Him. The far West stood hushed and silent as if conscious of the coming of that perfect One of whom some of its poets and philosophers had dreamed. And in the fulness of time the Son of man came. The babe of Bethlehem was the son and heir of all human hearts and hopes. After thousands and thousands of years, humanity had at last produced its perfect type; it had reached its flower and its fruit; it had seen its crown and consummation. For here all separate types of excellence were united; here all ideals were embodied; here all perfections were gathered together. Not in vain had humanity lived and suffered, since it had realized in history a character more beautiful, more noble, more exalted than the loftiest imagination had conceived. Its course, however often baffled, had not ended in defeat and failure. It had risen to victory, risen to triumph, to the fruition of its hope, to the satisfaction of its desire, in this child that was born, and this son that was given to it.

Nor is this all. We have not yet reached the full measure of Isaiah's joy. Had this been all, we could indeed look back to the past with reverence, but we could scarce look on to the future with hope. Christ would then be only the greatest name, the greatest power that has appeared in human history. Humanity would be like the fabled century-plant which flowers only once in a hundred years. Nay, it would not be like that; for we should have to find its analogy in some plant which flowers once, and flowers again no more. There is only one Jesus of

Nazareth. That character has been known once, and only once, in the annals of the world. He stands alone; He has no successors. If then He is to be our hope, and not merely our reverence, He must be something more even than the highest product of humanity. He must bring into humanity a life diviner than its own; He must inspire it with a spirit which shall transform it at last into His own likeness. But to do so, He must be not only the Son of man, but also the Son of God. This is the implication of Isaiah's words. He says, "Unto us a child is born, unto us a son is given: and his name shall be called Wonderful, Counsellor, The mighty God, The everlasting Father, The Prince of Peace." The implication, however dimly understood at first, becomes clear in the revelation of our gospel. For the angel in his annunciation said: "The Holy Ghost shall come upon thee, and the power of the Highest shall overshadow thee: therefore also that holy thing which shall be born of thee shall be called the Son of God." And St. John, too, opens to us the deeper mystery of this divine nativity: "In the beginning was the Word, and the Word was with God, and the Word was God. The same was in the beginning with God." "And the Word was made flesh, and dwelt among us, (and we beheld His glory, the glory as of the only begotten of the Father,) full of grace and truth." Here then is the full interpretation of the prophet's joy. For in this self-same glory— "the glory as of the only begotten of the Father"— we may behold the similitude of our own. For in the Christ, as has been nobly said, there is the manifestation of the divine origin and relations of humanity, and the eternal life which is given to it; in Him it overcomes the evil of the world, and is victorious over death, and in the power of His resurrection is risen with Him, and ascending with Him, is glorified with Him in the glory which He had with the Father before the world was!

Let us bow, then, in lowly reverence before this great nativity. Let us kneel in glad adoration to Him who is the Son of man, and the Lord of man also. We read that on the night when He was born Heaven itself broke forth into singing. Earth lifted up, to meet Him, her *Magnificat* and her *Benedictus*, and afterwards raised in His honor her great *Te Deum Laudamus*. Let not our own lips or lives be dumb. Let us welcome the "child" that "is born," the "son" that "is given," with some fitting offering. Let us sing, and make melody in our hearts, with psalms and hymns and spiritual songs. The world over, wise and simple, Magi and shepherds, are on their way to Bethlehem.

> See how from far upon the eastern road
>   The star-led wizards haste with odors sweet;
> Oh, run! prevent them with thy humble ode,
>   And lay it lowly at His blessed feet.
>   Have thou the honor first thy Lord to greet,
> And join thy voice unto the angel choir,
> From out His secret altar touch'd with hallowed fire!

III.

THE BENEDICTION OF PEACE.

[KINGSBRIDGE, CHRISTMAS, 1874.]

"And the peace of God, which passeth all understanding, shall keep your hearts and minds through Christ Jesus."—PHIL. iv. 7.

THE day which we have come together once again to celebrate is especially a day of benediction. It has for each and all words of blessing and messages of peace. The Glad Tidings run through all the earth. The voice of its great joy is lifted here, and there, and everywhere, in the different dwelling places of the common human family. For it has a universal and world-wide significance. Its good news knows no limitation, but belongs of right to man as man. No accident of birth, no misfortune of condition, no stain even of sin, can debar any who will from appropriating the consolation of its message. Once again the benediction of Christmas Day goes forth, and none so poor, none so far astray, none so tempted or lost, that he cannot feel that the great Father's arms are stretched out over him also in blessing. For to sinners it announces the birth of a Saviour who came to save them from their sins. To the homeless and the poor it brings the assurance of the sympathy of that divine wanderer, that heavenly Friend, who was born in low and mean estate, and who Himself had not where to lay his head. To the weary and the heavy-laden it tells of One who has promised to the weary and the heavy-laden rest. In the mourner's ear its voice is heard, saying, "Your sorrow shall be turned into joy." To the foreboding and the anxious heart its bidding is: "Fear not." Here again the tempted may read of temptation's victor; the sad and disappointed prodigal, of his good shepherd; the earthly pilgrim, of the way prepared and the door opened to the Father's house. The weary couch of sickness shall be gladdened by its returning message, the hope deferred revive again in the impulse of great joy, and waning faith be rekindled with fresh inspiration. Here may the seekers after truth find once more their guiding star; here again, as of old, may questioners and doubters come to see and to believe; and here, too, may the despairing read of One in whom is Life, and whose Life is the Light of men. The day belongs to all—to age and childhood and youth. It belongs to children; for He whose nativity it commemorates was once Himself a child, and afterward was wont to gather the children about Him, and bless them, and say: "Forbid them not, but suffer the little children to come unto me." It belongs to youth; for the Lord of life Himself, whose anniversary it is, did not disdain to drink the wine, and mingle in the gladness of youth's festivity, and by His holy presence to consecrate and bless its marriage day. It belongs to age; for to the failing energy, the waning strength, and the bereaved heart, which sooner or later age must bring. He and He alone can say: "I am the resurrection and the life: whosoever liveth and believeth in me shall never die."

I have said that Christmas Day is especially a day of benediction; and what deeper or more appropriate or more beautiful benediction could it have than the benediction of peace? That, as we read, was the burden of the angels' song, when the Judæan shepherds listened to the midnight strain which told of peace upon earth and of good-will toward men. That, too, was the fair scene, which, in prophetic vision, Isaiah saw, when he prophesied of Him who should come, and who should be called the Prince of Peace. And as we look back over all these intervening years and centuries, we can see how the promise has been slowly moving on toward its accomplishment. Perhaps it has moved so slowly that men have at times almost lost faith in it. But slowly it must move; nay, sometimes it must even seem not to move on at all, since the peace that is finally to prevail on earth is not man's peace, but God's. It can come from no compromise with wrong, no patched-up artificial truce, no neglect of duty, no compact with unrighteousness. Men and nations have sought peace again and again in their unhallowed ways, but God has as often "overturned and overturned and overturned," and brought all their devices to nothingness. The Prince of Peace himself says that He comes, bringing not peace, but as it were a sword, indicating thereby the toil and conflict and sacrifice through which all true peace must be won. And accordingly in the history of Christianity the gospel has sometimes been the occasion of wars and rumors of wars, and set nation against nation, as well as fulfilled the prophecy that a man's foes should be they of his own household. Great principles cannot arise with all the living issues that attend them; great truths cannot be put in jeopardy, without stirring, and stirring sometimes into fierce antagonism, the great national factors in the life of humanity. Swords have not yet been beaten into ploughshares, nor spears into pruning hooks; nor can they be until the hearts of men shall have been leavened first with the divine leaven. Yet none the less has the gospel slowly and silently been bringing the different peoples of the earth nearer and nearer together, and established that bond of unity between them, which leads them more and more to look on war not only as an evil, but as a sin. Certainly it is to Christ and His teaching that we must look for the final passing away of those battle-fields with all their attendant miseries, which once made up the glory of human history, but are now more justly regarded as man's reproach and shame. The gospel, and the gospel alone, can accomplish this. Self-interest cannot do it, for self-interest does not always make for peace; and even when it does, vindictive passion will overbear, as it has always overborne it. Christian faith and principle and fellow-feeling—these things are the leaven, the divine leaven, which shall renew the nations, and realize for this scarred and war-worn world of ours the benediction of peace. We know that no jot or tittle of the Lord's word shall fail; and as often as we commemorate His Advent, we are reminded and have the assurance of that blessed consummation which His Advent yet shall bring.

And as with the warring nations, so also with the warring elements of society. Perhaps, to some, the benediction of peace may seem more hopeless in the latter case than in the former. The growing antagonism of classes; the bitter jealousies and conflicting interests; pride and insensibility on the one side, hate and envy on the other; fires smouldering inwardly everywhere, and in some places not smouldering inwardly, but bursting out into a fierce, wild flame—this is the problem which our wisest thinkers foresee will be more and more the problem of the future, and foreseeing, have yet no hopeful solution of it. This is the dark cloud in the distance, perhaps no bigger than a man's hand, but which broods so ominous and threatening over all the pride of our modern civilization. Are the nations, then, not to learn war any more, simply that the rage of battle may be turned inward on themselves? Are dynastic struggles to pass away, that newer and more dreadful ones may be inaugurated? Are human communities to divide into hostile camps, maintaining at the best but a hollow truce, and ready on occasion to join in a life-and-death conflict with each other? Then were the last state of humanity worse than the first. Yet all the contrivances and adjustments of man, all the schemes and theories of his busy brain, seem powerless to avoid the evil that shall come, if not upon us, upon our children or our children's children. Nor can it be averted in any of these ways. Natural, social, economic laws, in and by themselves, drive and must drive the weaker to the wall; and in that alternative, labor, when once it comes to know the strength of numbers, and learns better how to wield that strength, will not always consent to be the weakest. True, the desperate remedy may end, nay, will end, in some other form of that very same enslavement from which it sought to work itself free; but what a chapter of woes, what sorrows and sins, must follow and wait upon each recurring struggle! And yet the remedy, the effective remedy, the true solution of the whole matter, is all the while in our own hands. This gospel of ours, this plain, simple, old-fashioned gospel, speaking to rich and poor alike of their respective duties; consecrating for each alike their different lot in life, and referring back to God's appointment the vocation wherewith they each are called; bidding the one to be mindful and considerate and helpful to the other, and the other in turn to put away envy, jealousy, and discontent, thus binding both together, if they will only consent to be thus bound—and if men profess to accept the gospel and to practise it, how can they disannul these marriage bands? this gospel, I say, binding both together in a bond of mutual sympathy and service, may dispel for us, if we will, this darkest cloud that obscures the fair promise of the modern time. And that it will dispel it no Christian man should doubt. Here, too, the gospel shall breathe its benediction of peace. Our children and our children's children, let us trust, shall have a deeper faith and a better practice than their fathers, and the civilization which shall be the product of a more Christian future shall be lifted above and out of the dark and seemingly hopeless problems which have beset an unchristian past.

But we turn now from communities to individuals. Let us try to take the benediction of Christmas Day to our own hearts and homes. This seems to have been the thought of the apostle when he bade his disciples rejoice in the Lord alway, and added the assurance that the peace of God, which passeth understanding, should keep their hearts and minds. It was, as it were, his Christmas message, for he spoke it looking back to the advent which had been, and looking on to the advent which was to be, of Him whose nativity we commemorate. And what a strange, sweet, beautiful message it is! Peace, God's peace, the peace which passeth understanding, shall keep our hearts and minds. Can we not, some of us at least, in some dim way, realize the need and enter into the consolation of this wondrous benediction? We do not expect childhood to do so. For children now and always let this be "merry" Christmas still; let smiles and laughter still be their inheritance; the gay heart, the light thought, which is beautiful in them, which knows not yet, and which as yet should not know, of any deeper need. Enough if we can teach them to associate their gladness with the Child that has been born and with the Son that has been given; enough if we can lead them in their merry-making to feel some childish sort of gratitude to Him. They, too, assuredly, shall share in His benediction, but in that same incomprehensible way in which they shared it when once, long ago on earth, He stretched out His hands over them to bless. Nor is it to be expected that youth, with bounding pulse and bright, onlooking eyes, should chiefly dwell upon and linger over this tender apostolic benediction. Youth, except in some strange, unnatural way, cannot anticipate the later experience of humanity. Yet that experience, with its record of toil and conflict, is essential before the need of peace can be fully felt, or its consolation adequately appreciated. Enough if we can enlist the young in the Master's service, if we can win them to consecrate their strength and energy and high, brave hearts to Him. In the establishment of His kingdom there is the call for zeal, fervor, enthusiasm, and it is theirs to feel and furnish that. In the Christian life, as in all life, the chief need of youth is work; some high purpose to call out and employ all its strong activities. But when life has reached its maturity, or is on its decline, then man begins to have some deeper perception of the necessity of peace. Then he listens, as if the words had some strange, new meaning in them, to the assurance of a peace, a peace of God, a peace that passeth understanding, a peace that shall keep his heart and mind. Has any such benediction as that entered into his experience? Does not his gaze go back rather over years of distracted feeling and troubled thought, the very antithesis, as it were, of this serene tranquillity? Whatever else he may have gained, can he count this among his possessions? And if not, must not the worth of all the rest lessen to him day by day? He has heard at last, or rather his ears have at length been opened to the message of an unspeakable gift—a gift which all his toil and conflict have fitted him more and more to appreciate, and if that may not be gained, all other things turn to vanity and nothingness. Were he to relive his life, would he place any other object in a moment's comparison with this? Would he not search for it, as for hid treasure, this divine, beautiful gift of God, which shall keep his heart and mind? Is it, then, possible to be won, and may the peace which passeth understanding yet come even to him? Our Christmas Day is the assurance that it may; for Christmas tells of Him in and through whom the apostle says God's peace is given. Thus Christmas answers year by year more and more to the later and deepening necessities of our human experience. Its glad tidings we meet and welcome first; its hope and promise we lay hold on afterward; but we come with tears and tenderness to listen to its solemn, consolatory blessing last of all.

"He that hath an ear to hear, let him hear." To all who have begun to feel the need of peace, and to all whose troubled lives whether of thought or feeling have enabled them in some sort to appreciate its blessings, Christmas Day is the witness that God's peace may be won. We may have, if we will only seek it, a peace that shall keep our hearts and minds. These wild, wayward passions, these unruly affections, these inordinate desires, which have made our hearts to heave and beat at times so fiercely, and then again to ache with the very bitterness of disappointment; or more woeful still, to be, as it were, dead in the disgust and weariness of sheer satiety—all these may be put away, or so transformed and ennobled in their consecration, that we shall be no more tempest-tossed, but be upheld and guarded in God's own holy, calm, divine tranquillity. Man's poor, deluded, blind, ignorant, self-deceiving heart may stay itself on One who can interpret and answer its deepest necessities, and in whom it shall find the fruition of its hope and the satisfaction of its desire. And for his troubled thoughts, his sad doubts, his perplexed questionings, here also shall he find rest. The revelation of truth is given him in Him who is Himself the Truth, the Life, and the Way. Looking unto Jesus, the author and finisher of his faith, he shall not be driven to and fro with every wind of doctrine; he shall not be taken captive of some strange delusion; but shall stand like a rock in the uncertain sea. Hopes which are, and must remain, open questions to others, shall be assured certainties to him. Doubt and disquietude may visit other minds, but as for his, the peace of God shall keep it.

"The peace of God, the peace which passeth understanding, shall keep your hearts and minds." How can I help dwelling on, and lingering over, this divine beatitude? Surely no more tender or sweet or more reassuring promise was ever given to man. Are we not led to reiterate, and repeat the words over and over again, as if in the repetition something of this strange, beautiful peace might descend upon and visit us? What a wonderful benediction it is! To think that in this world of ours—a world of sorrow, sin, and shame; a world in which our path is beset with snares and temptations on the right hand and on the left; a world in which we seem sometimes to be the mere sport of circumstance, and given over as a prey to the discordant, warring elements within us; and not only that, not only that, but a world of intellectual doubts, moral bewilderments, and mental perplexities; a world of uncertain seekings and more uncertain answers to our search; a world in which it appears often as if no truth that would stand could be found—to think, I say, that in such a world as this, the peace of God, if we will only suffer it, the peace that passeth understanding, may keep our hearts and minds! Shall we not, then, on Christmas Day lift up our voice in adoration and thanksgiving for the Saviour, in and through whom God's peace is given? And as we go on now in His worship, to the Communion of His body and His blood, shall not our prayer, our chiefest prayer, be this: that some portion, at least, of this solemn, beautiful, consolatory benediction of the apostle may be ours? that the "peace of God," in very deed and truth, may "keep our hearts and minds"?

IV.

HOME AND HOME'S TEACHINGS.

[KINGSBRIDGE, JAN. 5, 1873.]

"And the shepherds returned, glorifying and praising God for all the things that they had heard and seen."—ST. LUKE ii. 20.

THE holy Christmas-tide has not yet all gone by, and on this present Sunday, therefore, which is its last lingering day, it is still a Christmas scene and still a Christmas lesson that are brought before us. The Gospel that has been read to you this morning takes up the story of the shepherds where Christmas Day had left it, and completes for us that strangely beautiful and sweet and simple tale. For of all stories in the world it is perhaps the simplest, the sweetest, and the most beautiful. The new evangel— an evangel embracing such mighty themes as wisdom, righteousness, sanctification, and redemption—opens with a fair, idyllic picture such as might have belonged to the long-gone days of human innocence, or to some childlike, pastoral age of which history has no record, and tradition no remembrance; a picture painted, too, with such simple pathos and power, that all succeeding generations have been moved and melted before it. It has come with us to assume a kind of representative character, to symbolize, as it were, at the outset, the fair, childlike spirit of Christianity; and although our gospel, as it goes on, becomes sombre and sorrowful, and deepens at last into the world's darkest tragedy, still with every returning Christmas-time we read once more this story of the shepherds, we are reassured again by their human and angelic voices blended in loving unison, and feel that this sweet idyl of the evangelist, reviving, as it does, man's dream of his own innocence, and holding, moreover, the suggestion of a still nobler innocence that shall return to him again, stands, and must always stand, as an essential part, and that part in the very forefront, too, of a gospel whose glad message is, "Peace, good-will toward man." Men have dreamed many beautiful dreams, and the human imagination has reached some of its highest flights in those myths or legends in which the religious sentiment of various ages and climes has found expression and embodiment, but the difference between the most elaborate pagan and the simplest Christian idyl is this: they have only a local and temporary significance—a significance which has passed away, either wholly or in part, with the age or nation that gave them birth, while our Christian stories have a meaning for all men always and everywhere. It is the difference between fancy and inspiration; the difference between the baseless fabric of a dream and the tale which, however poetically and beautifully told, is none the less a tale of truth and soberness. Certainly this story of the shepherds has passed through the crucial test of many centuries, and remains as fresh and fair and sweet for us as for our fathers. Time, which tries all things, has tried this too, and yet has detracted nothing from its strange, persuasive influence. Nay, as our years increase, we love to linger more and more over this gentle prelude to our gospel. Either the literal narrative of the evangelist, or the familiar words of the Christian hymn, are inseparably associated in our thought with the very name of Christmas. The believer believes in it more deeply with every returning festival, finding in it, perhaps, some new and deeper comfort for some new and deeper need. And as for unbelievers, how many of them, did we know their secret thoughts, linger with strange yearning on the old familiar strains, and wish that the story and the song, so sweet and so beautiful, might be for them also, as for others, equally comforting because equally true.

It is not my present purpose, however, to dwell upon this story of the shepherds, but rather to call your attention to a single incident of it. The lesson for Christmas Day left them listening to the angelic song: "Glory to God in the highest, on earth peace, good-will toward men." To-day the Gospel tells us how, when the angels had gone away into heaven, the shepherds said one to another: "Let us now go even unto Bethlehem and see this thing which is come to pass;" how they went and saw and "found the babe lying in a manger;" how they "made known abroad the saying which was told them concerning this child;" and how they returned again, "praising and glorifying God for all the things that they had heard and seen."

Whither was it that they returned? And why did they return at all, or at least so soon, and not linger longer about the sacred nursery at Bethlehem? They reappear no more on any page of the New Testament. Are we to conclude, then, that this first and only mention of them was the beginning and the end of their connection with the nativity?

The answer to our first question is, that they returned to their own homes—to what at least was the equivalent of home to them—to the tent or cottage which held their little household; to their fields and flocks; to the simple occupations of the day, and the lonely vigils of the night; to their own place, as it were, in a world where every man has his own proper avocation and abode; to all those familiar scenes and associations which made up the substance of their quiet, uneventful life. And this answer is the solution, also, of all the other questions we have asked. They returned, and returned so soon, because, in a sense deeper than they could realize, it was necessary for them that they should go back. The necessity of which they were conscious might be only this: the neglected flocks at home, needing their renewed diligence and care; the necessity of which they, perhaps, knew little or nothing was a necessity of their own nature. We shall understand it better if we recall for a moment the several incidents of their story, and try to imagine ourselves, as it were, in the same position. Their life had indeed been a singularly quiet and uneventful one, as far removed as it is possible for any earthly existence to be from all the stirs and commotions of the world. We can well believe that into the seclusion of their solitary plains an outside voice would seldom enter, and scant tidings reach them of the strifes of men, of the great hopes and fears which mark the epochs of human history. Kings and kingdoms, philosophers and their schools, the passing away of the old and the incoming of the new, the political and religious movements that were going on round about them—all these things would have for them a dim and far-off sound; they would be among the things which concerned them not. For the life of an Eastern shepherd was as childlike as any human life could be—childlike in its simplicity, in its ignorance of ambition, in the even tenor of its way, in its freedom from all disturbing influences, and yet childlike, too, in its singularly imaginative and impressionable character. And to these simple yet most sensitive minds there had come, on one memorable night, a wondrous revelation of glory. The angel of the Lord had come upon them, and the glory of the Lord had shone round about them; the heavens themselves had burst forth in angelic strains, and they had heard tidings in comparison with which the fate of states and empires was as dust in the balance. We read that they were sore afraid. We can well believe in their affright, their perturbation, their exaltation of spirit. We can imagine, too, the eager excitement with which they hurried on to Bethlehem to find this divine child which had been foretold to them; the awe and wonder with which they looked upon Him as He lay there in the manger; the disturbance of their thought amounting almost to confusion and bewilderment of spirit as they recognized the sign of which the herald angel had spoken; the wild, disordered way, perhaps like men, as it were, beside themselves, in which they repeated over to others the words which had been told to them; the ecstatic character of their praise and thanksgiving as they glorified God for all the wonderful things that they had seen and heard. Unless we are to suppose that they were supernaturally freed from the control of those laws which inhere in the very nature of man, we must believe that they would lose, as in like circumstances all men would lose, that accustomed balance of mind, that equipoise of spirit, that serenity of heart, without which wonders may be seen and heard indeed, but never adequately realized or appreciated. It was, therefore, necessary for them, and no necessity could be deeper, to return to those familiar scenes and associations, to those fields and flocks, to those night vigils and daily avocations, to those homes and households in which alone these conditions of mind and heart could be recovered. There the confusion would disappear, and the excitement pass away; things would shape themselves into order and distinctness; and there would come again that calm, meditative thoughtfulness in which the wondrous tidings which they had heard would sink deep into their souls. Thus their return homeward, although the evangelist mentions them no more, was not the end of their connection with the nativity; it was the beginning, rather, of their true and deeper relation to it, for these shepherds did not and could not return the self-same men that went away. A change had passed upon them which they themselves, perhaps, could but dimly understand. Yet, nevertheless, the change was there. The heavens, peopled of old only by the stars, were peopled now, for them at least, by angelic visitants. The very air would seem to breathe an echo of the celestial strain. They had been brought into communion with the unseen—communion in which the spiritual world had assumed substantial form and reality. As they watched again their flocks by night, how would they meditate and ponder over all that they had seen and heard? Through repeated vigils and slow succeeding days, how would they become insensibly more and more prepared to meet and greet the Saviour that had been born to them? Some thirty years should come and go before that Saviour should summon men to forsake all and follow Him, to leave their homes and gather to his side. And meanwhile, not only in the shepherd's tent, but in many a humble household in Galilee and Judæa, there was going on that quiet preparation which should fit men to hear and answer the call when the divine voice should indeed be lifted, and the word go forth: "The time is fulfilled; behold, the kingdom of heaven is at hand!"

Thus the moral of this story, or at least that part of it which I have specially dwelt upon, a moral not perhaps directly taught, yet certainly suggested, is this: Each man's home, or its equivalent, is to be for him in some real and deep sense the measure, the interpreter, and the appropriation of truth. It is to be the place in which he shall realize best the conditions of a calm and deliberate judgment; in which he shall be more open than elsewhere to any message that God may send him; in which he shall appropriate, as he could not otherwise do, the great lessons of life, and make them part of his own personal being. For by home, I mean not merely a man's house, but his household; not merely the four walls of his habitation, but the family that fills it; nor only this, but also and as well those scenes and associations with which he has been long familiar— the friends and neighbors among whom he dwells, the ordinary avocations of the day and the accustomed vigils of the night, the joys and sorrows, the hopes and fears, the labor and repose which make up the sum of his own separate existence; in short, that lot and condition of life into which it has pleased God to call him. This, then, is the place in which he is to meditate and ponder over wonders whether seen or heard; the school in which he is to gather his lessons of deepest wisdom; the sphere within which those lessons are to be applied and wrought out. Home has been given him as a kind of vantage ground on which to arrange and adjust his thought; a bond connecting him in the great realities of his own nature with things unseen and eternal; a vocation, individual but not exclusive, in which the highest truth he knows is to find expression and embodiment. It is the point on which his lever must be laid if he would work his way into the mysteries of man's life and the secrets of God's universe.

For, first of all, the home life is essential to that serenity of mind and stability of character which are the necessary conditions of every calm and deliberate judgment. There must be some sure, certain footing beneath our feet if we would give all our thought to the mysteries that are overhead. We must have a foundation to stand on if we would see with clear mind and no tremulous eye. But in scenes strange and unfamiliar, where new worlds, as it were, are opened before us, and where we ourselves are necessarily to some extent out of relation with ourselves, we are apt to lose, in less or greater measure, that balance and equipoise, both of mind and character, without which truth fails, and must fail, of all its proper relations and proportions. Thought becomes disordered and confused; strange doubts and bewilderments intrude themselves; things appear often to be dark and contradictory; we seem incapable of rearranging and readjusting them, and realize the Psalmist's expression of the "mire where no ground is." Our incapacity is in the fact that we have lost the props and supports which home and home's surroundings bring us. It may not be very flattering to our pride to realize how dependent we are upon these self-same surroundings, to know how largely the mind itself leans upon the props and supports which place and circumstance give it; but one can never put them aside without danger, and seldom without disaster. Probably we are all familiar with instances of people, sober-minded enough and sufficiently well conducted at home, who, nevertheless, when far away, have suddenly undergone strange transformations, either of thought or character. And this was due, doubtless, not so much to any new evidence brought to bear upon the mind, or any outcropping of some latent vicious characteristic, but simply to the loss of their mental or moral equilibrium. The fact is, it was meant that we should live at home, that we should judge of truth at home; that here and not elsewhere we should seek and find it. Or if, indeed, our seeking lead us, as perhaps it sometimes may, into paths and surroundings in which we feel ourselves to be strangers, it must, nevertheless, be in our own homes again that we shall bring to it the fittest and most profitable meditation. Here, by the aid of those helps which God has put about us, and which have their necessity not in the infirmities only, but also in the nobilities of our nature, clouds shall clear and misgivings pass away, and in the quiet thought of our own spirit we shall learn more of truth than even any pilgrimage to Bethlehem could teach us.

For home is not only the place where the conditions of meditation are best realized, it is the place also in which we are brought into the deepest and most living relations with truth itself. This holds good of all truth, but it is pre-eminently so of religious truth—the truth which has to do with heaven and God. For it is in a man's own home that we come upon the great realities of his nature. It is there that he strikes his roots deepest into unseen and spiritual things; there that he reaches out after things eternal. The divinest thing about him is his home. If we question him for proofs of his immortality, for qualities in him worthy to be immortal, the most convincing answer he can give us is to point to the household in which his nobler nature is developed and expressed. His intellect, however far-reaching it may be, is nevertheless perplexed before the simplest mysteries of nature, and after all its striving must fain confess itself incapable of solving the problems which concern it most. His imagination in its fairest flight bears traces of the earth-born. The works of his hands, mighty as they sometimes are, are nevertheless seamed all over by decay, and yet even they have a permanence which belongs not to him. The pages of history, and the great volume of the world itself, when we seek in them for confirmation of our hopes, are more often than not disappointing and unsatisfactory. It is only when we get at man's affections, when we come upon his pure, disinterested love, upon his capability of self-devotion and self-sacrifice, upon all the hidden sweetness, gentleness, and tenderness of his nature, that we seem to find in him qualities in any way worthy of an immortality. And these are the qualities which belong pre-eminently to his home. It is in his home, therefore, that religion must find him, if it would take him in his softer mood and more impressionable character. The mere wanderer and wayfarer on the one hand, or the mere cosmopolite and citizen of the world on the other, has but few avenues of approach by which the divine voice may reach him. There is little or nothing in his life to speak to him of things eternal. For ourselves, therefore, is it not wise to welcome religion into our inmost privacy, to carry back her words with us to our firesides, to give her a place in the household where she shall find us more susceptible and docile than elsewhere, to open to her, and open gladly, that side of our nature which looks, as she looks, to hopes which go beyond the earth, and can find their fruition only in the hereafter?

For, finally, home is the sphere above all others within which the truths of life are to be applied and expressed. Few men only are called to play a part in the great world, and if we knew all the danger and disadvantage of that part, we should scarcely envy them. For most of us life moves, and is meant to move, in a quiet routine, an uneventful round. Yet that round so quiet and uneventful, in which the days and years succeed each other, as we sometimes think, so wearily and monotonously, has room and abundant room for the development of noblest character, for the accomplishment of worthiest work, for the building up in our lives of something that shall stand. Nothing shall stand, we know, that cannot abide the test of the last day, that has not in it the true elements of endurance. Yet how little of man's outside work can lay claim to that! I said just now that history and the great world were more often than not disappointing; to some minds they are so disappointing and so sad that they are constrained to take refuge from their own doubts and misgivings in the beauty and the worth of common things. Yet the refuge is no deceitful one, for the testimony of Scripture is, that common things are the divine things. Some time or other, perhaps, we shall realize this truth, and take to ourselves all the comfort and the ministration of it. Then this spectacle of man going forth to his labor in the morning, and returning to his home again for refreshment and repose at night, will not seem to us the dull, tame picture that we have been disposed to think it. We shall see in it, instead, the normal order of human life—the way, in God's appointment, in which fair and beautiful things are fashioned. What worthier work, in the great Father's sight, was going on in Judæa than the silent preparation of the shepherds in their own homes for the Master's call when He should summon them to His side? Year after year went by, and long before the summons came some of them doubtless had fallen asleep. Yet dead or living it mattered not, the preparation had been made, and they should be counted among His chosen. We too, brethren, have our preparation to make, that we may meet Him when He shall come again in glory. This is our life work. And where can it better be accomplished than in the households which God has given us?—glorifying Him indeed for all wonders seen and heard, but none the less faithful in daily duty and common endeavor, as we meditate upon His truths in the secrecy of our own homes and hearths.

As you have followed, brethren, the drift of this discourse, you have perhaps anticipated the single word of a personal character which on this occasion I would say to you. It is to your liberality and kindness that I owe it that I have been permitted, under singularly favorable circumstances, to see many wonders of nature and man's works, and when all other books were closed to me to read somewhat in the great volume of the world. I have returned, not as successful as I hoped in the immediate object of my going, but not without some lessons gathered which have been profitable to me, and which I trust may be no less profitable to you. One of these lessons has found imperfect expression in my discourse this morning; namely, the use and worth, the beauty and divineness of a man's own home, be it the shepherd's tent, the peasant's thatch, or the noble's palace. This truth has grown upon me as nothing else has grown. Often, when away, thinking of dear friends, of familiar scenes and faces, I have longed for my own home again with a longing deeper, I think, than any instinct, and which amounted almost to a spiritual necessity of my nature. For I was led to realize, as I never realized before, how dependent I was upon home and home's equivalents for all the great assurances of man's heart; how little there is in all the world beside to speak to him of things unseen and eternal. It is with deep thankfulness, therefore, a thankfulness for which I have no adequate expression, that I have been permitted to return again to my accustomed place, and minister once more at our own altar. Here, for me at least, must truth be pondered on, appropriated, and wrought out. It is not to be expected, perhaps, that with all the thoughts expressed or suggested to-day you should fully sympathize; yet my testimony, I trust, may not go all for naught. And that testimony, so far as it can add anything to line upon line and precept upon precept, is simply this: For the human witness to our immortality—I am not speaking now of a supernatural or scriptural one—for the human witness to our immortality we must look to the affections of our own hearts; and as for the great realities of life, the things worth living and worth dying for, they lie one and all at your own door.

V.

THE AUTHORITATIVE CHARACTER OF THE SERMON ON THE MOUNT.

[KINGSBRIDGE, 1870.]

"And it came to pass, when Jesus had ended these sayings, the people were astonished at his doctrine: for he taught them as one having authority, and not as the scribes."—ST. MATT. vii. 28, 29.

THIS is the account given by the evangelist of the impression produced upon the people at the first hearing of the Sermon on the Mount. These sayings of Jesus, fragmentary in appearance, yet forming in reality one coherent and connected whole, are the earliest abstract of his teaching of which we have any record in the gospel narrative. They were propounded to the disciples and the multitude somewhat after the manner of a set and formal discourse. Seated on an eminence, with the open sky above, and the spell-bound audience gathered round about Him, He gave utterance in unbroken succession to those remarkable and ever memorable words which were destined to influence so largely both the thought and practice of mankind. There fell from His lips, one after another, a series of exalted truths and principles, such as no other teachings disclose, and which have confessedly become the standard, the measure, of all true religion and virtue. The Sermon on the Mount we call it; and what a sermon it was! How famous it has since become! No words can fitly characterize it, and in connection with it eulogy falls scarcely short of impertinence. It transcends our praise, and is as absolutely above it as it is absolutely without parallel or comparison. It is the one sermon of the world, the one matchless discourse, in connection with which the collective wisdom, the most exalted utterance of human-kind, is not even to be named. As we read it, and with every reading realize its inexhaustible instructiveness the more, the day and the scene of its delivery become sacred. The spot and the hour are hallowed, and made forever memorable, by such words as these. We wonder how they felt who were first privileged to hear them, whether they suspected what an epoch they would make in human history. There are many famous scenes in the New Testament—circumstances which appear as crises or turning points in man's destiny. Such, for instance, was St. Paul's discourse at Athens, when he stood on Mars' hill, and in the very citadel of Grecian paganism declared the unknown God whom they ignorantly worshipped. But sublime as that incident was, and inspiring as are all its associations, it is yet as nothing in comparison with that other scene when Christ sat down on the mount, and opened His mouth, and taught His disciples, saying, "Blessed are the poor in spirit: for theirs is the kingdom of heaven." This was His opening, His first general or inaugural discourse. We have read already, in the narrative, of His birth,

His baptism, His temptation. We have heard Him sounding out the call to repentance. We have seen Him summoning one and another disciple to His side. On various occasions, here and there, He has been preaching to the people and healing them. His church has been instituted, and a following gradually collected; and now, when his fame has gone abroad, and there come to Him multitudes from Galilee, and from Jerusalem, and from beyond Jordan, He formally defines, as it were, His position, and sets forth as a clear and connected whole the divine principles of his ministry. He enumerates one after another the great moral and religious truths, in the recognition and application of which, He says, man's true life consists. He tells over to His audience the notes or characteristics of that holy society which He would establish. He lays bare the propositions to which He is committed, and to which he expects they also will commit themselves. Thus the Sermon on the Mount is the inaugural of the kingdom of heaven. It is an abstract, an epitome of the Gospel. It is a general and compendious statement of the principles which Christ proposes to illustrate in His own life, and which He proposes also to enforce upon the recognition and practice of his disciples.

St. Matthew has preserved to us a record of the impression produced by this remarkable discourse on those to whom it was originally delivered. He says that, when Jesus had finished these sayings, the people were astonished at His doctrine; that is, they were surprised and amazed at the character of his teaching; and their astonishment, their amazement, seems to have been chiefly provoked by the *tone* which He assumed. "For He taught them," in their own expression of it, "as one having authority, and not as the scribes."

There were, indeed, many things to wonder at in this Sermon on the Mount; many things which must have appeared strange and new and altogether unprecedented to those who heard it. They had never listened to the like before. Whether they considered its scope or spirit or the general impressiveness of its utterance, it might well fill them with astonishment. But the one thing beyond all others which excited their surprise was the conviction which it forced upon them as to Christ's authority. Elsewhere and later, we read that on another occasion, men marvelled at Him, saying, "How knoweth this man letters, having never learned?" There the subject of amazement was, that a man who was not professedly a scholar, who was notoriously of humble extraction, and had never been trained in the discipline of the schools, should yet exhibit in his speech the results of the very highest culture. But it is not this which makes the multitude about the mount marvel now. They are not thinking of the learning or the eloquence or even the wisdom of the sermon which they have heard, but of its authoritative character. This for the time is the one predominant and overpowering impression. The voice which had been speaking to them had, in their own despite, extorted from them an acknowledgment of its unqualified and unequalled right to speak. In comparison with that, every other seemed unauthoritative, a mere conjecture or commandment of men. "For He taught them," they said, "as one having authority, and not as the scribes."

Now this contrast becomes still more significant when we consider who and what the scribes were, and what were their legitimate and generally recognized pretensions. They were, as it is well known, a body of scholarly men who were universally respected and esteemed in the community. They held, as we would say, a kind of official position. They were the authorized and accredited teachers of the people. Their opinions were largely deferred to, their traditions and expositions of the law were held in profound veneration. They were mostly identified with the Pharisaic party, which was the ruling and representative party of the nation. Their place as a body in influence and position was second to none in the commonwealth of Israel. It would be difficult to imagine a class of men more favorably situated for imposing laws on the thought and practice of society. Their authority, so far from being questionable, was of the most comprehensive and indisputable kind. For they had in the first place the weight which rightfully attaches to great learning. They were the scholars of the Jewish people. All that philosophers and wise men are and were to other nations, the scribe was to his own. Then again their authority was fortified by the official or semi-official character of their position. We are naturally disposed to defer to the opinion of a man in matters which are confessedly within his special jurisdiction, and it was the province of the scribe to investigate and determine all disputed points in morals and religion. The scribe, moreover, had at his back the whole weight of the Jewish hierarchy. He was the recognized exponent of its faith and practice. He could plant himself upon venerable, immemorial traditions, and summon to his aid all the influence that would come from the moral indorsement of the Church. And above and beyond all this, to him belonged the interpretation and exposition of the law. He held in his hand that sacred book, the object of every Jew's profound and even superstitious veneration, and the voice which commented on the sacred page, which elucidated and expounded it, was as authoritative as any human voice could be. Nor was this authority merely illusory and artificial, something which had no foundation in realities. On the contrary, our Lord himself expressly says that it is to be respected. To a certant extent He gives it the weight of His indorsement. He was careful to impress upon His disciples the obligation of deference which they owed it. "The scribes," He says, " sit in Moses' seat ; whatsoever, therefore, they command, that observe and do." Learning, official character, churchly tradition, the authorized interpretation of the law—all these in His estimate did not go for naught. In these later days we may be disposed to attach very little importance to them, to push them all aside at the mere bidding of a private judgment. But the Master taught otherwise. He would not permit men to disregard such authorities in His own day, and the plain inference is, that neither will He sanction such disregard in ours. Yet, while we accord to them all due and proper respect, we must, nevertheless, acknowledge that in comparison with Christ's, all other authorities seem to us as nothing and less than nothing. It was so with these Jews who made up His audience at the mount. They had been trained from infancy in deference to the scribe. All their associations, all the influences about them, tended to keep them submissive at his feet. He spoke, and they expected him to speak, in the imperative. But when a greater than he began to speak, when they listened to such discourse as no scribe had ever uttered, then in the astonished recognition of this new and overshadowing authority it seemed to them as if the scribe in comparison with the Master taught with no pretence of authority at all.

Thus the more we consider the original impression produced by the Sermon on the Mount, the more remarkable does it become. We, indeed, also recognize and bow to its authority; we, too, are astonished at its doctrine; but it must be borne in mind that we come to its perusal with certain predispositions in its favor. We have been trained to reverence, beyond every other name, the name of Christ. It was otherwise with the multitudes who listened to Him. He stood before them a comparatively unknown man. He had neither the prestige of learning, nor office, nor ecclesiastical recognition. Whatever weight his words should have must be inherent in them. And yet this discourse of His impressed

His hearers, above all other things, with the conviction of His authority. What then was the secret of this? What was there in this sermon which led the people to consider Him with their venerated teachers the scribes, and contrast Him with them to their disadvantage?

I. It was, first, its eminently personal character, the strong self-assertion that pervades it. This is expressed or implied from beginning to end. In every sentence, in every successive statement of doctrine, the personal pronoun appears or is understood. The authority of the scribe was prescriptive. He enforced his teaching with such a formula as this: "It is written," or, "It hath been said." He stood upon tradition and the law, and beyond that he could not go. This was the limit of his authority. But Christ simply said: "*I* say unto you." He referred to His principles as "these sayings of *mine*." He asserted an exclusively personal claim. He dispensed with all the usual and venerated indorsements. He did not appeal to the schools. The verdict of the learned was nothing to Him. He quoted no great names. He did not intrench Himself in traditions. He did not rest His authority even on the Scriptures. In some instances He even asserted it against them. "Ye have heard that it hath been said," etc., "but I say unto you," is an expression which we meet with continually in this discourse. In respect to the law of oaths, the law of retaliation, the law of love and hatred, and various other laws, He avowedly proposed to modify or supersede the commandments of Moses. We cannot adequately realize how immense this assumption appeared to those who heard it, what an unparalleled, unprecedented claim He seemed to them to be setting up. We know, indeed, that He expressly disclaimed all *irresponsible* personal authority; that He says, on the contrary: "I do nothing of myself, but as my Father hath taught me, I speak these things." Before Pilate He defined His mission as simply that of a witness to the truth, but, nevertheless, asserted that it was regal, kingly in its authoritative character. So identical, indeed, were the truth and the witness to it, that it became a necessity of His later ministry to preach openly, as He here preaches inferentially, Himself. The self-assertion which runs as an undercurrent through the whole Sermon on the Mount, appears farther on in the Gospels in a more definite, and, to the Jew, a more offensive form. Yet this was only the development, the logical sequence, of that which had preceded it. He, whose usual formula was simply this, "I say unto you," would, of necessity, sooner or later also say: "I am the Life, the Truth, and the Way. No man cometh to the Father but by Me." The Jews at last came to look upon such pretensions as blasphemous; but, as yet, they were rather awed, and, in spite of themselves, impressed by them. There is but a step between the sublime and the ridiculous, a step between what men adore and what they deride. The same personal self-assertion which, in its later statements, so infuriated His countrymen, was the occasion now, in no slight measure, of their recognition of Christ's superior authority. It seemed to them that one who could speak thus must have some mysterious, indisputable right to speak—a right which transcended and put to shame all ordinary claims. They were surprised and overpowered by the personality of Jesus. He had impressed Himself irresistibly upon them. They were for the time being His captives, held by the spell and fascination of His speech. "He taught them," they said, "as one having authority, and not as the scribes." And this same personal element we recognize as an essential characteristic from beginning to end of the Gospel now. You cannot in any degree eliminate it. It is hopelessly, inseparably identified with the whole body of His teaching. The personal claims which He sets up are so continuous, so consistent, and so unprecedented, that we have no alternative but to account Him an impostor or to account Him divine; no alternative but to deny to Him all authority whatsoever, or to confess that authority to be simply illimitable.

II. Another element in the impressive character of this discourse was the manner of it. Christ's very attitude was, as it were, authoritative. It was not simply that He asserted His authority, but the way in which He asserted that authority, that enforced upon others the recognition of it. Manner is one of the most subtle, the most indescribable, and yet one of the most potent of all influences. Most often we can give no satisfactory account of it, it defies all attempts at analysis, and yet we are profoundly conscious of the depth and reality of the impression which it makes upon us. Not infrequently it is the one grand distinguishing characteristic between men. With little else apparently to separate them, this alone forbids comparison, and puts them immeasurably apart. For manner is, perhaps, the surest index of the inmost character, and is sometimes the only way in which that character can find adequate expression; the only way in which it can gain a perfect method of communication between itself and others. The great names in human history are all in a greater or less degree associated with this species of influence. A succeeding generation reads, perhaps, the bare record of some famous leader's life, the mere dry statistics of the chronicler, and wonders at the vast, undisputed sway which this man so long exercised over their forefathers; but some lingering contemporary, when you question him, replies, " No description can give you the faintest conception of what our great leader really was—it was the tone, the look, the manner of the man that so inspired us; these things are incapable of representation; you would not wonder at his sway had you ever known the personal magnetism of his influence." It is so in almost every reference. The power and value of a thought are to a great degree dependent upon the mode and circumstances of its presentment. The great things which men have said have been made great chiefly by the manner in which they said them. The poem, the nation, the teachings of the masters, which live and which will live always, have in their measure, each and all, this same subtle, mysterious, indescribable fascination. The world's book of wisdom is a book in which personal characteristics look out at us from every page.

Even in the most ordinary and common affairs of life

we recognize the importance which invariably belongs to manner. We credit or discredit the assertion of a man often for no other reason than the way in which he makes it. The tone, the look, the gesture, the whole attitude—these are the things which, more or less unconsciously perhaps, we mainly rely on. There is a certain ring about truth, and the way in which one will speak it, which distinguishes it almost unmistakably from falsehood. One good, searching look into a stranger's eyes is generally worth more to us, as far as an impression of trustworthiness is concerned, than any amount of second-hand, hearsay evidence as to his character.

Now, just what manner is, in all these various ways, it was and is in the doctrine of Christ. There was something in the way in which He asserted His authority which constrained others to recognize it. There was an atmosphere about Him which you could not enter without feeling it. It is quite conceivable that this impression had sometimes little if anything to do with the substance of His teaching. We read, for instance, that on one occasion the Pharisees sent out certain officers to effect His arrest. It is not likely that these officers were at all favorably disposed, or that they had often seen or heard Him before. Nor going now upon such a commission would they be likely to appreciate all the deep significance of His words; but in a general way they were profoundly impressed nevertheless. They returned without their prisoner, and the only explanation they could give of the matter was, that "Never man spake like this man." They had felt the spell of His manner, and that was enough. And what happened on this occasion may illustrate the impression produced as to Christ's authoritative character upon all. His clear, strong, persistent self-assertion could not, in itself, have led to this. Others have been self-assertive enough, but have only provoked thereby the equally persistent denial of men. His claims, indeed, are so unprecedented that they do not admit of any thing of self-deception. We must either account Him an impostor or account Him divine; but the unprecedented character of those claims does not in itself determine which side we shall take in the alternative. It is the manner of Christ, His tone, His attitude, the subtle and mysterious influence of His character, that goes such a long way in the demonstration of those claims and the vindication of His authority.

Now this manner is distinguished first of all by an ineffable calm. It has about it the halo of perfect, unclouded serenity. The Sermon on the Mount opens and continues and closes with measured movement and in solemn state. The sentences rise and fall uninterruptedly in the recurring cadence. The emphatic repetitions, "I say unto you," those assertions of personal authority, are as calm and serene as all the rest. Even when superseding various regulations of the law, and setting His own authority above it, Christ's speech has the same unruffled repose. There is in it no excitement, no discomposure, nothing of that overstrained emphasis and vehement reiterated asseveration which makes us suspect a speaker of being conscious in his own mind of the vulnerability of his position, or at least of the insufficient, inconclusive evidence that he can adduce in its behalf. Christ asserts His authority as quietly and simply as though that authority could be neither questioned nor gainsaid, or, if questioned or gainsaid, had in reserve for its own vindication some overwhelming and incontrovertible testimony. He has the repose and calm which belong only to the absolute truth ; and we are disposed, therefore, to credit Him with the possession of that truth. He seems to us to teach as one having authority ; because, among other things, we believe that without authority it would have been impossible for Him to teach in the serene, ineffable way in which He did.

Nor can this calm serenity of self-assertion be associated in the remotest way with any suggestion of arrogance. It stands at the very antipodes of that. Sometimes there is a quiet assumption, a complacent self-assurance, which mimics the serenity of indisputable authority. But every one who reads them will confess the singularly tender, nay, even pathetic gentleness of Christ's words. While asserting to the utmost the authoritative character of His mission, He once and again disclaims all thought of exalting Himself. "I seek not mine own glory," He says ; "if I honor myself, my honor is nothing." And with a seemingly beautiful—but nevertheless only seeming—inconsistency, He invites us to submit to His authority on the very ground of this inherent humility of nature—" Take my yoke upon you, and learn of me ; for I am meek and lowly in heart."

Christ's manner, again, was distinguished not only by the singular calmness and humility of it, but by the impression of certainty in respect to its own convictions which it produced upon every listener and beholder. The Master seems always absolutely sure of Himself. Neither in this discourse nor in any other do you ever come upon any trace of doubt, hesitancy, irresolution. We see Him in the Gospels walking in His solemn, heavenward way with a step that never falters. It is so at the opening of His ministry; it is so also at its close. There is no moment between the two that betrays any hint of indecision. Always it is the same assured, incomparable, yet meek and lowly, self-confidence. His words, He says, "shall never pass away," and against the work which He has wrought "the gates of hell shall not prevail." In a world of doubt and uncertainty, He moves as the only one in whose heart doubt and uncertainty have no place and cannot enter. In this respect He stands apart—a character solitary and unique in human history. There is absolutely no one with whom we can compare Him. Since His day there arose in the East one who claimed to be a prophet, and whose claim, though repudiated by us, is recognized, it is said, by a hundred million of believers. But if we contrast the lives of Christ and Mohammed, what an unspeakable difference, in this single reference, is revealed between the two! One who writes of the Koran enthusiastically enough to make us suspect him almost of a partial discipleship, points out as the very charm of the book the rapid, sudden transitions of feeling. "There rings through what may fairly be considered some of the very last revelations, ever and anon, the old wild cry of doubt and despair, or the sermon turns abruptly into a glowing vision, or a curse, fiery and yelling as any of the hottest days, is hurled upon some unbeliever's head." It is needless to say that there is no such charm in the gospel of Christ. There are no lightning-like transitions, no wild, occasional outbursts of doubt and despair there. Yet everywhere else, even in our own Bible, we may meet with them. We come upon them not only once or twice or thrice, but again and again in the words and deeds of Moses, Samuel, Elijah, and Isaiah. The Baptist, than whom there was no greater prophet among woman born, comes in his imprisonment to doubt the actual presence of that kingdom of heaven which he had before so confidently proclaimed. And even St. Paul, whose name in the history of Christianity is second only to that of his Master, betrays sometimes that uncertainty which is inseparable from the vision that sees through a glass darkly, and the mind that knows now only in part, not as yet as it is known. No; in the sureness which never falters, Christ stands absolutely and unapproachably alone. And this, I think, beyond all other things, is the secret of our unlimited confidence in Him, our irresistible conviction of His authority. We feel that here, and that here only, we plant our feet upon the rock. We put our hand in His as the one and only guide that we have heard or known or read of, whose calm, unalterable confidence in Himself can inspire the same confidence in others. In the midst of deadly peril, sometimes, when all hearts are failing for very fear, men turn with new hope and reassurance to some leader whose collected mien, unclouded gaze, and clear, decisive utterance, constrain them into sudden, mysterious submission and trust. And we in like manner, amid the oscillation and uncertainty of all other men and things, turn with joy and peace unutterable to that one form which stands out so grandly calm before us, that one voice which rings as no other rings upon our ear, "Though heaven and earth pass away, no jot or tittle of my word shall fail."

III. The authoritative character of the Sermon on the Mount was due, in the third place, to the substance of it, and here we return again and limit ourselves exclusively to this discourse. Christ appealed to man's religious intuitions, to his verifying power, to the witness which he has within himself. He called into exercise that faculty which when it does respond to truth responds authoritatively. The burden of the scribes' teaching, on the contrary, was in the very nature of things incapable of any such verification; it did not meet, and it could not meet, with any such necessary authoritative response. His maxims, rules, regulations, precepts, might be enforced by learning, argument, and churchly tradition, but after all these had been brought into requisition they might remain open to controversy and be doubtful still. Learning is a double-edged weapon, and more than that, its testimony with the majority of men must practically go for naught. No argumentation can be absolutely demonstrative. And as for churchly tradition, we are ready enough upon occasion to question the validity of that. All this is, as it were, outside of a man; it may silence him, but it does not necessarily convince. Nay, such convictions as it does enforce, are not the convictions of our whole nature. They are only the opinions of the intellect, conclusions which we have reached in various ways, positions to which we may zealously enough commit ourselves, but which may and do sometimes fall absolutely away from us. Stronger argument or additional testimony or more weighty authority may lead us to modify or repudiate them. All teaching, therefore, which in the very nature of things is incapable of a man's own verification, cannot be, in his recognition at least, in the highest sense of the word authoritative. For, no matter what the authority may be, as long as there is no inner witness to it, it cannot amount to an irresistible, overwhelming conviction. Were an angel from heaven to testify to us of the binding force of certain rules and regulations, or the truth of certain dogmatic propositions, we are so constituted that it would be, and it could be, only outside testimony after all. It would be indeed authoritative, but not authoritative in the deepest sense in which we are open to the impression of authority. There is a distinction here which it is well not to lose sight of. The non-concurrence of our private judgment can never of itself invalidate a legitimate authority, but neither can that authority without it be to us all of which we are capable. And therefore it is that all speculative systems of doctrine, all the traditionary and expository lore of the scribe, can never impose upon us that conviction which admits of no dispute. Human authority in whatever shape it comes, however venerable and sacred, is necessarily subject to doubt and limitation. The strongest chain of testimony we may suspect has a missing link somewhere, and should it prove to be so, the whole is comparatively worthless. The world has never seen an organization so marvellously adapted to impress its members with the conviction of its authority as the Roman Catholic Church, and yet no intelligent Romanist believes, except in a transcendental sense, in the dogma of the infallibility. That only is literally and truly infallible to us which constrains us into its recognition, and makes the outside voice find an echo in our own. For there is an intuitive faculty within us, a moral and religious sense, which, though it may not be able to discover truth, can nevertheless bear witness to it when it is revealed. And this witness within its own sphere is absolutely authoritative, and compels the assent of our whole nature. It is to this that Christ makes His first and last and reiterated appeal. For they who are of the truth, He says, will hear His voice. And in this Sermon on the Mount, from beginning to end, He deals only with eternal and universal principles—principles which come within the sphere of this verifying power within us. His teaching, therefore, in this discourse at least, we recognize at once as absolutely authoritative. When Christ says, "Blessed are the poor in spirit: for theirs is the kingdom of heaven; blessed are the pure in heart: for they shall see God; blessed are the merciful: for they shall obtain mercy;" do we need any additional testimony to confirm to us the reality of these beatitudes? Were there twelve legions of angels in the skies to re-echo them, could the conviction of the words go deeper? The truth speaks, and if we are of the truth we cannot help but hear the voice and answer it. And so, again, when He passes to the characterization of sin, and affirms that the violation of the commandment is not only in the letter, but also in the spirit, is there any one who doubts the guiltiness of intention—the adultery of the heart? Or when He would enforce upon us the obligation of returning good for evil, and says in the way of illustration, "Your heavenly Father sendeth His rain upon the just and upon the unjust," are we not constrained, whether we will or no, to assent? To all these principles of the Sermon on the Mount the answering witness within us bears its own conclusive testimony. They seem to us now self-evident, indisputable propositions, and our chief wonder is, that no voice was found to gather them together and enunciate them before. To Him, therefore, who did enunciate them, to Him who in their utterance draws unto Himself the conviction of our whole nature, we turn; and, as often as we listen to His words, confess the absolute, indisputable, transcendent character of His authority.

It was said of those who first heard the Sermon on the Mount that "they were astonished at the Master's doctrine, for He taught them as one having authority, and not as the scribes." We, too, one and all, will be content probably to have the same account given of us. For if the principles of this divine discourse do not seem so authoritative, it must be either because we are radically, hopelessly vicious, or because our moral sense is so imperfectly developed that we constitute an unenviable exception among men. Let it be taken for granted, then, that this Sermon on the Mount, in the admission of all, is confessedly authoritative. What follows from that admission? Are we to contrast it, as is sometimes done, with the other discourses of the Master to their disadvantage? Are we to pick it out, and dilate upon it, as if it were the only intelligible and satisfactory portion of the Gospel? Are we to point to it and say: " This is the sum and substance of my religion ; what lies beyond in the New Testament pages I accept with many grains of allowance"? Are we, in short, to confess Christ to be authoritative here and deny Him to be authoritative elsewhere? Yet this is the curious inconsistency of many who in various fashion call themselves by His name. The Sermon on the Mount, that is well enough—we all agree on that—but there are infinite disputings beyond. It is indeed true that when we pass on from this discourse, the teaching of the Master becomes mystical and deeper, and takes us, at first sight at least, beyond the sphere of the verifying witness within us. But was not that to be expected, or could it be otherwise unless the human were commensurate with the divine? Should not our Lord's opening words, instead of being contrasted in this invidious way with the others, be taken to be confirmatory of all? From the confessedly authoritative character of the Sermon on the Mount, the plain inference is, that all Christ's teaching is equally authoritative. That discourse, as we have said, was in some sort the Master's inaugural. The substance of it was, and was intended to be, within the scope and apprehension of all; within the jurisdiction of the verifying power of the human spirit. It was to furnish a common ground, a common starting point, a common pledge and assurance for Christ's disciples. They were to follow Him wherever He might lead, and trust implicitly to His authority, on the strength of the convictions which had taken possession of them at the mount. There might be much that they would not at first understand; much that might fail at first to call out an answering response and enlist all the sympathy of their nature. But here, in the way of reassurance, at the very outset of their discipleship, were words which they recognized as indisputably authoritative. They might trust the Master then on the basis of His inaugural discourse. As Nicodemus said of His works: "Rabbi, no man can do these miracles which thou doest, except God be with him," so might His disciples say of His words, "No man can speak these things which thou speakest, except he be from God."

The Sermon on the Mount, if we rightfully consider it, has great, the very greatest, evidential force. It is confirmatory of our Lord's whole mission—a kind of demonstration in advance of every claim that He puts forth. We speak sometimes of the unsatisfactory character of miracles as corroborative evidence, and complain that no amount of traditionary testimony can counterbalance the fact that these miracles do not come within our own personal observation and ken. But here in this inaugural is a moral miracle—something which our own ears hear and our own eyes see. We cannot escape from the conviction of its authority. There is something in us, each and all, which necessarily, inevitably responds to that. May we not believe that as we follow the Master humbly, reverently, trustfully, into the deeper mysteries of His teaching, the same response will not finally be wanting? Doubtless we shall come upon some hard sayings; doubtless we shall be tempted sometimes, like others before us, to turn back and walk no more with Him; doubtless He forewarns us, as He forewarned His first disciples, "I have many things to say unto you, but ye cannot bear them now." But may we not believe that of these hidden things, no less than of the things which are already open, we shall have, each man, as we go on in faith and patience, the witness in himself?

VI.

THE INCREDULITY OF GAIN.

[KINGSBRIDGE, 1868.]

"If they hear not Moses and the prophets, neither will they be persuaded, though one rose from the dead."—ST. LUKE xvi. 31.

THIS saying of the Master is among the most memorable and significant of His ever memorable words. It enunciates, in the terse brevity of a single sentence, that hopeless incredulity of unbelief which is due not to unfavorable circumstances, but to moral defects of character. It declares, in the most striking and emphatic way, that no miracle, no evidence that can be named or asked for, will bring conviction to a man whose heart and mind are not open to conviction. It has passed into a principle of general and universal application. There is nothing now more widely recognized among Christian apologists than this: that it is useless to multiply demonstrations of truth to those whose perverted will and affections will not admit of its reception. St. Paul, in another connection and in equally startling words, asserts substantially the same thing. "If our gospel be hid," he says, "it is hid to them that are lost." Philosophical difficulties may be overcome, the scepticism which is purely intellectual may yield to additional evidence and accumulated proofs, it may be able to see and recognize the truth from another point of view or in a more comprehensive presentment, but the unbelief which comes from an evil life and evil dispositions is simply invincible. By no argumentation or testimony can you make one believe what he does not wish to believe, or bring him to the realization of facts from which his gaze is persistently averted. Thus the moral condition invariably determines the capacity of faith. Those only can see and hear who have the eye to see and the ear to hear. But neither of these can we have, on the contrary we must continue in a moral and spiritual sense both deaf and blind, so long as the heart and the conscience are not right. To believe in truth, we must be true; in purity, pure; in integrity, honest and sincere. Thus the believer in the implication of St. John has the witness of his faith not so much without as within himself. Our Lord tells us that if we "do the will" we shall "know the doctrine;" that if we regulate our lives and desires in accordance with God's commandments our minds will come in time, however slowly, yet surely, to the apprehension of God's truth. And again, in the reverse statement of this proposition, He declares that the moral obliquity, the evil and perverse condition of a man's nature, which will not be convinced by sufficient evidence, neither will nor can be convinced by men. "If they hear not Moses and the prophets, neither will they be persuaded, though one rose from the dead."

But while the saying of the Master legitimately admits of this general and universal application, it had in the first instance a more particular and special one. Its immediate reference was not so much to speculative unbelief, to the scepticism which touches the eternal verities of the faith, as to that practical unbelief which consists in a failure to realize in one's life and conduct principles whose truth is nevertheless conceded. The religion of a man, as far as profession goes, may be theoretically irreproachable, but in his daily walk among men he may be guilty of practical infidelity to each and all of its precepts. If we fail to live out the influences and consequences of our creeds, then no matter how often and solemnly we may repeat them, as far as any use or worth is concerned, we might as well have no creeds at all. If, while giving to religion an intellectual acceptance, while admitting its heaven and hell hereafter, its better and its worse estate, we still take no heed of its commandments, its moralities, its charities ourselves, or sneer at and deride those who do, be sure our real condition is one of sheer and hopeless scepticism. And out of that virtual, practical atheism there is no spell in heaven above or earth beneath to raise us. If there is nothing in the present circumstances of our life, or in the opportunities which we have enjoyed, to make us realize our duty, then most likely in no circumstances and in no opportunities shall we find anything that will. If the Providence of the past has not guided us to better thoughts and ways, we need not count with any confidence upon a more constraining guidance for the future. If the words of truth and soberness have not availed already, then it is more than probable that neither they nor any other words ever will avail. If we "hear not Moses and the prophets," if their warnings and exhortations do not lead us to repentance, to a change of mind and heart and life, then in all likelihood neither shall we repent, however marvellous the sign or significant the miracle displayed. If the monitors which God has given us, His common and familiar oracles, cannot win us to a life noble, holy, charitable, and unselfish, then neither will we be persuaded by any prodigy or portent, any extraordinary and unprecedented occurrence; no, even though it were a message from the grave and a resurrection from the dead.

The statement which sets forth so strongly the inveterate obduracy of man's heart, the invincible character of that incredulity which comes from the moral perversion of his will, occurs at the conclusion of the parable of the rich man and Lazarus. It is the point or moral of that parable, the startling truth which it was intended to enforce and illustrate. We shall appreciate its practical significance best from a brief consideration of the circumstances which were the immediate occasion of its utterance.

Somewhat earlier in the same discourse, our Lord had been urging upon those about Him the duty of a faithful use and administration of worldly wealth. His exhortation on that occasion had taken the form of an appeal to man's higher self-love and self-interest. The motives He advanced were purely rational and prudential. He sought to show that charity, liberality, philanthropy was, to say nothing more, a wise and provident thing; that the dedication of wealth or a portion of it to God's service, the employment of it in works of mercy and beneficence to others, would be found at last to have been in reality a future provision for one's self. He maintained that the shrewdness and forethought of worldly men in their ordinary and sometimes disreputable transactions, the energy, prudence, and sagacity displayed by them in securing their temporal well-being, should admonish "the children of light" to be at least equally wise in heavenly things; should lead those who believe in the future to live for the future; to lay up some treasure there; to make that investment of money, time, and service here which shall yield a sure and large return hereafter. As a practical enforcement and illustration of His meaning He tells them the story of an "unjust steward" who, finding himself about to be turned out of his stewardship, contrives so to use his brief interval of authority as to make his lord's debtors, on his expulsion, receive him into their own houses; and, bidding them imitate the one point in the steward's character which alone was worthy of imitation, namely, his prudence, He exhorts them to make with their wealth friends who shall receive them after death into everlasting habitations. He concludes the whole subject with the assertion that the services of God and mammon— the religious life, and the life whose god is money, whose idolatry of gold consists either in a selfish hoarding or an equally selfish expenditure — are simply and absolutely incompatible.

How the majority of those who heard these exhortations received them, we are not told. Probably with much of the same mixed feeling with which a Christian congregation listens to their repetition now. A few, possibly, went away to act upon these precepts, resolved henceforth to be wiser in their generation. Many, doubtless, assented, yet hesitated with more or less reluctance to reduce their assent to practice. It is a curious fact that even those of us who are accustomed to depreciate the temporal and magnify the eternal can be stirred to enthusiasm on any other subject sooner than on this. In other matters we are not always wary, and one may take us in an unguarded hour. We can be brought, heavy and mundane as we so often are, to applaud a "counsel of perfection" to the echo. We can be entranced by love, enamoured of holiness, carried away and lifted above ourselves by the portraiture of a life unselfishly consecrated and devoted to the service of humanity. No grace so fair, nor virtue so heroic, that in our hearts its aspiration may not be kindled But the argument that touches the pocket forthwith excites caution, uneasiness, distrust. At once we descend to earth again with all our faculties alert and ready. It must be a faultless logic and an incisive rhetoric that can reach us there. In practical experience it is found to be easier to part with almost anything than it is to part with money. The faith that can face martyrdom comes sometimes before the faith that can face the depletion of its exchequer. The commandments we can keep; the one thing lacking yet, the distribution out of our abundance to every good work, often remains lacking to the very end. Many a man is capable of fanaticism in a cause, who is nevertheless incapable of liberality towards it. It has always been so, it will always be so. To keep all we've got and get all we can, seems to be the first and most inveterate instinct of human nature. The majority of those who heard Christ probably illustrated anew His charge of inconsistency by acquiescing in all He said, recognizing the wisdom and prudence of His counsels, and yet, while looking on to the better life hereafter, continuing as of old to make only scant and reluctant provision for it, sending on before the fewest possible "friends" that might suffice to "receive them into everlasting habitations."

But there were some who by no means approved of the Master's teaching in this reference, who repudiated His counsels, and refused even a silent acquiescence in His precepts. On the contrary, they received this doctrine of "investments for the future" with incredulity; they met His illustration of it with a sneer; they replied to His warning against mammon worship, the idolatry of wealth, with scorn and derision. The evangelist sets their position and character before us in a single phrase when he says that "The Pharisees, who were covetous, also heard all these things, and they derided Him." Singularly enough, the very class which might naturally have been supposed the most ready to follow out and enforce His injunctions was that which alone repudiated them with contempt. For these Pharisees confessedly comprised the chief moral and religious elements in the community. They held to the doctrine of the resurrection, and believed in retribution—a system of rewards and punishments hereafter. They advocated and observed the obligation of tithes, and were ostentatious even in the distribution of alms. But the one sin which went far to neutralize their religious faith, to make it a mere doctrine, and not an actual, practical life, is found in the fact that as a rule and as a class they were " covetous." The greed of gain, which was fast eating into the vitals of the nation, had in them its worst manifestation—all the worse because its true character was in a manner hidden from themselves and others by manifold hypocrisies. In witness of the real covetousness of their character, it is only necessary to refer to our Lord's subsequent denunciation of them for " laying burdens upon men which they themselves would not touch with one of their fingers; for devouring widows' houses, and for a pretence making long prayers." Thus their ostentatious alms-giving in one direction found an ample compensation in avaricious and discreditable acquirements in another. True charity or liberality they had not. They were essentially mammon worshippers, devotees and idolaters of gold. Thus their actual religion in any practical reference differed widely indeed from their speculative faith. The hard materialism of their character made them intrinsically earthy and of the earth. They knew well, none knew better, the value and omnipotence of wealth. They were quite convinced of the superior worth of " a bird in the hand " over " two in the bush." They were not in the least disposed to emulate the thorough-going measures of the " unjust steward " as applied to eternal things. It is not at all difficult to understand with what disgust they would hearken to the counsel to part with money and lands here in order to secure for themselves "friends" and "heavenly habitations" hereafter; or with what scornful incredulity they would receive the assertion that it is impossible to reconcile the services of God and mammon, to live for this world and to live for the next, or even to strike a safe balance somewhere between the two. To their strong, earthly common sense, with its tenacious grasp on the visible and the temporal, doubtless Christ seemed a mere visionary, a fanatic, who had no sufficient authority either in reason or revelation for the exhortations and warnings in which He was so freely indulging. Volumes could not tell us more of their contemptuous rejection of Him and His impracticable precepts than is found in the simple statement that "the Pharisees derided Him."

But Christ had an answer to that derision. They thought His counsel visionary and illusive, a thing to mock at; and for reply to that they shall behold, as in a mirror, their own moral perverseness, their own fatal incredulity, the dulled ear, the closed eye, the hardened heart, that will not let them feel, nor see, nor hear. Hitherto He had addressed the multitude in general, now He directs His discourse exclusively to them. "Ye are they which justify yourselves before men, but God knoweth your hearts; for that which is highly esteemed among men is abomination in the sight of God." Once again He clothes his speech in parables. He will tell them of one who neglected to make "provision" for the future, who "laid up" no "treasure" there, who sent before him no "friends" who should receive him into a heavenly habitation. "There was a certain rich man, which was clothed in purple and fine linen, and fared sumptuously every day: and there was a certain beggar named Lazarus, which was laid at his gate, full of sores, and desiring to be fed with the crumbs which fell from the rich man's table. And it came to pass, that the beggar died, and was carried by the angels into Abraham's bosom: the rich man also died, and was buried; and in hell he lifted up his eyes, being in torments, and seeth Abraham afar off, and Lazarus in his bosom." There is nothing said, you observe, of the depravity of the rich man, no crime or iniquity is laid to his charge; the whole implication of the story is that his perdition was due simply to his neglect to make with his wealth "a friend" of the beggar at his gate. Convinced at last of his own fatal improvidence, the result of his wilful incredulity, and realizing, too, the hopelessness of his condition, his thought now is for his "brethren." He is anxious that they should be warned in some extraordinary and unprecedented way; that some further evidence and confirmation of the truth should be given to them than had been vouchsafed to him. "I pray, thee, therefore, father Abraham, that thou wouldest send Lazarus to my father's house: for I have five brethren; that he may testify unto them, lest they also come into this place of torment. Abraham saith unto him, They have Moses and the prophets; let them hear them. And he said, Nay, father Abraham: but if one went unto them from the dead, they will repent. And he said unto them,

If they hear not Moses and the prophets, neither will they be persuaded, though one rose from the dead."

Thus the answer of Christ to the derision of the Pharisees was substantially this: " You set at naught and mock my words, you scorn and deride them, you think them visionary and fanatical, not because they are not sufficiently authenticated in your sacred books, the oracles which you profess to respect and acknowledge, not because they have not their witness both in reason and revelation, not because they are not in themselves entitled to belief, but because of the stubborn incredulity and inveterate covetousness of your own hearts; your scorn, your contempt, your derision, has its source and root there, and you will continue in your unbelief, you will still mock and deride me, no matter what proofs I might produce or what miracles I might display. You have not heard Moses and the prophets, you will not be persuaded though one rose from the dead."

This answer should bring to each and all of us, in the hurry and the rush of life, a pause of earnest consideration. It is the most emphatic declaration of which words are capable, that the duty which has not succeeded in commending itself to us in ordinary ways may, and in all probability will, never be commended—never, until it is too late. Conviction will not come, no matter how great the pressure that is brought to bear, if we stop our ears, and close our eyes, and steel our hearts against it. We must give every statement of truth and duty a fair and impartial hearing before it is safe to turn away. We must be sure we meet it with an unprejudiced mind, and a judgment not warped by mean passions or self-interest. It may be worth our while, therefore, to re-open many a question which for some of us, perhaps, has long been closed. The wisdom of liberality in its eternal reference, that is a theme for every man to think on. The impossibility of serving God acceptably and at the same time giving ourselves up to mammon-worship, a practical idolatry of gold, that is another subject for reflection. We will say nothing more of the duty or wisdom of liberality now, leaving it, however, with this single remark, that its vindication can be found only in its practice. Let us once begin to give, and we shall need no other argument for giving. Then perchance our eyes will be opened to many things which before were not dreamt of in our philosophy. Life will take on nobilities which before it knew not, and earth will borrow a beatitude from heaven. To be charitable is to be eternally wise. Its occasions meet us everywhere. We need not go far away. For often it will prove that the "friend" whose welcome and reception we shall need on high is none other than the ordinary beggar at the gate.

But this other consideration of mammon-worship, with its idolatry of gold, is not one to be dismissed merely with a word. We live in times in which, despite Christ and Moses and the prophets, it is well nigh impossible for any one to "hear" or "be persuaded." When the Master spoke, the greed of gain was already wanton in the land. The chief men of the nation, the most moral and religious, sad to tell, were the most covetous of all. Even then the Jewish traders were scattered up and down the whole length and breadth of the Mediterranean coasts, and gathered to themselves more and more the traffic and profit of the world. The influence was not slow to cast its baleful spell on all the people of Judæa. Sorry subjects they, for discourses against mammon. Yet it may be doubted whether either then or later, when their insatiate avarice became synonymous with their ancient and once honored name, they presented more unfavorable conditions for paying heed unto the warning than our own age and land afford. The centuries have not belittled, but dignified, nay, canonized, the pursuit of "the main chance." The democratic movement of the times, breaking down hereditary and other distinctions, has yet helped to enthrone one distinction over all, has made wealth more coveted and imperial. Riches now are the Ultima Thule of our desires, and he who gets the most is the best man and the greatest. They bring to their possessor dignity and honor, but to lose them is to fall lamentably in social consideration. Modern civilization, too, with its appliances and comforts, has made man's needs the greater, and assuredly the stimulus to gratify them not the less. We must be clothed, each and all, in purple and fine linen, and fare sumptuously every day. The Master's counsel, to take no thought, to be not over-anxious for the morrow, seems of all things an impracticable requirement. Poverty, or what we esteem as its equivalent, is the one thing to be dreaded. Many forms of suffering have been alleviated or removed, but now as of old the poor man goes always to the wall. What wonder, then, that we are wedded more and more unto our idols; that we bow down more and more before the golden calf? Were the denizen of another sphere to visit this, could he have a moment's doubt as to what the absorbing nature of our quest might be? Or, were the knowledge of the true God to pass away from earth once more, should we not change again the glory of the Incorruptible into an image of gold or silver graven by art and man's device, but building our temples and raising our statues not to Jupiter or Mars or Dionysius, but to almighty and universal Mammon? There is needed a poet to sing of the omnipotence of wealth; prose is all too common-place and tame. True, there are other judgments in the Bible, that antiquated book, but with our hard, stern materialism, they only seem to us like idle tales. We dispose of the authors of these sayings as visionaries, enthusiasts, fanatics—men who had no common sense. Such warnings, too, meet us in the churches; but the preacher, dimly conscious of his own practical inconsistency, is half-ashamed to speak them, and the pews account them among the stock platitudes, the harmless vaporings of the pulpit. Transcendentalisms about "heavenly habitations" with such-like ethereal abodes, and other castles in the air, may do for Sundays, but we have no time to amuse ourselves with such matters in the week. Then our concern is with brick and mortar, wood and stone, something real, something substantial, something that we can see. Treasure garnered up on high is all very well as a mere metaphor, but the treasure in which we are chiefly interested, the only treasure in fact that we believe in, must be in our own coffers or the bank. And the saddest thing of all is this: that there seems to be no influence anywhere, no possible evidence that can be named or asked for, that may avail to free us from the blindness that has come upon us. The man that died last night, what to him are his possessions now? Yet were he sent from the grave to testify unto us, who would believe his testimony? Who would cease to make a god of gold? Who would be convinced at last that unseen things alone are real and permanent, that the visible and the temporal are only fleeting and illusive? How much easier, rather, to disdain the superstition of ghosts, and to deride the vanity of dreams! But what need to argue more? Has not Christ died and risen again, and put the seal of His resurrection on the everlasting verity of His words? And yet in the fulfilment of His own prophecy, neither have we been nor will we be "persuaded."

Nevertheless the fact remains, "Ye cannot serve God and mammon." For the conviction of that we need no arguments, no evidences, no miracles, no proofs. Were they multiplied ten thousand fold, they would be utterly unavailing. The difficulty is with ourselves. The conclusion of the whole matter is in our own hearts. First take the beam out of thine eye, and then shalt thou see clearly. Let us once begin to serve God with something like zeal, earnestness, and unreserve, and then we shall not be long in realizing that no other service is compatible with His. Let us strive in all sincerity to be the children of our Father, and then the children of this world we cannot be. Let us consecrate ourselves to Him, not in words, not in professions, but in deed and truth; and then, as one by one our idols fall away, we shall see and know that there is none other God beside Him!

VII.

THE FEEDING OF THE FIVE THOUSAND.

[YORK, PA., 1877.]

"Then those men, when they had seen the miracle that Jesus did, said, This is of a truth that Prophet that should come into the world."—ST. JOHN vi. 14.

ONE of the most impressive of our Lord's miracles, so far as its effect upon the people was concerned, seems to have been His feeding of the five thousand. There are certain things about it which give it a kind of representative character, which make it the key to the right apprehension of the others; just as Jesus Himself says that the proper understanding of the parable of the sower is the necessary condition of the proper understanding of all parables. It may be interesting, therefore, as well as instructive, to consider the moral and spiritual significance of this miracle, and the various lessons which grow out of the several incidents connected with it.

Now, in regard to the Christian miracles, one general principle is this: They are distinguished from all pseudo miracles, whether ancient or modern, by their moral and spiritual content. In other words, they have an ethical and religious meaning which justifies them to man's heart and conscience. They are not primarily evidential; this is not their first and foremost aim—not, at least, in the sense in which the word "evidence" is commonly understood. In the very nature of the case they do acquire great evidential worth, but this follows as a consequence, almost as an incident; it does not express the purpose which informs them. They are not presented to us primarily in the character of proofs, evidences, credentials. If our Lord Himself ever seemingly consents to this view of them, it is a kind of weary concession to that grossness of heart, that slowness of understanding, which cannot recognize a divine word, but which may, perhaps, recognize a divine work. As simple marvels, mere signs and wonders—things which, if they accredit a teacher at all, accredit him quite irrespectively of the moral and spiritual character of his mission—this conception of His miracles Christ repudiates peremptorily and altogether. How strange that both the defenders and the assailants of the miraculous should have lingered so long in this unworthy misapprehension when the Master so often went out of his way, as it were, to disparage mere signs and wonders! And St. Paul has left on record his testimony, that even an angel from heaven, irrespective of the purport of his message, is not to be believed. The Christian miracles are mainly modes and methods of manifestation. They are the epiphany, the manifestation, the setting forth of Christ. Through them, as through some hieroglyphic, some larger kind of speech, He discloses, reveals Himself to the world. Assume

Him to have been what He claims to have been, and He must have embodied in some such acts His relation to and His work among men. Thus His miracles, in their primary significance, become, not so much evidences, proofs, credentials, as grand expressions and illustrations of His redemptive ministry.

Now, the feeding of the five thousand is a most felicitous and striking instance of this general principle. It had, as was said before, a singularly impressive effect upon the multitude. But its primary object was not the exhibition of supernatural power; it was not wrought by the Master with the direct intent of constraining, compelling men to believe in Him; its purpose was moral, religious, spiritual. It came as the supplement, the complement of something which had gone before. It was only another way of saying and doing over again what Jesus had but just now said and done. It was not a capricious, arbitrary display; the occasion demanded it as its moral consequence. The great, comforting truth which had been set forth, but which no words could adequately express, needed the larger exposition of its divine symbolism. Let us trace briefly its history.

All the evangelists tell us that the occasion was one on which Jesus had withdrawn for rest with His disciples into a comparatively desert place. The multitudes, assembled in the neighboring cities, according to the implication of St. John, by the approaching Passover, follow Him into His retirement. Whereupon Jesus comes forth to meet them, and seeing the "great company," according to Matthew and Mark, He is "moved with compassion toward them."

The sight of this large concourse of men and women and little children fills Him with divine pity. A great multitude may be to us a very grand or a very sad spectacle, according to the mood we are in, and the point of view from which we look at it. It may help us to realize our humanity in its collectiveness, its ideality, for the race is larger and greater than the individual; and then the sight becomes noble and inspiring—something which lifts us out of ourselves, and overpowers us with strange, uncontrollable emotion. Or we may abstract ourselves from the crowd, and look down upon it, and individualize it; we may tell over in our thought all the sorrows, miseries, and sins of the several units who compose it; we may realize how deceptive all this parade of life is, how brief a time before all these eyes will be closed and all these lips dumb, and then the spectacle is made a sad and touching one indeed. It seems to have been in this latter way that the Master regarded it. He is moved with compassion. He is filled with pity. St. Mark tells us why. Because "they were as sheep not having a shepherd." As Jesus lifts up His eyes and beholds this great company that had come to him, His first and controlling thought is their ignorant, benighted, uncared-for condition. They are blind, and have only blind leaders of the blind. Like the silly sheep themselves, they are liable at any moment to go headlong to destruction. They are the sport of circumstance—creatures of mere fitful, wayward, irregular impulse. Here are immortal souls with no one to minister to their divine needs. Jesus pities them, is moved with compassion toward them, yearns with tenderness over their condition of moral and spiritual destitution. They require a shepherd and have none. Now one of His most cherished conceptions of His own office, as we know, was that of the Good Shepherd, and therefore on this occasion He proceeds to fulfil it. If His pity leads Him, as in the parable, to seek and to save the one sheep that had gone astray, what compassionate solicitude will He not feel for many times the ninety and nine who have done likewise? He ministers to the spiritual hunger and thirst of these famishing human souls. St. Mark says, He began to teach them many things. We can imagine what these "many things" were; how the moral and spiritual truths of the gospel, which centuries have made familiar to us, were here first opened to them. We can imagine how the words of life were given them—words which, as the Master Himself says, are meat and drink indeed. But as the day wears on, the physical necessities of this multitude begin to be sadly apparent. They had come from far, had fasted long. The body no less than the soul needed pasturage, feeding—some attention of the Shepherd's providential care. He had ministered already to the greater need, He now ministers to the lesser one. It is to the physical necessities of this shepherdless flock that, with the closing day, He in turn addresses Himself. He takes the loaves and the fishes, and feeds the five thousand; that is, He completes, He supplements, the feeding of the spirit which had gone before, with this feeding of the body which now follows it. This is the moral and religious justification of the miracle. It is no wanton, capricious, arbitrary display of power. There is, on the contrary, as we see, a logical, moral, spiritual sequence in it. The occasion involved it by a kind of religious necessity. It became, and it was intended to be, the symbol, the expression, the manifestation of Christ in His relation of Shepherd to men.

But how differently was this manifestation received! How far and wide apart were the various effects produced by it! Those who witnessed it were made up of different grades of moral character, all degrees of religious sensibility. This act, like all Christ's acts, served to bring out their several characteristics into special prominence. The gospel was, is, and will always be a kind of moral touch-stone. It shows what men are; it makes each one known to himself and to others. In this instance it disclosed the little faith of some, the unworthy motives of others, the captious spirit of more, while yet it bore witness, and most reassuring witness, to the simple, honest, docile receptiveness of our common humanity.

1. It brought out, first, the slowness of apprehension, the "little faith," of the disciples. Jesus had manifested forth His glory to these same disciples at Cana of Galilee, in that beginning of miracles when they believed on Him. Subsequently on several occasions He had done the same. Even at this very time and place, according to Matthew's and Luke's accounts, he had healed some of this multitude of their infirmities. Yet the disciples are slow to see in the present instance any call or appropriateness for the exercise of Christ's power; slower still to

believe in any power until after it has again been manifested before them. In order to lead them to this apprehension the Lord Himself puts a suggestive question to one of them: "Whence shall we buy bread that these may eat?" It has been suggested that Philip is selected here because his spiritual apprehension was especially slow, as appears elsewhere in his questioning about the Father. The inquiry, we are told, was put to prove him. Will he rise to its requirement? Will he see what the Good Shepherd can and will do? No! with him the true order and relation of things is hopelessly inverted. It is nothing, no manifestation of divine power, to feed famishing souls; to feed famishing bodies, that indeed would be divine, too divine even for his divine Master. The thought of it does not even occur to him. He is busy telling over in his mind what large supplies of bread it would take. He answers: "Two hundred pennyworth is not sufficient for them." Just then Andrew, another disciple, coming up, has nothing better to say. He turns, indeed, to the boy with his five barley loaves and two small fishes, but asks: "What are these among so many?" Later on all the disciples advise Jesus to send the multitude away. His answer is: "Give ye them to eat." It was a second suggestion that there might be a power of giving which they did not realize. But like the former one it goes unheeded. They only reëcho Philip's words. They cannot be made to share by anticipation in the Master's conviction and experience that "man doth not live by bread alone, but by every word that proceedeth out of the mouth of God doth man live." And so only a little while afterward they are affrighted on the sea because, as Mark says, they considered not the miracle of the loaves and the fishes. They failed in this consideration to the very end, and it was not until after the Holy Ghost was given them that their faith became equal to the demands upon it. And so it seems to be with disciples always. Our trouble is the dull heart, the slow apprehension, the little faith. We do not "remember the years of the right hand of the Most High." We do not consider the providence which has its witness in our past experience. We fail to apprehend our Lord's meaning in the questions which our circumstances, our work in the world, our obligations and duties are continually putting to us. We miss the divine purpose in the emergencies, the exigencies, which from time to time confront us. Least of all do we suspect that they are opportunities of faith—occasions for the exercise of spiritual power. It is so with the Church; it is so with the individual believer. Missions, charities, social reformations, all the various forms of Christian enterprise —these things languish or fail chiefly because we, the disciples, cannot seem to get rid of the idea that man lives and must live by bread alone. We turn instinctively to secondary causes. We devise ways and means, but all our devising is of the earth, earthy. Our whole dependence is there. When that fails, we recognize no obligation to go forward. We forget Israel and the Red Sea waves, the widow and her meal and oil, the barley loaves and the five thousand. Yet faith is always the true conqueror. It, and it alone, is invincible. The mountains themselves are removed before it. From it have come all the triumphs of the past; from it must come all the triumphs of the future. When our faith is what faith should be, then will the Lord's word be fulfilled, and we shall indeed ourselves do even "greater works than these."

2. The second lesson is a very humiliating one; for the only effect of the miracle on some who witnessed it, or heard of it, was to give them an unworthy motive for attaching themselves to Christ. Instead of exaltation of thought and feeling, it brought them small and pitiful considerations. Thus the grandest revelations are often lost, the noblest lessons perverted and degraded. Men again and again miss the significance of a great act or a great utterance, and seize upon some mean, selfish use to which they can apply it. They did so now. For the next day, it seems, some of this multitude followed and sought out Jesus at Capernaum. Why? With any wish for further instruction, any desire to hear somewhat more of the many things which He had taught them, or to tender Him an allegiance that honored Him, and such as He might accept? No! with neither and none of these; for He meets them with the rebuke: "Ye seek me because ye did eat of the loaves, and were filled;" and adds the solemn admonition: "Labor not for the meat which perisheth, but for that meat which endureth unto everlasting life." It is almost incredible that these men should have missed all the moral and spiritual meaning of the late scene in the wilderness, and have followed Christ only for such an unworthy end as this. Yet so it was. We

can understand now why they had even designed on the day before, as John tells us, to "take Him by force, and make Him a king" over them. Their idea of a king was a king who should feed them gratuitously. In the same way and for the same reason they were ready to hail Him as Messiah, just as the Roman populace was ready to hail as Cæsar any one who gave them circus-shows and bread. But Jesus will have no such royalty; He will accept no such homage; He will tolerate no such following. Let us remember this. For we, too, may be tempted to attach ourselves to Him from unworthy motives—motives which He will reject. There is such a thing, you know, as religion on false pretences. Social considerations have a good deal to do with some people's piety. The constraint of respectability sends no inconsiderable number to church. Others show outward deference to Christianity because they consider it useful, a kind of conservative force, a good thing to have in the community. A superstitious man may be led to call himself by the name of Christ as a sort of religious insurance against adversity, or as a provision in the hour of it. We all of us may be too much inclined to say with Peter: "We have followed Thee, what shall we have therefore?" Prudential considerations for our supposed interests here or hereafter may be, unwittingly, our chief motive in seeking Him. Let us realize, then, that all these motives simply in and by themselves are unworthy. They must bring upon us the Lord's rebuke and admonishment. They are not the stuff out of which true adherents are made.

3. A third class seem to have made this miracle not a help to faith, but an occasion of offence. They too met Him the next day at Capernaum, not to recognize His claims, but to question and discredit them. They furnish us with a notable instance of that curious mixture of superstition and rationalism which has found so many illustrations in our own age. Extremes meet, and the man who believes everything and the man who believes nothing are often only reverse sides of the same character. They may pass into each other without any shock or even consciousness of inconsistency. This third class appears to have been of that order of mind which, on the superstitious side, is always seeking after signs, and on the rationalistic is always demanding some sensible proof or logical demonstration, before it will believe. It is a habit of mind which, in both aspects of it, the Lord rebukes and will not encourage. He will not pervert and degrade His divine power in the exhibition of signs, nor will He appeal chiefly to the formal logic of the understanding, rather than to the verifying faculty of the human spirit. He will not, because in either case it would be wrong; it would be the substitution of an inferior, and, therefore, an unworthy kind of evidence for a higher and nobler one. The substitution, moreover, would do no good. For though He will give no sign in answer to the demand for it, yet, in the course of His manifestation of Himself, the sign comes. But what use do these men, and such as these, make of it? They turn it into an objection, and disparage it. They contrast to its disadvantage the feeding of five

thousand with what seem to them the still more wonderful works of Moses. "Our fathers," they say, "did eat manna in the desert: as it is written, He gave them bread from heaven to eat." According to them, Jesus at the most had only fed a multitude with a few loaves and fishes, but Moses had fed a nation with nothing; he had given them bread from heaven. If Christ expects to win their recognition He must do something to equal or surpass that. And so they say again, "What sign showest thou? What dost thou work?" And this is the outcome of the over-credulous or over-sceptical process always. Even the required evidence, when given, becomes to the perverted mind a hindrance, not a help. In the very nature of the case, one sign or demonstration needs another to confirm it, and so on continually. It is not wisdom, but folly, to turn from the moral and spiritual verification—the witness in one's self—and demand a kind of proof which is inconsistent with God's order and ways. For the proof we crave, the proof which we imagine would be so satisfactory, so conclusive, even were it given, would not avail. The superstitious or captious mind would soon see reason to disparage, to decry it, to proclaim its insufficiency. Once enter on that path, and you find no end in wandering mazes lost. You become only another illustration of the Master's law: "If they hear not Moses and the prophets, neither will they be persuaded, though one rose from the dead."

4. It would be sad, indeed, if the general effect of this miracle had no more positive or hopeful lesson;

sad, indeed, if its only moral were the little faith of the disciples, or the unworthy motives of selfish followers, or the persistent scepticism of captious opponents. Classes of men, individuals, may fail us; they are often utterly disappointing, but humanity as a whole is true to itself, and always presents to us something to reverence and believe in. Let that be our consolation. It was so with the multitude on this occasion. The selfish men, the clever men, the superstitious men were not satisfied, but the people were. The great heart of that assemblage responded to the manifestation of the Christ which had been given it. It did not miss, but apprehended at once and intuitively, the moral and spiritual significance of the miracle. However it might be with others, the people were open to its special revelation and disclosure. It made known to them the Shepherd whom they needed, the Teacher who should feed their souls. St. John says: " Then those men, when they had seen the miracle which Jesus did, said, This is of a truth that Prophet that should come into the world."

Let our reassurance be here—a reassurance which we cannot find even in the disciples. Let us rejoice in, and reverence, and bow down before the general receptiveness, the simple, open, ingenuous heart of our great collective humanity—that humanity which is in God, and answers to every revelation of Himself; which is guided and inspired by Him; which is of the truth, and, therefore, hears the truth's voice. Christ may be rejected by our culture, our philosophy, our science, our superstitions, our religions even. Yet, in the true conception of them, all these classes are only fragments— mere mobs of the passing hour—in and by themselves they are nothing. The ideal man is not of them nor is he in them. He is in the great collective organic life of the race—that humanity which knows no respect of persons, no separate classes, no individual men. And of this humanity, as through the ages past, so through the ages on, the Christ will be accepted. He is come, and " unto Him shall the gathering of the people be!"

VIII.

THE UNJUST STEWARD.

[KINGSBRIDGE, 1868.]

"And the lord commended the unjust steward, because he had done wisely: for the children of this world are in their generation wiser than the children of light. And I say unto you, Make to yourselves friends of the mammon of unrighteousness: that, when ye fail, they may receive you into everlasting habitations."—ST. LUKE xvi. 8, 9.

THE parable which is known by the title of "the unjust steward" seems to stand alone in the Gospels in the peculiarity of its construction, and the apparently doubtful character of its moral. In the interpretation of other parables there are many differences in point of detail, but here the dispute touches the significance of the main body of the illustration itself. So widely have commentators differed both as to the substance and the incidents of this story, that scarcely any two agree in either reference, while the various explanations that have been attempted are so numerous as to hinder rather than help one towards a satisfactory appreciation of its meaning. The general reader either carries away with him only a vague and confused sense of its significance, or, if he stop to give it closer examination, is surprised to find his investigation result in still greater perplexity. Under these circumstances it would be presumptuous to advocate over-confidently any particular theory, and I simply propose, in the brief comment that I shall make, to put those of you who may not be already familiar with it in possession of that interpretation which commends itself most to my own mind, and which seems to have in its support some of the best critical authority.

Though it cannot be called a peculiarity of this parable, it is certainly most emphatically true in respect to it, that the more closely we fix our attention upon the *details*, the *incidentals*, the mere *accidents* of the story, the more apt are we to be entangled and bewildered by them, and consequently lose our hold upon its *aim* and *drift*. In this, doubtless, is to be found the occasion of very much of the perplexity which is involved in this passage. The early or patristic mode of interpretation, whose influence has continued in no small degree to our own day, delighted in minute and subtle analogies, in finding an exact moral and significance, not only for the parable itself, but also for every incident and circumstance of it. Thus the machinery of the story, the filling-up, and the ornamentation became quite as important in this estimate as the story itself. It was thought to be quite as necessary to find parallels and applications for the one as for the other. But it is evident that if we start out with this preconception we must sometimes go far astray. For it is certainly reasonable to suppose that while some of our Lord's parables may have been wrought out with that exquisite care which allowed and required not only an interpretation for the *whole*, but also for *each* of the *several parts*, others again were limited to *one general application*. Thus, in the parable of " the sower " there are legitimate analogies which run all the way through, and a clear and distinct moral follows upon each step of the illustration. But in that of " the unjust steward " the case is entirely different. Here a story is told us with a *single definite purpose*. It does not concern us to find a parallel, that is, a definite interpretation and application for the " steward," or for his " lord," or for his lord's " debtors." We have nothing whatever to do with the *moral* character of the steward's transactions. Nor is it of the least importance to determine whether in a moral point of view his lord's commendation of his conduct was or was not justifiable. All these are questions *entirely aside, absolutely distinct* from the one purpose of the parable. Our business is not with any of the *parts* of the story, but with the story as a *whole*. It is told as one might narrate an incident within his own observation or experience, to illustrate a single solitary fact, and that fact is the thing and the *only* thing which concerns us.

Now what is this *fact* which claims our exclusive attention? What is the *point* illustrated by this parable, and what *lesson* did Christ propose to enforce by it? If we turn to the words which immediately follow its conclusion, and which, therefore, may be taken as a kind of summing up and application of it, we find Him exhorting those about Him to a faithful use and disposition of whatever of worldly wealth they might possess, telling them that he who should prove himself unfaithful in that would thereby demonstrate his unfitness for any higher trust, and warning them that a covetous, selfish idolatry of wealth was incompatible with the service of God. "He that is faithful in that which is least is faithful also in much: and he that is unjust in the least is unjust also in much. If therefore ye have not been faithful in the unrighteous mammon, who will commit to your trust the true riches?" "Ye cannot serve God and mammon." These words were spoken, like the parable, to His disciples—the Pharisees "who were covetous," and others, standing by. Plainly, then, our Lord's purpose was to urge upon them who heard Him the *faithful use and administration of the wealth* with which God had intrusted them; holding out to them as a *motive* for so doing, that they should thus prove themselves worthy of eternal riches, of nobler and heavenly things. Nor are we at any loss to understand what Christ meant by a faithful use and administration of wealth. He meant the charitable employment of it in works of mercy and beneficence to others; not a covetous appropriation of it to one's self whether in the way of hoarding or expenditure, but a generous dedication of it to the manifold service of God. This He tells them shall not go unrequited; it will bring with it a sure and great reward. Everything given, therefore, in good faith; every alms bestowed upon the needy; every contribution to a good work, is, *in reality, an investment for the future, is treasure laid up in Heaven.* But while all men of religious convictions know and feel this, few or none fully act up to their convictions;

few have the promptitude, and none the liberality, which the circumstances require. The prudence which they observe in other matters fails them here; here alone they miss the golden opportunity, and hesitate or neglect to make that investment which brings with it a hundred-fold increase. They do not *act* upon the truths they believe in; they are not *consistent* with their own principles; they do not follow them out with the *energy and promptitude and unreserve* with which men of lower and different principles follow out theirs. For "the children of this world are in their generation wiser than the children of light." And thus sometimes and in some things a bad man may even become a good man's teacher; the forethought and providence of the one in evil things may serve as an example of providence and forethought to the other in things not evil. The parable of "the unjust steward" is an *illustration* of this fact. Our Lord, in order to impress more vividly upon the minds of His disciples the contrast between the *worldly prudence* of a *worldly man* and the *religious imprudence* of a *religious man*, tells them the story of a dishonest agent accused to his master of wasting his goods. The agent is called to render an account of his stewardship, notified of his proposed dismissal, and meanwhile has a brief consultation with himself as to what he must do. He is unfitted for labor, he cannot dig; too proud to trust to chance and uncertain charity, to beg he is ashamed. He resolves to make the most of the one opportunity that remains to him, to guard by his last official act against that destitution which confronts him. The accounts of his stewardship have not yet been rendered; it is yet in his power, perhaps, to put his lord's debtors under that personal obligation which will in itself insure him an effectual future provision; he assembles them, and in collusion with one and another, changes the several amounts of their debts. And his lord commended him, because he had done wisely. The commendation, of course, is not a *moral* one, it is only a recognition from the *standpoint of the steward* of the wisdom or prudence of his act. Putting aside moral considerations, in his circumstances and with the end he had in view, the steward had shown shrewdness and forethought; he had been wiser and more prudent in his generation than are the children of light. He had made *the most* of the opportunity which he had in hand, which they often fail to do; he had made that provision for earthly shelter which they neglect to make for everlasting habitations. He comes upon the stage and passes off again without favorable or unfavorable comment. With his honesty or dishonesty, we have nothing to do. His *worldly prudence* is the one fact in his character and history which at present concerns us. And accordingly our Lord selects *that* as the one point on which His exhortations turn: "And I say unto you, Make to yourselves friends of the mammon of unrighteousness; that, when ye fail, they may receive you into everlasting habitations."

Thus when we withdraw our minds from the secondary and comparatively unimportant *incidents* of the story, from the *mere drapery and setting* of the parable, and fix our attention exclusively upon its general *aim or drift*, we see what a forcible illustration it was of the fact that worldly men are, as a rule, more *consistent*, more *fertile in resources*, more *prudent* and *wise* in their pursuit of worldly things, than religious men are in their pursuit of heavenly things. Here was a dishonest man on the point of being turned out of a position of trust and emolument which he had long held. His future prospects were of the darkest and most gloomy character. His past life had unfitted him for ordinary avocations, and fostered that pride which revolts from the mere suggestion of beggary. Now, what was this man to do? Remember, the whole implication of the story is, that he has no moral principle whatsoever ; honesty or dishonesty is with him simply a question of policy; his ideas do not pass beyond this world ; he cares nothing for the approval or disapproval of God, or conscience, or society; his concern is this, and this only, to employ the last hours of his stewardship to such advantage, to make such effectual use of his remaining opportunity, as will insure him that welcome reception among his lord's tenants and debtors which will in itself be a refuge from both work and poverty. He takes his resolution on the instant, therefore; suggests to each and all of these debtors false returns ; connives at them ; and turns his expiring authority and responsibility wholly in their favor. And *in his theory of life*, with *his ideas and principles*, we must admit that he did wisely ; we are forced, as it were, to *commend* his promptness, prudence, and sagacity. For if it be true that this world is all in all, if moral distinctions amount to nothing, if we are indifferent to or disbelieve in God and conscience, if the great thing for a man to do, here, is to insure himself against work and want, why, then, in the circumstances of "the unjust steward," the only thing for one *to do*, is to do precisely what "the unjust steward" did. But if we (religious men and Christians) are constrained to admit that he acted wisely, prudently, *on his principles*, are we not convicted at the same time of foolishness, of imprudence and improvidence *on our own?* We, too, have a stewardship which sooner or later will be taken from us. Are we making the most of it while it lasts, and employing the responsibility intrusted to us to our greatest possible advantage? We, too, have a golden opportunity which hour by hour is passing away. Are we making such effectual use of it, now, as to insure ourselves a future provision, not for time, but for eternity? We profess to believe in God and conscience. We recognize moral distinctions as permanent and immutable; our thoughts *do* pass beyond this world. We look on, we say, to "the house not made with hands, eternal in the heavens;" but who, as a rule, can commend either our wisdom or prudence or sagacity in seeking it? We assent to the proposition that "a man's life consisteth not in the abundance of the things which he possesses," yet how poor our contrivance, and how slow our forethought in the attainment of those things in which it *does* consist! Here are stewardships of various sorts everywhere about us, talents of one kind or another intrusted to all, opportunities of service greater or less in the hands of each; yet of whom can it be said that he has done *wisely*, if we test the use of these things by the principle of a judicious employment and adaptation of the means to the end? The life of a religious man is of all things the *most irrational and contradictory*, it is of all lives the most *imprudent and unwise*, if, believing in the future, he yet makes little or no provision for the future; if, while expecting great increase hereafter, his investments here are only scant and pitiful; if, seeking the riches which neither fail nor fade, he seldom or never casts that " bread upon the waters " which shall " return to him after many days "; if, hoping for heaven, he yet lays up no treasure there; if, looking at death, and that which lies beyond death, the earthly tabernacle so soon to be dissolved, yet he sends no " friends " before to greet and welcome him to the great Father's house. In him what a sad witness and verification of the Master's comparison; " The children of this world are in their generation wiser than the children of light."

Our Lord sums up the moral of His parable in the application already quoted: " And I say unto you, Make to yourselves friends of the mammon of unrighteousness; that, when ye fail, they may receive you into everlasting habitations." The peculiarity of this expression has occasioned no little perplexity. Just as in the story itself one is at first somewhat bewildered at finding the Master apparently holding up a dishonest man's act to His disciples' imitation, so here again the bewilderment is repeated at finding them bidden to make to themselves friends of " the mammon of unrighteousness." But as in the first instance the difficulty disappears as soon as we recognize the fact that the *prudence* of the steward, and *not his dishonesty*, is the *point* on which the moral turns, so also in this second instance our perplexity is lessened when we come to understand what the phrase, " mammon of unrighteousness," *really means*. It does not mean, at least in this connection, ill-gotten gain. In that case Christ would have commanded its *restitution*, not its investment as a provision for eternity. We can dedicate to the Lord's service, we can employ for the good of others, only that which is *rightfully* our own. God will neither accept nor take knowledge of an unrighteous offering. The phrase, " mammon of unrighteousness," is evidently the equivalent of the " unrighteous mammon " which is spoken of farther on, and which our Lord represents as intrusted to men for their faithful administration. "If ye have not been faithful in the *unrighteous mammon*, who will commit to your trust the *true riches ?*" Both expressions, *i. e.*, " mammon of unrighteousness," and " unrighteous mammon," as they are here used, mean simply worldly wealth of any and every kind. The peculiarity of the phraseology arises out of the not unusual practice of speaking of the *general or ordinary character of a thing as commensurate with the thing itself*. Thus in Scripture, wealth is often associated with "mammon," or wealth-worship; not because the two are *identical and inseparable*, but because the possession or desire of wealth is *generally* found to lead to its practical idolatry. So, also, wealth is, as a rule, characterized as unrighteous; not because it is *inva-*

riably or *necessarily* ill-gotten or ill-applied, but because, on the whole, that is its *ordinary and prevailing* character. The Bible warns us against the love of money as the root of all evil; not because the desire for wealth is *in itself always and necessarily evil*, but because it *so often results in evil*. It follows, therefore, that the phrase, " unrighteous mammon," " mammon of unrighteousness," as it is employed in Scripture, *may mean*, and sometimes *does mean*, simply wealth, apart from all considerations of its acquirement or use. This, at least, seems to be the fair interpretation of it here. And thus our Lord *points* His parable with the direct and legitimate application: So use your wealth, so employ the opportunity of your stewardship, that ye may make with it friends who, when ye die, may receive you into everlasting habitations.

The statement, that by the benevolent and charitable disposition of the means in our possession we may make to ourselves friends who shall stand us in good stead at last, is no new one in the Gospels. The best confirmation, as well as the best illustration of it, is found in the Master's revelation of the great judgment, and the principles which shall determine it.* In that solemn vision which He there calls up, that august scene which He discloses, these " friends " who shall receive us are found to resolve themselves at last, each and all, into *Christ Himself*. We discover and rediscover the Lord Jesus under an infinite variety of disguise. " Come, ye blessed of my Father, inherit the kingdom prepared for you from

---

* See St. Matt. xxv. 31-46.

the foundation of the world: for I was an hungered, and ye gave me meat: I was thirsty, and ye gave me drink: I was a stranger, and ye took me in: naked, and ye clothed me: I was sick, and ye visited me: I was in prison, and ye came unto me. *For inasmuch* as ye did it unto one of the least of these my brethren, ye did it unto me."

Thus this parable, from its opening to its close, is an exhortation to liberality, charity, benevolence, as the *rational and logical consequence* of our religious faith. It appeals throughout to *prudential considerations*. It illustrates, by the forethought of a worldly man in worldly things, what should be the forethought of a Christian man in heavenly things. It seeks to demonstrate the fact, that if it be *wise* to make provision for time, it must be *most unwise* not to make provision for eternity. It meets us on the *lowest ground* we can select, and, leaving out of view all higher and nobler considerations, proves to us beyond dispute that, if we believe in a future life at all, it is the part of *wisdom and prudence* to lay up some treasure there. It commends liberality on the ground that what we give here shall be returned to us hereafter with a hundred-fold increase. It holds up benevolence before us, not because it is *divine*, but because it is *profitable*. It exhorts us to the charitable use and employment of wealth, not because it is *beautiful and Christ-like so to use and employ it*, but because *in the long run it is the best investment of it that we can make*. It is, perhaps, the most remarkable instance in Scripture of a *purely prudential and rational appeal*.

It has been sometimes objected against Christianity, that it deals at times so largely and unreservedly in such appeals, that it does not confine itself exclusively to more disinterested considerations, that it does not set before us goodness of whatever kind more for its own sake, and less for the happiness and rewards which shall wait upon it. And if the gospel dealt only in the prudential motives, if it had no nobler incentive and inspiration than they hold, the defect would indeed be fatal. But while our Bibles contain the Sermon on the Mount, to say nothing of innumerable passages of a kindred spirit, the objection seems scarcely just. It is indeed true that the consideration that, in the long run, honesty is the best policy, never made, and will never make, a sincerely honest man. The goodness that can live and thrive only in the expectation and assurance of its *reward* is neither of the finest nor of the most enduring texture. The self-sacrifice which has in it nothing *spontaneous*, which has its gaze fixed always upon an *ultimate gain*, misses the grace which can alone make it divine. The liberality which finds its controlling motive in the conviction of a *future compensation* is not the spirit out of which the noblest benefactions come. By the soiled way of *self-interest* the fairest virtues and graces do not pass. To give, simply that we may *receive again*, is not to be in very deed and truth "the children of our Father." The charity which goes not beyond *that* can know nothing of the munificence of His nature. To be perpetually balancing our accounts with God, and as it were scoring up our claims against Him, is not the way to be a graceful or a cheerful giver. Even the meanest beggar on the streets detects at once the difference between the alms bestowed with the view to a *future investment*, and the relief which comes from human *sympathy and fellow-feeling*. There was a saying of the Lord Jesus, "that it is more blessed to give than to receive," but if while *giving* we are thinking only of *receiving*, the *secret* of that "blessedness" can neither here nor hereafter be disclosed to us. If our philanthropy, our liberality, our charity, is prudential and *only prudential*, we can know nothing of the beatitude of those "who give, hoping for nothing again."

But, while all this is true, still the fact remains that Christianity *does* appeal to the prudential motives, and appeals to them at times freely and without reserve. I take this to be one of the surest witnesses to its divine and universal character. A merely human philosophy or religion, if it could have attained to the spirituality of the gospel, and realized its highest ethical expression, would inevitably have excluded all inferior considerations, and in its refinements about "goodness for its own sake," emptied itself, as far as mankind at large was concerned, of all practical worth and force. But Christianity is as many-sided as human nature itself. It takes men as it finds them, and becomes in turn "all things to all." It has the loftiest inspiration, the most transcendent counsels of perfection, for those who have the ear to hear. It has other and lower considerations and motives for those who have not yet reached up so high. Let us be thankful that

God in His revelation has condescended to meet us in our weakness, that He has made our very instinct of self-love an opportunity of moral and spiritual advancement. If, for instance, we have not yet learned to give simply and solely from the pleasure of giving, from an experience of the divineness and the blessedness of it, let us still give out of "respect unto the recompense of the reward," hoping that we may attain to a nobler and more disinterested liberality by and by. That recompense is set before us in this parable and elsewhere as a motive, and it should be allowed all its use and worth. Christ did not fear to give it a place in His gospel, we need not fear to leave it there. Indeed, upon this point the language of the Master and His disciples could not well have been stronger. Our Lord Himself says: "Make to yourselves friends of the mammon of unrighteousness, that when ye fail they may receive you into everlasting habitations." And again St. Paul: "Charge them who are rich in this world, that they be ready to give and glad to distribute; laying up in store for themselves a good foundation against the time to come, that they may attain eternal life." Christianity comes even to the most sordid and selfish of us, even to those into whose souls the greed of gain has entered deepest, and asks us to interest ourselves in the necessities of our fellow-men, to take part in every noble and philanthropic enterprise, to contribute our share towards the support of every kindly and Christian charity, on this ground, if on no other, that we shall thereby secure to ourselves an exceeding great reward. The shrewdest and most worldly of us will admit that the problem which concerns him most is this: how to invest his means most safely, and where it will yield the surest and largest return ; and for answer to that, Christ points to the " heavenly habitations," to the "hundred-fold increase," and to the " treasure laid up where neither moth nor rust doth corrupt, and where thieves do not break through nor steal."

IX.

THE SINFULNESS OF LITTLE SINS, AND THE WORTH OF LITTLE VIRTUES.

[KINGSBRIDGE, 1869.]

"He that is faithful in that which is least is faithful also in much : and he that is unjust in the least is unjust also in much."—ST. LUKE xvi. 10.

THESE words which follow immediately upon the conclusion of the parable of the unjust steward seem to set forth a supplementary moral, as it were, to the main drift of that illustration. Our Lord had been commending the prudence of the steward to the imitation of His disciples, but before leaving the subject He draws from it another lesson, and proceeds to impress upon them the importance of an exact and scrupulous faithfulness. Every incident, of course, has several sides on which to look at it, and its more prominent meaning does not preclude lesser though related ones. The counsel to make to ourselves friends of the mammon of unrighteousness is followed by the assertion of the ultimate significance of our action, even in apparently slight and trivial respects. It implies our fitness or unfitness for larger spheres and greater trusts. If we have been found wanting in the one, the presumption is that we shall be found wanting in the other. The key-note of character once sounded, you may predict with tolerable certainty what it will eventually result in. This steward, it seems, had been accused some time before of mal-administration. His derelictions of duty, most probably, had been in the way of small pilferings, but they indicated well enough the untrustworthy character of the man, and his readiness, upon occasion, to resort to those fraudulent transactions which are afterwards recorded of him. His moral status was determined by the wasteful course of his stewardship quite as much as by the wholesale collusion and fraud which signalized its close. The end was the natural and logical result of the beginning. For "he that is faithful in that which is least is faithful also in much: and he that is unjust in the least is unjust also in much."

The principle is an universal one, and holds good in whatever reference we may apply it. It goes far beyond the particular instance of it here given, and finds its illustration in the whole course and conduct of human life. It is one of the postulates, the fundamental axioms of Christian ethics. It brings before us in a compact and striking form the sinfulness of little sins and the worth of little virtues. It asserts that in seemingly trivial matters, as well as in confessedly great ones, there is a sure test and revelation of character. This assertion is repeated over again and in many different ways in the gospel, and our Lord on one occasion and another seems to have dwelt with special emphasis upon it. In the closely related parable of the talents He represents the good servant as thus commended of his master: "Because thou hast been faithful in a very little, I will make thee ruler over ten cities." And in Himself submitting to a rite which others supposed might have been dispensed with, He begins that example which He has left us, by showing us how "it becometh us to fulfil all righteousness." Throughout His whole teaching He lays the most significant stress upon things which often go with us for unimportant details. His moral code, sublime and unapproachable as it is, soaring so far beyond even our ideal goodness, condescends, nevertheless, to the most minute particulars. It has condemnation for the wayward thought and the idle word no less than for sins of greater magnitude, and its benediction is not only for saints and confessors, but for the considerateness of the poor woman also, who "hath done what she could." He commends the widow's mite, and rebukes the discourtesy of His Pharisaic entertainer. He tells us how the cup of cold water shall in no wise lose its reward, and assures us that the omission which came of mere thoughtlessness shall not therefore go unpunished. By practice and precept, in direct statement and in the illustrations of life, He enforces upon us these two and corresponding truths; namely, that little sins are none the less sinful because of their littleness, and that the minor virtues are not without great worth in the sight of God, because with men they are so often made of no account. In the divine estimate, however it may be with the human one, "he that is faithful in that which is least is faithful also in much: and he that is unjust in the least is unjust also in much." We are warned against the thought that we can habitually commit little trespasses and yet be true to duty in greater matters; and we are encouraged by the assurance that the fidelity which approves itself on slight occasions will approve itself equally on momentous ones.

That, however, is not a view which obtains common acceptance among men; not, at least, when it is applied to our own personal experience. Simply as an abstract proposition, we may not be disposed to dissent from it, and in our estimate of others there are times when we are ready enough to take it into account. Every sagacious man, every one who is at all conversant with human nature, knows that the best index of character is in the ordinary and everyday affairs of life. Those who have occasion, in one way or another, to commit to subordinates positions of responsibility, if they are as careful of their own interests as men are apt to be, are pretty sure to scan and scrutinize the most trivial incidents in the conduct of the persons whom they propose to confide in. No wise merchant, for instance, would take an agent into a confidential relationship, or intrust him with powers which, if abused, might result in the ruin of his employer, without first informing himself of that agent's antecedents—all the minute circumstantial details in his previous history. No matter how capable the man might be, or what special qualities he had to recommend him, if that merchant, in the course of his investigation, came upon some questionable, though insignificant, transaction, he would not venture to put himself unreservedly in such hands. And he could not safely do so. For the integrity which one can rely on must be above suspicion; it must vindicate itself in the most unimportant things. And that is the best sort of vindication it can have, for it must be an almost superhuman hypocrisy that fails to betray itself in some careless and unguarded hour. The more circumspect we are in seemingly trivial matters, the more carefully we heed the very slightest indications that we meet with, the less likely are we to be deceived in our estimates of character. The fact that so many persons are deceived, that mistakes are so often made, is mostly due to their own heedlessness and the partial, insufficient evidence that they go upon. It requires no great penetration, if we only take pains and time enough, to discover what this or that man really is. And as a general thing, when the interest at stake is an important one, the pains and the time will be taken. In making up our opinions of other men, we, for the most part, recognize and act upon the principle which our Lord lays down; namely, that faithfulness or unfaithfulness in that which is least implies in the long run faithfulness or unfaithfulness in that which is much. But the moment we turn our eyes inward upon ourselves, we ignore the principle altogether. By some strange freak of mental and moral perversity, we shift on the instant our entire position, and abandon, without the least suspicion of inconsistency, the test which we had so shrewdly applied in other instances. Our own peccadilloes, our own laxities, our own little derelictions of duty, we pass over complacently enough with the self-comforting reflection that they are of no particular importance one way or the other. We are not always conscious of the permanent impress they have left on the character; and, as we none of us profess to be faultless, we imagine that the worst that can be said of them is that they indicate the common infirmities of human nature. As long as we have done nothing flagrant, nothing that an outraged conscience, however dull, cannot help but visit with moral censure, our self-estimate, on the whole, is tolerably comfortable and satisfactory. Especially is this so in spiritual and religious matters. In the world, so much abused of pious people, you nevertheless meet, not infrequently, with a very nice and scrupulous sense of honor, something that is daintily and almost fantastically exact in the very minutest particulars; but in the Church, a corresponding scrupulousness is more rarely met with. Here we feel ourselves licensed, as it were, to be somewhat remiss. If we avoid the greater sins, we need not be so circumspect about the lesser ones. If we control our passions, it is not of so much consequence whether or not we always control our tempers. If we fight persistently against the world and the flesh and the devil, we may be indulged, perhaps, in an occasional or habitual truce with vices which seem hardly formidable enough to belong to either. It would be scandalous for a Christian man to lie or steal or blaspheme, but he may be vain or proud without forfeiting his self-esteem. It would be a disgrace to him to neglect the more prominent offices of religion, but he can disregard with no blush of shame its less obtrusive behests. He is expected to square his conduct by the Ten Commandments, but surely he is not expected to stand guard over every thought and word and act. And so in innumerable instances we try to persuade ourselves that little sins are not so very sinful; indeed, in a broad, common-sense view of them, no sins at all. It is a somewhat similar procedure that we adopt in our estimate of the worth of little virtues. We account them of scarce value enough to give us any particular concern. We are disposed to despise "the day of small things." Our ideals are lofty and noble, and did our circumstances permit of it or call for it, we could give ourselves with enthusiasm to heroic matters. But the practice of daily and familiar duty is quite uninspiring. We could consecrate ourselves to a great cause; we could make vast sacrifices were a mighty principle at stake; we could be a saint, a hero, a martyr; but a simple, ordinary kind of goodness, to be merely faithful and diligent and circumspect in one's walks and ways, this seems scarcely worth our endeavor—a very dull, tame, and commonplace affair. In that warfare to which we all are called, every disciple's experience will verify the fact, in the words of the poet, that:

> "If this tedious battle could be fought,
>   With Sparta's heroes, at one rocky pass,
> One day be spent in dying, men had sought
>   The spot, and been cut down like mower's grass."

But it is with reluctance and weariness, and only half alive, that

> "We skirmish with our foe long hour by hour."

Yet this estimate of ours is contradicted not only by the assertion of Christ, but also by every revelation which God has given us of Himself, and by all the lessons which are written on His moral and material universe. Throughout the Bible, from its opening to its close, He always appears as one who takes equal account of small things and great. He is not more solicitous for the whole human race itself than He is for the single, solitary individual; and we may infer from the law and the prophets, no less than from the gospel, the joy there is in heaven over one sinner that repenteth. The elder dispensation is characterized by minute and almost wearisome details. The divine Lawgiver did not content Himself with laying down a few broad principles for men to steer by; He did not simply point out to them the cardinal virtues, and leave other and lesser things to their own discretion, but hedged His people round with all manner of particular, and sometimes even seemingly trivial, provisions. These, in His view, were none the less important than the immutable principles of morality itself for the attainment of that growth and stature of a righteous man to which He would bring them, and accordingly the transgression of them was punished with a scarce inferior severity. The indulgence of Noah, and the consequent disrespect of his son, was visited with an awful and far-reaching curse. The longing backward look of the woman fleeing from the cities of the plain, petrified her into a pillar of salt. One deceitful act of Abraham well-nigh brought ruin on himself and the Egyptian kingdom. And for a petulant word, Moses was not permitted to go over into the promised land. The instances are innumerable, and one might go on recounting them through all the pages and chapters of that famous history. Nor are the illustrations of the worth which God puts upon the minor virtues, a comparatively unappreciated sort of goodness, less numerous and remarkable. When the widow of Sarepta sheltered a persecuted man, she won from God the restoration to life again of her son. Because the descendants of the house of Rechab kept with filial reverence a certain prohibitory injunction of their ancestor, the Lord said of them that they should not want a man to stand before Him for ever. Ten righteous persons would have saved Sodom. And the patriarch, when he kindly entertained some wayfaring men, entertained angels, and received a blessing unawares—a type, as it were, of that other blessing which shall one day be given, in those memorable words: "Inasmuch as ye did it unto one of the least of these, ye did it unto Me!" The same truth, namely, God's equal care and appreciation of the least as well as of the greatest, is seen not only in His word, but also in His works, in the whole order and composition of His universe. Science tells us that there is no mote or particle on which the wealth of Omnipotence has not been lavished. The stately harmony of the planets is not ordered with greater concernment than the laws which govern the meanest thing that is. The elaboration that is expended on Nature's more imposing forms is the same, neither more nor less, that clothes the grass and arrays the lily. But these illustrations are too familiar to linger on. It is enough to say, that the divine Maker, in His care and concern for each, shows no distinction of great and small between the things which He has made. We may suspect, therefore, that with Him there is absolutely no such distinction. He is Himself so immeasurably above and beyond the sum of His creation, that our relations and comparisons become as nothing in His sight. It were manifestly a poor conceit to suppose that He who fills immensity, so that the heaven of heavens cannot contain Him, could look down on this earth, this mere waif of ours, and speak of one thing as little and another big. And we should realize this especially when we pass to the moral order of human history. Those crises, those battlefields, those social revolutions, which fill the pages of the chronicler, do not cast into the shade with the omnipotent and omniscient One, as they invariably do with us, those obscure, insignificant, individual forces, which in their collectiveness become ultimately the occasion of them. The great man of one and another nation's idolatry is morally with God of no more account than the nameless and undistinguished units in the throng who are applauding him. The captain of an embattled host weighs no more in the scales that weigh him than the sentinel at the door of his tent. The leader of a reformation is not distinguished in any way from the unrenowned co-worker in it. Each has his place, and the places are of equal worth with God. It is absurd, in any divine reference, to apply to such things contrasts and measurements of superiority. The terms are indeed necessary terms with us, but they become meaningless and inappropriate when we hold them up before the infinite Mind. The only distinctions that God makes, the only distinctions that are eternal, the only distinctions that obtain beyond this sublunary sphere, are distinctions in goodness. And a man's goodness is greater or less, not according to the position that he fills, but according to the measure of his performance of the duty that is involved in it. You can do no more than your circumstances admit of; but doing that, you do all that an archangel could do.

This principle, then, that he that is faithful in that which is least is faithful also in much, and he that is unjust in the least is unjust also in much, is a principle which has its verification everywhere—in the Bible, in nature, and in human life. In the practical application of it, it resolves itself into a warning and an encouragement—a warning against little sins, and an encouragement to the performance of little virtues.

1. We are warned against little sins, because, in the first place, it is in them that our chief danger consists. They take us by surprise and unawares. It happens to us, as to all careless combatants, that it is our fate to fall sooner or later before some unworthy and insignificant foe. The self-confident disdain we feel for these trivial antagonists is sure to lure us at last to our ruin. Even in secular affairs the mistakes that men make, the mistakes which as they look back are seen to have been fatal to them, are mostly small mistakes. And these came about, because at the time the matter in hand did not seem important

enough to command any particular attention. In undisguised emergencies the veriest trifler takes a leaf from the book of wisdom, and becomes on the instant deliberate and full of circumspection. And so as a rule these emergencies are passed safely over. In our religious life the contrast is still more significant When we feel a great temptation upon us, we sound the alarm, and set the battle in array, and summon up all our powers. When we consciously stand on the brink of some moral precipice, there is an instinctive recoil; we hesitate, go down on our knees, reach out our hand for the stay we know we can depend on, and we are saved. But the little pitfalls which are everywhere around us we take slight heed of. We think that, even if we have the mishap to fall into them, it does not much matter. At the worst it is only an affair of bruises and soiled clothes. Yet a mere stumble has cost many a man his life. And in our daily walk, how often do the best intentioned of us stumble thus. We would scorn to tell a positive untruth, or commit a downright fraud, or avenge ourselves of an injury in any brutal or unseemly way; but nevertheless we can, upon occasion, resort to some trifling prevarication, or take some slight though illegitimate advantage of our neighbor, or indulge after some moderate and civilized fashion the quiet spite we may chance to cherish. Perhaps the most curious fact connected with the whole matter is this: that just in proportion as a man's sphere is a narrow and contracted one is his danger of unfaithfulness. It would not at first seem so. For we might naturally suppose that in the absence of greater responsibilities, he would give more circumspection to those other and lesser ones which concern him. But experience proves the reverse. He thinks these little matters unworthy of him, and will not condescend to labor with the same diligence that he imagines he would display in more imposing circumstances. In that parable of the talents before referred to, the unfaithful servant is not he to whom were committed ten talents, nor he to whom were committed five, but he to whom there was committed only one.

2. Again, we are warned against little sins because they invariably and insensibly lead to greater ones. No man breaks the commandments all at once. The road to ruin is a gradual slope, a well-paved and even way. You may reach your destination with a facility that involves no exertion or fatigue, and that occasions you in the end a very genuine surprise. What a reiterated tale, true in that instance and true in all, is Hogarth's delineation of the rake's progress! How many intermediate steps between the youth whose fair countenance is marred only by the shadow of an impure thought, and that unsightly premature age, reeking with debaucheries. It is a gross instance, but its parallels are not the less vile because they are more decently habited. And look where you will, you find its moral analogies everywhere. Many a disgraced and ruined man once prided himself upon his integrity, but he was not scrupulous in little things, and in course of time he found that his integrity and the reputation of it had gone from him. How is it that so many sincere Christians become

gradually indifferent, and at last wholly irreligious men? Can they not each and all trace their defection back to the inroad of little sins—sins of temper and appetite and indolence and various indulgence? The only place to make a sure and certain stand against the assault of sin is in its beginnings. If we let that opportunity pass, it is only a kind of moral miracle that can save us.

3. And still again, we have this impressive warning, because little sins, no less than great ones, indicate a character out of sympathy with Christ and God. If there were in our lives that holy self-consecration which is required of us, if there were in our hearts that love which alone can make us acceptable with the Father, we should be anxious and solicitous, even in the most trifling things, to please Him. Indeed, there would then be with us, as with Him, no distinctions between things great and small. Every duty, viewed in its divine relations, would have such supreme importance in our eyes, that all comparisons would be simply idle and superfluous. We should be as much ashamed, and repent as sincerely of our habitual, daily trespasses, as of those darker transgressions of which we are occasionally guilty. We should feel that both were a cloud between us and God; and that if the greater and occasional sin indicated a wider separation, the lesser and habitual sin indicated a more settled alienation from Him. He who has the mind of Christ will not limit the example of his Master to its more striking features and incidents. He will be equally careful of those unobtrusive graces which attend its silent walk. He will

go forth with his Lord not only to death, or whatever dangers may await Him, but he will keep as closely to His side in the unheroic scenes of his patience, humility, self-restraint, and common, everyday fulfilment of "all righteousness." If he fail of that, or at least make no endeavor at it, it must be, and it can only be, because the mind of Christ is not in him.

Yet this principle is not more full of warning than it is of encouragement. For, if to be unjust in the least is to be unjust also in much, we have to remember, on the other hand, that to be faithful in that which is least is to be faithful in that which is much, also. This truth, it is at once apparent, invests the most humble and obscure life with the deepest and noblest significance. One of the last lessons to learn here below, and yet the lesson which is worth all others, is the glory of common things. •When once a man has mastered that, life to his eyes becomes transfigured. There is a halo about duties, homely enough and unattractive before; and virtues which were wont to go in faded guise, are revealed at last in radiant light. How beautiful the lives of some men and women are, not those we read of in the books, but those whom now and then we chance to meet with! Simple, quiet, without ostentation or parade, unconscious of anything in themselves to merit notice or applause, they win upon and hold us, not so much by anything they do, as by the latent, luminous goodness shining through them. Such persons, wherever they are found, are powers—more efficient powers than many a noisy martyr and talkative saint. They do not need high tragedy to make them interesting; they must not have an audience, the glare and the glitter of the stage, before they will condescend to play their parts. Their parts are played, often with the slimmest or no audience at all to mark them, and the scenic pageantry is only the bare walls of their own closets. They have not found it necessary to be great in order to be good, or to have an extended sphere before they think it worth their while to be virtuous. There is a benediction on such lives, a benediction which extends even to the beholder. We are the better as we look at them, and something of their own beauty seems reflected back upon us. It is a calm and quiet beauty; something which comes, as it were, unsought. "They toil not, neither do they spin: and yet Solomon in all his glory was not arrayed like one of these." It is the beauty of character, the beauty which consists not in what a man has, or in what he does, but in what he is. Let us learn from them the dignity and worth with which every life, however humble, if it be only true to itself, may be invested. It is a great and comforting and encouraging thought to anyone who can receive it. It is something to know that every sphere, every duty, every virtue, no matter what it be, has a glory of its own, and needs not to shine by any borrowed radiance. It is something to know that these little frets and trials, which so often and so sorely vex us, and which seem to lack the stimulus that comes of greater things, are not unheeded or unregarded of the Lord, but hold equal balance in His sight with those heroisms which we applaud with loud acclaim. The lives of most of us, and probably of all, will be made up of little things; there may be nothing extraordinary in them; there may come no grand occasions, as we term them, in our way; still, if we are faithful in that which God has intrusted to us, we shall hold in His estimate no second place; and to us, as to others whom in their larger range we may be disposed to envy now, shall Christ fulfil His promise: "Him that overcometh will I make a pillar in the temple of my God, and he shall go no more out: and I will write upon him the name of my God, and the name of the city of my God, which is new Jerusalem, which cometh down out of heaven from my God: and I will write upon him my new name. And to him will I grant to sit with me in my throne, even as I also overcame, and am set down with my Father in His throne. He that hath an ear, let him hear what the Spirit saith unto the churches." *

* See Rev. iv. 12, 21, 22.

X.

THE WEDDING GARMENT.

[KINGSBRIDGE, 1869.]

"And when the king came in to see the guests, he saw there a man which had not on a wedding garment: and he saith unto him, Friend, how camest thou in hither not having a wedding garment? And he was speechless."—ST. MATT. xxii. 11, 12.

THE passage just read forms the concluding portion of the parable which is known as the marriage of the king's son. That parable has, as it were, two distinct though related lessons. It sets forth in the story the fate of those who reject the invitation of the gospel, and the fate of those who accept it yet who disregard the conditions on which it is given. It is a figure of the different ways in which men fail of the eternal good which God has set before them; they either deny that good and turn their back upon it, or else, while seemingly seeking it, they neglect and make light of the qualifications through which only it is won. These are the different representations which in the parable are brought successively before us.

And first, "The kingdom of heaven is like unto a certain king, which made a marriage for his son, and sent forth his servants to call them that were bidden to the wedding: and they would not come. Again, he sent forth other servants, saying, Tell them which are bidden, Behold, I have prepared my dinner: my oxen and my fatlings are killed, and all things are ready: come unto the marriage. But they made light of it, and went their ways, one to his farm, another to his merchandise: and the remnant took his servants, and entreated them spitefully, and slew them. But when the king heard thereof, he was wroth: and he sent forth his armies, and destroyed those murderers, and burned up their city. Then saith he to his servants, The wedding is ready, but they which were bidden were not worthy."

The most literal application of this portion of the parable belongs undoubtedly to our Lord's own time. It is a narrative and a prophecy of the reception which, in the first instance, His own invitation, and subsequently that of His disciples, met with. There were, indeed, some who believed in and followed Him, and many more who after His death and resurrection confessed their faith and were baptized in His name. But the great majority of the Jewish people, both during His earthly life and after it, rejected, and rejected with contempt, the salvation to which they were bidden. The parable is a very graphic picture of the manner in which the call of the gospel was at first received. It was prophetic, too, in a measure, of the reception which through all ages it should meet with. But it is more especially suggestive, and has, perhaps, its most solemn interest, when we try to realize for ourselves its literal correspondence to the facts in the ministry of our Lord and His apostles. We are sufficiently familiar with our own indifference and neglect, but it seems strange and almost inconceivable that there should have been neglect and indifference then. The novel and unwonted powers which were exercised, the marvellous and gracious words which then, for the first time, entered into human thought and speech, must have held spellbound, one would suppose, all who came within their reach. But every record speaks of the reverse of that. Strange as it may seem, while Jesus yet lived and spake, the mass of men heard Him at best with contemptuous unconcern. The vast proportion of those who listened to His earnest and repeated call simply refused to come. They met Him in the streets, in the fields, on the hillsides, and by the seashore, and made light of His persistent invitations. They went their ways—one to his farm, another to his merchandise. They paid as little heed to His entreaty as though it were a matter of no moment, as though the call of Christ were an insignificant and every-day occurrence. It disturbed not their ordinary pursuits, and left not even a ripple on the surface of their thought. They could hear Him who spake as never man spake, they could listen to the inspired words of His chosen disciples, and yet go their several ways with disdainful unregard. And that is not the worst which the parable and the Scriptures have to tell, for others resented the call with positive ill-will; they first crucified the Lord, and afterwards "entreated spitefully and slew" His servants. The history of apostolic martyrdom, as it is given in the Book of the Acts and the early ecclesiastical records, is the sufficient witness to the accuracy of this description.

These same records, moreover, recount the fulfilment of the vengeance that had been predicted. When Jerusalem was laid in ruins by the Romans, and her inhabitants put without mercy to the sword, then that word was accomplished which said: "The king was wroth, and sent forth his armies, and destroyed those murderers, and burned up their city."

But while this parable has its most literal interpretation in the time of our Lord and His disciples, it has had an interpretation also in every succeeding age. Now, as then, while some respond to the invitation of the gospel, others make light of it, take no heed of it whatever, or else contemptuously refuse to come. They set it superciliously aside for more substantial interests—the one for "his farm," the other for "his merchandise." Their several ways, each and all, are too important, too absorbing, too engrossing, to admit of their attendance at "the marriage." The idea itself seems often preposterous and impracticable. And so, though the dinner is ready, it is scarce half-furnished with guests. The majority of those who are bidden will not come. It is true we no longer, as a rule, spitefully entreat or slay the servants who are sent to call us. We accord to them a certain sufferance as long as they confine their message to a stereotyped phrase which, through long usage, has come to have no particular meaning; for we are not at all discomposed, or in the least discomforted, by its utterance. But if they step out of the prescribed limits, or infringe upon the articles of peace which have been tacitly agreed upon, then spiteful entreatment of some sort is pretty sure to begin. Persecution of one kind and another has not yet become obsolete, though in this age of the world it is seldom or never persecution unto death. Yet, nevertheless, our rejection of the gospel will surely be visited upon us, no matter how comparatively civil and undemonstrative our rejection of it may be. Society is sufficiently civilized now not to resent an unpalatable invitation with such a murderous disgust. However unwelcome the message, religious or otherwise, that may be proclaimed to us, it is rarely indeed that we should ever think of slaying or maltreating the messenger. But there may be little that is creditable to us in that. Had we been in the position of those unwilling guests, and had the wording of the invitation been as distasteful to us as it was to them, doubtless we should have emulated the example which they have left us. The substantial guilt of the gospel's rejection is in either case the same. The difference is simply a difference in temperament and circumstances. The Jew denied Christ with passionate vehemence, with all the wild fanaticism of his nature. We, when we deny Him, deny Him quietly and with perfect self-restraint. We care too little about the matter to get excited over it. We have found, moreover, that the most effectual way to silence a man is not to denounce him, but to ignore him. Those of us, therefore, who are repudiating the claims of Christ by simply taking no heed of them, must expect to be counted among His enemies, quite as much as more violent opponents; we have our place with those guests whom, though bidden, He pronounced unworthy;

who, since they would not partake of His supper when they could, shall not when they would.

The parable, however, after classifying those who openly reject the gospel, goes on to make a distinction between those who seemingly accept it. Though those who were bidden in the first instance refused to come, the marriage was not therefore to be without its festivities. The king commissions his servants to go into the highways, and as many as they shall find to bid to the marriage. "So those servants went out into the highways, and gathered together as many as they found, both bad and good, and the wedding was furnished with guests."

Our Lord seems to give here a distinct intimation of the call and acceptance of the Gentiles. The Jews as a nation had rejected the invitation which came first of all to them, and upon their rejection of it, it was offered throughout all the world to every creature. There is apparently no discrimination whatever in this second summons. All are asked whom the servants met with. There is no investigation made into their antecedents, no scrutiny of their personal qualifications. If they accept the invitation in good faith, and conform to the proprieties of the occasion, they are welcome. Naturally it was a miscellaneous company that was gathered at the board, and might be fitly described as made up of bad and good. It is so in the actual history of the kingdom of heaven as it exists in its present conditions upon earth.

The gospel does not require a man to have lived a

good moral life, to have, as it were, his credentials ready, before it will open to him the fellowship of the Christian Society. No matter what his past has been, it welcomes him equally with the rest. Its invitation is for the "publican and the sinner" no less than for those who, in our Lord's expression of them, "need no repentance." *But all who accept the invitation must comply with its conditions, otherwise their acceptance will avail them nought.* If we come to Christ we must "put off the old man and put on the new." We must appear before Him in the exercise of that faith and charity which He requires. We must conform ourselves to the habit of that Divine Society into which we have entered. We must be arrayed, in short, in "the wedding garment," for to fail of that is to insure sooner or later our own ignominious expulsion. And of this the parable forewarns us. For "when the king came in to see the guests, he saw there a man which had not on a wedding garment: and he saith unto him, Friend, how camest thou in hither not having a wedding garment? And he was speechless. Then said the king to the servants, Bind him hand and foot and take him away, and cast him into outer darkness; there shall be weeping and gnashing of teeth."

It may occur to us to ask here, is not the condition of this last as bad, if not worse, than the others? If we run such a fearful risk of final expulsion, is it not better not to go in at all? In point of fact this objection is often raised, and without any reference whatever to this particular parable. Very many who stand aside and altogether aloof from the Church justify to themselves, in some sort, their non-committal attitude, by enlarging upon the sad estate of those who have entered it, and at present remain in it, without complying with the gospel conditions. They speak of their position as a dreadful mockery and unreality; something which will bring down upon them a heavy weight of retribution at the last day. They themselves are not prepared to conform to Christ's requirements, and therefore they make a kind of merit of the fact that they have never formally acknowledged or recognized Him. They seem to think that this is a consideration which will not tell lightly in their favor at the final account, and will make their condition, whatever it be, preferable at least to that of the wedding guest without the wedding garment. But is there such a thing as preference in what in either case is utter and absolute loss? Is it worth our while to choose between positions, both of which are fraught with woe and ruin? True, the man in the parable was excluded from the banquet and cast into outer darkness, but were not the others who rejected the invitation altogether excluded? And if that banquet stand, as it must stand, for heaven, for eternal happiness, for divine felicity, how shall we draw comparisons between those who, from whatever cause, are shut out from any participation in its joy?

The fact, indeed, is not to be disguised, that our church-membership will avail us nothing, if we take no heed of its responsibilities; if we continue, in the scriptural use of the word, persistently unworthy. The time will come, when despite our apparent acceptance of the gospel's invitation, we shall be bound hand and foot and cast out. Though we cry, "Lord, Lord!" He will say that He "knows us not," that we are "none of His." But is there any assurance of comfort to be drawn from that for you who are without already, and seem to think it best to remain there? Is your position the more satisfactory because the false disciple, equally with yourself, shall be excluded from the kingdom of heaven? Or do you think it a plea that will better you in any way to be able to say before the Lord, that though you turned a deaf ear to His call on earth, yet you never made the faintest pretence of hearkening to it? that though you have despised and rejected Him, it is true, yet you were open and manly about it, and withal thoroughly consistent, for you never even once called yourself by His name? What a poor sophistry is that which can argue thus! All men have not the same sins; shall we excuse our own sin, therefore, because it does not happen to be our neighbor's? Let us realize the fact that we have to answer for ourselves, irrespective of what others may do or not do. The severity of their punishment will in no way lessen the severity of ours, and in such matters it is idle to conjecture which is the worse estate. If any one cannot make up his mind to acknowledge Christ, if he persist day after day in virtually repudiating and rejecting Him, let him at least not seek to justify his course by pointing out instances of Christian duplicity and inconsistence. They will be judged, there is no doubt of that, but will not you be judged also? However it may be with others, is not this at least sure, that your condition is perilous in the extreme—a condition which, if persisted in, can end only in utter ruin? Were it not better to make a venture of faith, and accept the invitation, and provide yourself with a wedding garment? It may be had for the asking, nay, it is given without even that. This whole story has an Eastern setting, and in the East, so scholars say, the custom was for the prince who gave an entertainment to furnish his guests with the robes that they should wear. The wedding guest was without a fitting vestment, not because it was difficult to get, but because, after it had been given, he did not deign, or would not take the trouble, to put it on. And Christ calls no man to His side to whom He does not impart the strength to come. His grace is freely given, bestowed before you seek it. If you will use and wear what you have of it already, you will find it sufficient to sustain you and keep you faithful to the end.

But perhaps the most significant lesson of this whole parable is the self-conviction of the wedding guest. When the king asks, "Friend, how camest thou in hither not having a wedding garment?" he is struck speechless. He seems to have nothing to say for himself—not a word of self-excuse. Yet, doubtless, he did not enter there with the clear recognition that his conduct was inexcusable. Had one questioned him previously, he would have had many a plausible reason to allege. It could not have occurred to him that the charge would find him utterly without defence. A moment before, his ongue could have justified readily enough, or at least palliated the seeming slight of his discourtesy. Perhaps he would have said that the garment was inconvenient, or that it did not please his fancy, or that he was too much interested to concern himself with such trifles, or that the whole matter seemed to him a mere idle conventionalism. But whatever his excuse was, it broke down utterly when subjected to the test. He could not force himself to speak it. He recognized it as worse than vain. It was one thing to make light of what he might choose to characterize as a mere formality outside, but in the presence of the king and the assembled guests, the manifest impropriety of his attire made him dumb. He is self-convicted, confounded as it were, by the witness against himself, which he finds in his own breast. He feels, despite all his recent self-assurance, that there is not one single word to say; and that feeling, whether he will or no, keeps him speechless. He is the picture of a man petrified into voiceless surprise.

And in him we have an illustration of what our own condition must one day be if we trust to the self-excuse which seems in some sort to satisfy us now. It will fail us at the last, and leave us self-convicted and self-condemned. Let us try to realize all that is involved in that. There are none who do not try to justify their conduct to others, and few, indeed, who do not seek some justification with themselves. Perhaps the most hardened and impenitent criminal never commits a crime without framing to himself some excuse or palliation of it. To enter upon any iniquity without first practising this jugglery of self-deceit would argue a nature more purely evil, more self-determinedly depraved, than we have ever met with or can conceive of. We seem to be so constituted, that in order to secure even a counterfeit peace, we must deaden, if we cannot wholly silence, the voice of conscience. It is curious to observe the process by which a man, when he has once determined upon wrong, gradually brings himself up to the commission of it. He argues the matter over with himself, and is as ingenious in his sophistries as though he were pleading before one who was really ignorant of his fixed intention. He urges everything that can be said in extenuation of that which all the time he is fully determined to do, and fortifies himself at every step in the argument with as much carefulness as though his purpose were not already a foregone conclusion. And then at last, having gone through this preliminary exercise, he goes about his will with a comparatively clear conscience. Not that he is ever in reality deceived; there is something within us that we cannot juggle. We know that what we are about to do is wrong, that the defence which we have made for it will not bear too close inspection; but still it seems to lessen our guilt somehow, and we delude ourselves with the idea that when we are arraigned for what we have done, we can plead that after all there was much to be said for it. Is not every human life conducted more or less upon this principle? Are we not continually trying to justify things which in our secret hearts we feel to be unjustifiable, and palming off excuses upon our conscience, which that conscience when allowed to speak authoritatively rejects? Yet so inveterate is the habit, that it is the rarest possible thing to find a man who under any conceivable circumstances cannot make his tongue run glibly in his own behalf. It must be a strange concurrence of adverse fates, something extraordinary indeed, that shall suffice to put him to silence. The more desperate our cause, the more desperately do we adhere to the sophistries with which we have fortified it. We repeat and dwell upon them until we almost succeed in convincing ourselves that we believe them. Yet even in this present life there are times when they seem to fail us. Many a plea which appeared plausible enough before sin, stands confessed in all its poverty after it. And the time is hastening on for each of us when our excuses will fail us altogether. Probably there is no one here who does not think that he shall have considerable to say for himself before the bar of heaven. We confess, of course, that we are "miserable sinners," and "acknowledge and bewail" without any hesitation "our manifold transgressions." But that is simply a general admission, a mere formal concession, which does not go for much. Let the charge, however, be made in reference to any specific offence, and we shall not be slow to repudiate or defend it. The moment we pass from vague generalities to precise and definite particulars, we are no longer miserable sinners, and not at all disposed to concede in any given instance our own unworthiness. There is nothing you can name, no omission of duty, no commission of wrong, that we have not, in our own case at least, something to say for. And yet, when we in turn come to stand before our Judge, we shall have nothing to say; we shall be absolutely speechless. The very conscience which we have drugged will awake again with all its terrors to condemn us. We shall find the plea, which so often we have urged before, die suddenly on our reluctant lips. All our well-conned excuses will melt into thin air. We shall be like those who rise from troubled dreams, or, rather, like those released from the spell of some enchantment, who have lived on deceptions and illusions. But before the throne of God no deception and no illusion can appear. We shall see all things, then, not as they have seemed, but as they really are. The cloud which here on earth half obscured the moral sense will pass away, and there shall return to the conscience the true and deep discernment which God originally gave it. And in that dread disclosure, that solemn self-revealing of ourselves, we shall be speechless, self-convicted, self-condemned.

It seems to be a provision of God's kingdom that the guilty soul should virtually pass sentence upon itself. In the parable the mandate of the king was but the fulfilment of the moral judgment which the wedding guest himself had given. His exclusion from the feast, and expulsion into the outer darkness, came as the necessary consequence of his enforced silence, the tacit admission that he was utterly without excuse. Thus he was made, as it were, his own judge and his own executioner. This is a necessary condition of the perfect and final triumph of righteousness. God is omnipotent, and can with a word crush all His foes; but even were they to be overpowered by a force external to and not within themselves, the vindication of his sovereignty would be incomplete. Should they, even in the moment of extinction, deny His goodness and justice and truth, they would be only half subdued. But "all things shall be subdued unto Him," "all things shall be put" at last "under His feet." None —no matter who he be—shall gainsay or quarrel with the justice of his sentence. For he himself shall be constrained by his own conscience, that witness within him which cannot die, to speak it. His speech may be, indeed, only a woful silence, but in that silence there is the vindication of divine justice; and in the confession of the wicked himself the ways of God are justified to man.

Since we ourselves, therefore, shall be made to bear witness in the future against all the evil that is in us, may it not be well to begin to bear that witness now? What does it avail to deceive ourselves so cunningly with the miserable sophistries of self-excuse, since the deception, even if it be partly successful in time, will fail us on the threshold of eternity? How idle to be so ready with our exculpations now, if we are to be stricken speechless then! How poor a preparation of defence to be cunning, and getting by heart the tales which we shall have no tongue to utter! How vain the hope of eluding God's discernment, if the day shall come when we can no longer elude our own! Would it not be better to enter upon that censorship of ourselves now upon which, sooner or later, we must inevitably enter? Would it not be more prudent to bring our lives to a searching test while we may, rather than defer it till we must? And wiser to judge ourselves here, rather than be judged by ourselves hereafter?

XI.

THE PENITENT THIEF.

[KINGSBRIDGE, 1868.]

"And one of the malefactors which were hanged railed on him, saying, If thou be Christ, save thyself and us. But the other answering rebuked him, saying, Dost not thou fear God, seeing thou art in the same condemnation? And we indeed justly; for we receive the due reward of our deeds: but this man hath done nothing amiss. And he said unto Jesus, Lord, remember me when thou comest into thy kingdom. And Jesus said unto him, Verily I say unto thee, To day shalt thou be with me in paradise."—ST. LUKE, xxiii. 39-43.

AMONG the many scenes and incidents which are brought before us in the different narratives of the Lord's passion and crucifixion, not the least significant or affecting is the story of the penitent thief. It takes its place with those other facts recurring every now and then in the ministry of the Saviour, which exhibit so touchingly the tender compassion of that friend of sinners, and witness so reassuringly to the marvels which are wrought in the human heart by a sincere and true contrition. We associate it in our thought with the story of the adulteress, the Magdalene who wept at the feet of Jesus, and the despised Zaccheus, the publican, at whose house the Master so graciously abode. It is recorded by only one evangelist, but he is the one whose gospel dwells more largely than the others upon the facts of grace and pardon, and who alone has given us the parable of the prodigal son. That parable and this story seem to be the complements of each other, and together serve to illustrate and enforce a truth more comforting to us, perhaps, than any other. The gospel would not be to us all that it now is had we never heard the words, " I will arise, and go to my Father ; " nor would it be all that it now is if in answer to that supplicating cry : " Lord, remember me when thou comest into thy kingdom," there had been no reassuring word : " To day shalt thou be with me in paradise."

Yet, in the interpretation of this story and the appropriation of its moral significance, we must be careful to bear in mind the probable character and circumstances of the subject of it. Without any wish to narrow down its meaning, but with the purpose rather to insist upon that meaning as far as it can legitimately go, still it is necessary to guard against the inferences that may be drawn from some popular errors in respect to it. Their best corrective, perhaps, is to be found in the simple statement of what may be considered as the results of the most fair and impartial criticism.

Thus the story is popularly known as that of the penitent thief. And here at the outset we are likely to be led astray in our estimate of the probable character of the penitent. The word " thief " in our usage designates the lowest and meanest class of social offenders; and while there are crimes darker far than thieving, still that seems especially to indicate a certain permanent and habitual viciousness of character. Before one is degraded to that, he has generally lost much, if not all, of the other native goodness that was once in him. But this man belonged to quite a different order of criminals. The word translated "thief" in the incidental reference of Matthew and Mark more properly means "robber;" and St. Luke, in his detailed account, does not call him a thief, but a "malefactor,"—an evil-doer. The distinction, perhaps, would not be of any particular importance were it not for some facts which are known concerning the character and circumstances of those civil offenders whom the Romans were accustomed to call "malefactors" and "robbers." Their offence generally originated in a participation in some of the many insurrections which were so frequent at that time against the imperial government, and which brought upon so many, even of the better class of Jewish citizens, the ban of outlawry and proscription. It often happened that a man of sincere but misguided purpose, joining in some one of these never-ending civil commotions, found himself suddenly without a home, hunted from place to place by the Roman soldiery, and compelled at last to take refuge with others, not always the associates of his own selection, in the mountain fastnesses of Judæa. There these bands of political outlaws led a precarious existence from day to day, subsisting as best they could. Under such circumstances, moral distinctions, nice discriminations in regard to property, are not apt long to survive; and, as a natural consequence, depredations upon the surrounding country and deeds of violence sooner or later followed. And thus a man who began by being simply what we should call a fanatic, or perhaps a patriot, ended by becoming more or less of a bandit and a robber. Yet it is not difficult to imagine that such an one might have had much of worth and goodness in him originally, and that something of it had outlived all the adverse influences of his lot. And if this be the history, as is probable, of the malefactor of Calvary, we can readily believe that there was working in his heart already some better remembrance of other days; some seed of goodness not all worn out, which predisposed him for his sudden and remarkable conversion. That he had been guilty of violence and wrong, that his conscience condemned him, is sufficiently proved by his own confession; but it is more likely than not that he had never become thoroughly bad, determinedly depraved, or suffered his heart to harden into that insensibility which at the last was so apparent in his impenitent comrade.

The immediate occasion of his appeal to Jesus seems to have been the peculiar malignity with which all His enemies were now exulting over the fallen Galilean. The spell which the great prophet had so long laid upon men was for the time broken; and priests and rabble, soldiers and scribes, were for once in full accord jibing and jeering at the crucified man of Nazareth. Even one of the malefactors at His side joined in that cruel mockery. Hanging on the cross, in all the torments of a lingering death, he too took up the taunt and scoff, and railed on Jesus, saying, "If thou be the Christ, save thyself and us." Hitherto, according to St. Luke, the other malefactor had been silent. Yet what thoughts must have been passing through his mind as he looked out upon that scene going on before him! What doubts and questionings, what hopes and fears, followed each other in quick succession, as his gaze went to and fro between priests and people, and the weak gentle, silent sufferer at his side—the Lamb dumb before His shearers, that opened not His mouth! What convictions of sin, what yearnings of repentance, were struggling in his heart, in the presence of that pure and perfect One! Was not "the body broken," the visage "marred more than any man's," leading him already to be the first of those who, in the fulfilment of the Lord's prediction, should be "drawn to Him when the Son of man should be lifted up?" As yet he had uttered no word, had made no sign. But when his fellow-robber joins in the railing of the mob, then at length he breaks his silence, first with an indignant rebuke to his comrade for his heartless cruelty, and then with a wondrous faith to cast himself upon the protection of the dying Nazarene.

It is important to notice here some of the indications which go to show how sincere and true this malefactor's repentance was. In the case of an ordinary death-bed repentance—repentance at the eleventh hour—we can seldom be sure that it is genuine. But in this instance there are considerations which seem to establish it beyond all doubt.

The first of these was his indignant rebuke: "Dost not thou fear God, seeing thou art in the same condemnation?" It was not so unnatural, perhaps, that these others, His enemies, should revile the Innocent, —these whom judgment had not overtaken, and who had no experience of their own by which to measure and interpret the sufferings of their victim; but it was something monstrous, indeed, that one similarly circumstanced, in the same condemnation, and who knew by his own agony what Jesus now endured, should thus turn upon and taunt his fellow-sufferer. This seems to be the force of the penitent's rebuke; and it is something—something which brings with it no uncertain revelation of character—that in the midst of his own torments he could pity the sufferings of another, and feel indignation at a gratuitous and unnatural wrong. Pain often makes us incredibly selfish; our own griefs often make us forgetful and heedless of all other woes. Had that malefactor been as self-observed as men generally are when writhing in agony, he would have been wholly indifferent to the mockery that was going on round about him. It was an evidence of grace, a kind of first-fruits of repentance, that he could forget himself to interpose and plead forbearance in behalf of another.

Another indication of his sincerity was his confession of sin and acknowledgment that his punishment was just. "We," he says, "are in this condemnation justly, for we receive the due reward of our deeds: but this man hath done nothing amiss." Now, perhaps the very hardest thing, the very last thing, that one can bring himself to do, is to say to himself and others, out of the midst of the judgment which has come upon him, that he is receiving only his deserts, reaping only what he himself has sown. It is generally a long time before we can make up our minds to the acknowledgment of that. We must first exhaust all the sophistries of self-excuse, we must first raise every possible cavil against human and divine justice, before we will admit it. And hence the Scriptures so often represent it as an evidence of grace, of regeneration, when a man suffers chastisement and murmurs not. This malefactor might have urged that he had done nothing so bad after all, certainly nothing worthy of crucifixion; and the bystanders, who sympathized more or less with the wild, lawless, insurrectionary spirit of the time, would probably have re-echoed his assertion. It must have been a profound conviction of sin, a deep realization and acceptance of God's eternal law that retribution shall wait upon transgression, that could lead him, while recognizing the innocence of another, to justify from his own cross the punishment of himself.

But the chief proof of his repentance was the wonderful faith that grew out of it. I do not know that there is any faith recorded greater, or so great, in all the gospel histories. Every circumstance seemed to repel and forbid it. Others had believed when they saw the Master's mighty works; but here His miraculous power had apparently deserted Him. Others had believed when He was in the height of His popularity, when He had no inconsiderable following; but here He was friendless and alone, the sport and the mockery of His enemies. Others had believed when His words seemed to foreshadow a temporal kingdom and earthly rule; but here His only symbol of royalty was the crown of thorns, His throne the accursed tree. It was a faith wonderful indeed—the more wonderful the more you think of it—that could trust in a crucified and dying man; that could turn with an appeal like that to one who hung by him, side by side, in the same condemnation. Side by side they hung, scorned alike, crucified alike, seemingly come alike to open shame and ruin. Yet the transgressor could see in this other, scourged and scorned and crucified like himself, something divine, immortal—something that could not die. That was what the disciples—the chosen twelve themselves—could not do. Long before, they had forsaken Him and fled, and now stood afar off with the women, beholding the things that were done. Deserted of His friends, alone among His enemies, the dying Christ had yet gained a new and later witness, one who could acknowledge Him before them all—this outlaw, this malefactor, this hill-side robber of Judæa. May not the explanation of Christ's immediate, free, and unhesitating response to his appeal be found in the marvellous faith of that dying robber's heart? How nearly were they drawn together—these two, the Master and His latest disciple—in the few hours that remained to both. Surely it is not a mere fancy that has invested the words of one with a certain pathos—a wail almost—the pathos of simple, childlike trust: " Lord, remember me when thou comest into thy kingdom ; " and given to the reply of the other the tender accents of ministration, something of the tone with which one soothes a suffering child with the assurance that the pain and grief will soon be over: "Verily I say unto thee, To day shalt thou be with me in paradise."

I do not think that we can ever sufficiently value this story for the testimony that it gives to the worth, the reality, the acceptableness, even of a late contrition, of a repentance that has its birth in "the eleventh hour" of death. It witnesses, as perhaps no other fact can witness, to the forbearance, long-suffering, and inexhaustible mercies of God. It is the fulfilment, almost beyond any other, of the assurance of the Saviour: "Him that cometh to me I will in no wise cast out." We needed at least one such fact, when a godless, wasted, mis-spent life is hurrying to its close, to keep us from despairing of ourselves and others. It has brought hope to many a heart that otherwise must have been hopeless, and has helped many a sinner, as the shadows of death began to gather round him, to offer to his God the acceptable sacrifice of a broken spirit, a broken, humble, contrite heart at last. It has been the comfort and the consolation of sorrowing relatives and friends as they stood by the dying bed of one unworthy indeed, yet nevertheless so dear, and listened to that tardy confession of sin, those broken ejaculations and faint mutterings of prayer on lips that seldom or never prayed before. We could not have borne, we could not have endured, to be present at the death of some whom we have known and loved; we could not have had the heart to think of them after we had laid them in the grave, had it not been for the secret hope which this penitent thief has encouraged us to cherish. True, the story may be, and has been, and will be abused.

True, that dependence has been put upon it, and will continue to be put upon it, which will be found at last to have been only a broken reed. True, that there is danger in the reading of it, danger sometimes so fatal and disastrous that many have been led to look upon it as a snare, and have sought to explain away its application, to separate it absolutely from all other human experience. But with the limitations which the circumstances of the story themselves imply, it has a meaning, a significance, an encouragement for all. Christ was not afraid to give it a place in the most prominent and well-known portion of His ministry. The evangelist was not afraid to record it in his gospel. Surely, we need not fear to let it stand. As I said before, we need it, it answers to a necessity of our nature. There is nothing in it, moreover, to which we cannot find a parallel of some sort in well-authenticated religious experience. Sudden and radical conversions are the exceptions, not the rule; but, nevertheless, they have occurred, and do. Even the great apostle of the Gentiles, St. Paul himself, underwent a change equivalent to a new creation in the space of a single day, nay, an hour. It is more than probable that a death-bed repentance will not be genuine, will not be sincere, but it may be. Let us thank God for that possibility; let us thank him that we are never wholly in the power of circumstances, never absolutely bound by the limitations of time. Let us not try through prudential considerations to reason away the faint, struggling, uncertain hope that has been given us. Rather let us rejoice—yea, though it be with fear and trembling

—that even in a dying sinner, impenitent before, that contrition may be conceived and born which shall be found acceptable before God. And even if we scarcely dare, as well we may, to think of this in connection with ourselves, let it at least be a consolation to us in our thoughts of others—some whom we love and care for, and who yet are on the downward path, and we are powerless to arrest them. Let it be a comfort and a hope, I say, that some time before all is over and the lamp has ceased to burn, the prodigal will call upon his Father; that that cry: " Lord, remember me," will go up from the malefactor's wild, wayward, sinful heart, and that it will not go up in vain.

It would not, however, be doing justice to our subject, were we, while recognizing its legitimate encouragement, to leave it without a brief reference to some considerations which should deter us from its abuse. How often it has been abused, how often men have sought to silence their conscience, to solace their fears, to put aside the monitions of duty, to keep themselves in countenance from day to day and year to year in the protraction of a godless, impenitent life by the remembrance of it, we very well know. It is no uncommon thing to hear men whose only resemblance to the penitent thief is that they are "in the same condemnation" quoting his case with much easy self-complacency, and comforting themselves with the assurance that they have only at last to echo his prayer to find entrance also into the paradise of God. And may we not all be convicted, more or less, of this perilous procrastination?—convicted, even though to ourselves we care not to confess it, of building more or less consciously upon that foundation,—a foundation which in our case may not, and in all probability will not stand?

For let any one who looks forward to a death-bed repentance remember, first of all, that the deliberate entertainment of such a purpose tends of itself to produce that moral and spiritual insensibility which makes honest, true, genuine, sincere repentance practically impossible. For what is that which you are doing? Nothing less, when you come to analyze it, than this: you are deliberately shutting yourself out from every influence that should soften and elevate and ennoble you now, closing your eyes and your ears against all the regenerating instrumentalities which God has set about you, encasing yourself in that impenetrable armor of indifference which becomes the more invulnerable the longer it is worn; and all this with the expectation, wonderful to tell, that in an hour, in a moment, in the twinkling of an eye, your sinful soul shall be converted, your steely insensibility melt away, and your leprous "flesh" come again to you "like the flesh of a little child." Can human infatuation go beyond that? Can any one thus self-deluded have any idea at all of what repentance really is? The shame, the grief, the agony of soul which it involves? Granted, that repentance is always, invariably accepted; but what assurance have you that at the last you either will or can repent? Have you considered how the will itself is formed day by day and year by year? How it hardens under impiety into almost hopeless induration, into more than adamantine firmness? If you postpone contrition until death, the experience of the other malefactor more likely will be yours,—imprecations and curses rather than prayers and penitence upon your lips. True, you *may* repent and be accepted, but how tremendous will be the odds against you! And what kind of a God is this to whom you propose to give nothing but the vain oblation of your dying breath? Yet we read that "God is not mocked." Should not one live in heathendom rather than in Christendom to face Him with such a thought? And indeed it is the half-pagan, half-Christian Roman emperor that has become for us the most notable instance of a deliberate death-bed repentance; one who postponed his baptism, believing that baptism could wash away sins, until the death-hour, and meanwhile employed the time to commit follies and cruelties and crimes without number. And what was that late baptism, that late repentance, worth— baptism deferred, repentance postponed, to give him time to sin? Yet that is what we, in our lesser degree, are doing when we resolve not to seek God or repent until we must.

Again, we have to remember that though the hour of death will come, the *opportunity* of repentance may not. How many pass away suddenly, with no premonition, no sign or note of warning! A blow, an accident, a sudden turn of secret disease, and all is over. At sea, on land, at home, abroad, how often does the angel of death come with his immediate summons: "This night, this hour, *now*, thy soul shall be required of thee!" Is it not pitiful to think of the many, many souls that go out in darkness, no time allowed even for a hurried prayer—one despairing cry? And even when the ordinary course of nature is not broken, how often do there come days and weeks of stupor, when the man lies in a kind of dreamless lethargy like one already dead, heedless alike of earth and heaven, of all things past, present, and to come; or, worse still, when delirium maddens the brain, and sins forgotten or only imagined reappear, and clothe themselves in hideous shapes, and a hell begun in the man already "feeds the fires and whirls the lash of its incessant woe!" Oh, if repentance has been postponed till then, if no cry has before gone up to God, then it can never, never, go!

And though your own experience may be different from all this; though we will suppose that your hour will not come suddenly, and that when it comes there will be no moral insensibility, no physical stupor, no mental delirium, but that, instead, there will be ample time, a clear vision, and a steady brain; that there will be the exhortations of friends and the ministrations of religion; that you will say your prayers, and confess your sins, and think yourself at peace with God,—what assurance have you that all this will not be a mere mockery, a delusion, a miserable self-deceit? Repentance, let it be again repeated, is always, invariably accepted when it is genuine and sincere, but seldom can an hour or a day or a week bring with it any sure conviction of that. What is it that you repent of, your sins or your imprudence? What is it that you shrink from, your guilt or your punishment? What is it that you desire, your impunity or your purification? Are these the questions that are to torment you in the last moments that remain to you of earth? And can these last moments fit you, do you think, for the bosom of Abraham and the paradise of God? Would not that be a moral miracle, possible indeed, but still improbable? Remember the malefactor's repentance was sincere. In his case every circumstance tended to forbid it, to repress it; but in your case every circumstance will tend to produce excited feeling and imaginary experience. Are we not becoming familiar with that, and disgusted with it too, in the scarcely edifying exhibition, so frequently given us now, of the last hours of criminals before execution—men guilty of the most atrocious crimes, and yet each one so very confident of heaven, piously exhorting the spectators, and only doubtful, as it would seem, whether his auditors shall meet him there? And I tell you, I tell you that those scenes of the gibbet are re-enacted in many a curtained chamber and on many a bed of down. The oftener one sees a death-bed repentance, the harder it becomes to believe in it.

While, then, we refuse to shut out the hope which this story of the penitent thief has given us, let us not build upon it over much. Better if we draw from it a consolation in our thoughts of others, than suffer it, however indirectly, to postpone the preparation we should make to meet our God. The future is not our own. We cannot tell how soon or in what form the summons may be. Of the present only are we sure. "Now is the accepted time;" but the day may come when "no place shall be found for repentance, though we seek it diligently with tears."

XII.

THE CRUCIFIXION.

[KINGSBRIDGE, 1868.]

"Likewise also the chief priests mocking him, with the scribes and elders, said, He saved others; himself he cannot save."—ST. MATT. xxvii. 41, 42.

THE subject that is brought before us again to-day is the tragedy of Calvary, the passion and crucifixion and death of Jesus Christ. We are called once more to the commemoration of that fact which has given its symbol to Christianity, which has become the power of the gospel, and which penetrates the human heart with a wondrous and incomprehensible efficacy. The thoughts that are suggested by it are thoughts of mingled joy and sadness, thanksgiving and shame. We look back with reverent adoration to that love, "than which no man hath greater," that could "lay down its life for its friends;" and we recall with sorrowful conviction that common sinfulness of which we all are partakers, and which found its darkest expression in this one unparalleled crime. The various feelings which that scene calls up, the emotions which follow on the recital of it, are too numerous and too deep to be put into words. No language can express all the significance that is contained for us in that uplifted cross; all the hope, love, gratitude, self-accusation and remorse that are associated with it. Yet we would fain make some acknowledgment of our debt, would fain testify by some outward act that we are not wholly insensible to its appeal, and in the setting apart and religious observance of this day have sought to render a slight but not unmeaning tribute to its worth. Let the day be consecrated to solemn thoughts; let it be a day of contrition, of prayer, of humiliation; yet a day, too, of peace, of joy, of most comforting assurance. For if it is the day which gives most emphatic expression to our sin, it is the day, also, which gives most emphatic expression to our redemption.

I have selected for a brief exposition, and commend now to your attentive consideration, one or two aspects of the cross of Christ, which show that cross to have been not an accident, but a moral necessity; and which serve to illustrate the fact that the work which the Saviour had assumed of seeking and saving the lost, from its beginning to its close, implied and could admit of no other alternative than the final sacrifice of Himself. The words in which this truth has found, perhaps, its most significant and startling expression, is the reiterated taunt of those who reviled Him: " He saved others; Himself He cannot save."

All the four narratives of the crucifixion have given with more or less particularity what can scarcely be otherwise characterized than the fiendish malice with which His persecutors exulted and gloated over the dying agonies of Jesus. So deeply was this terrible remembrance impressed upon the minds of the disciples, that the first three gospels give an almost disproportionate space to the storm of blasphemy and mockery which for some hours assailed the meek, unresisting sufferer on the cross. It would seem as if these bitter enemies of the man of Nazareth could not contain themselves, could not preserve the semblance even of common decency and humanity in that fierce, satanic joy with which they at last beheld Him nailed and dying there. A kind of diabolical glee appears to have been their predominant and undisguised feeling. Ordinary conspirators generally draw a veil over their real sentiments, and, when they have compassed the destruction of their victim, suffer him for appearance sake, if for no better reason, to die in peace. But not so these Jewish murderers. Every other consideration for the time is lost in an intense, malignant satisfaction. High and low, officials and rabble, vie with each other in that dreadful mockery. The mob, forgetful of that pity which in the quick revulsion of feeling sometimes takes possession even of a mob, hoot and jeer as fiercely as they had cried out before the judgment-seat of Pilate. The chance passer-by must stop to have his scoff. And priests and scribes, men of learning and position, heedless alike of every propriety, of all dignity and decorum, join in and encourage the coarsest railing of the populace. They were determined, it would seem,—these enemies so ruthless and relentless,—not to spare their victim one conceivable pang, not one single drop in that cup of agony which they had pressed upon his lips. We are reminded, as we read, of the words of St. Jude, and apply to them the description which he applies to others: "Raging waves of the sea are they, foaming out their own shame."

Must it not have seemed to a chance stranger there, one ignorant of the character and history of the Master, that they had all gone mad alike together in a delirium of triumph over some hated and execrable foe? "Who is this?" he might have asked, "and what crimes, what unspeakable atrocities hath this man committed, to be thus shut out from the common sympathies of humanity?" Had such a question been put to that miscellaneous crowd about the cross, it would have puzzled many there to answer it. The replies would have been various indeed, and, perhaps, somewhat contradictory. Crimes, in any ordinary sense of the word, could not be charged upon Him. As for atrocities, His life had been singularly gentle, beneficent, and inoffensive. Everything which He had said and done in those three years or more of His public ministry had been subjected to the most searching investigation; false witnesses, too, had been suborned, but even that unrighteous expedient had failed to substantiate anything worthy of accusation. The charge before Pilate had been that of sedition—that he was a rebel against the authority of Cæsar. But no one believed that fabrication, least of all those who made it. And even had it been true, it was certainly not the proud Jews, or their prouder priests, who would have been eager to bring a champion of their oppressed nationality to judgment. Some would have alleged, with greater sincerity, that He had spoken blasphemy—that He claimed divine attributes and prerogatives. Others would have asserted that He was a dangerous and irreligious teacher, undermining the whole Jewish law and polity, sapping the foundations of the ancient hierarchy, respecting neither priests nor temple nor scribes nor Sabbath days. And still others would have said that, while putting forth royal pretensions, claiming to be the predicted King of Judah, the promised Messiah of Israel, He yet was essentially unkingly, and positively refused to enter upon that work of political deliverance and conquest which they considered as necessarily messianic; that He had raised hopes and expectations only to bitterly disappoint and betray them. And in all these accusations, when thoroughly sifted, there would have been found some germs of truth. Christ *had* claimed, with more or less directness, divine attributes and prerogatives, which claim the chief priests and rulers in all probability did consider blasphemous. He *was* undermining that corrupt hierarchy, that worn-out ecclesiasticism which had outlived its time, and preparing the way for that new society, the Christian Church, which was to supersede it. He *did* disregard the authority of scribe and Pharisee, denouncing, with the most withering invective, the hypocrisy of the one and the formalism of the other, and had, consequently, made implacable enemies of both. He *did* bitterly disappoint the hope and expectations of the people. Yes, and of His own disciples also; hopes and expectations which had been raised at the first announcement of his character and mission, and which up to the last, almost, they fondly believed were about to be fulfilled. And so all these who had their different enmities to settle—furious people, vindictive scribes, outraged Pharisees, and fanatical priests—were gathered now about His cross, gloating over the revenge which together they had wreaked on Him.

There is a consideration which, perhaps, may explain in some measure the frantic joy and glee which belittle even their enmity on this occasion, and which betrayed men so careful of appearances as the Pharisees invariably were into the most unseemly demonstrations.

Shortly after the baptism, in all the narratives of the evangelists, we come upon the fact of the Lord's possession and exercise of miraculous powers. The exhibitions of the supernatural might with which He was clothed are not very frequent, indeed, but neither are they simply occasional. They occurred often enough to make the fame of them very widely known. Probably many thousand people both in Galilee and Judæa had seen one or more miracles of the Master, or were personally acquainted with some who had. Some of the chief men and rulers had themselves been present on several of these occasions, and we never find them denying the supernatural character of these works or their reality, though they do not hesitate to attribute the derivation of such power to Satan. It could not well be that any of the elders or people at Jerusalem were ignorant of the Galilean prophet's remarkable gift. It was noised abroad everywhere. Even Herod had heard of it; and when Jesus was brought before him, we are told that he was "glad," for "he hoped to have seen some miracle done by Him."

Now the question occurs to us, how was it that priests and people, knowing what they did, ventured upon the arrest and persecution of One necessarily so formidable? A recent writer has given great prominence to the fact that the Lord always exercised His supernatural power under a self-imposed restraint; limiting Himself to deeds of beneficence, and putting Himself on a level with the weakest, for purposes of hostility or self-defence. This will be found, upon consideration, to be generally if not strictly true; and it may be, as he suggests, that this fact was now almost universally recognized. Yet we cannot conceive how His enemies up even to the last could fail to be more or less apprehensive. When the order went forth from the Sanhedrim for His arrest, it must have been with no little uncertainty as to the result. They felt it necessary to employ treason to accomplish their object. And even then the "great multitude" that "went forth with swords and staves to take Him" would seem to imply an expected and formidable opposition. Naturally enough they could not foresee that the Master would quietly suffer Himself to be led away to execution. Even His forewarned disciples could not believe that. Once before they had called upon Him to destroy His enemies with fire from heaven, and now doubtless they expected that the time had come. And for one moment it seemed as if the expectation were about to be realized. When the officers and band and crowd approached Him, and in reply to their inquiries for Jesus, He answered, " I am He," we are told " they went backward and fell to the ground," smote down as it would seem, by a word. But in the next moment He delivers Himself to their will. Can we not appreciate the incredulity, the bewilderment, the dismay of the disciples? Had the Lord, then, become indeed suddenly powerless? May not this suspicion account in part for their instant desertion—desertion of one to whom but a brief while before they had pledged such firm, resolute, unfaltering devotion? And must it not have been a mingled feeling of triumph and apprehension with which the rulers looked upon their prisoner—triumph gradually becoming more and more predominant as the conviction grew upon them that He was indeed delivered to their will—yet the apprehension not dying all away until they saw Him securely nailed to the cross? Then at length there remained no fear to cloud their wicked joy. The great Prophet was indeed overthrown. It was a thing incredible to them that He should suffer Himself to be crucified, if He had the power to prevent it. The unspeakable magnanimity, the marvellous self-restraint of Jesus was something which their thoughts could never, never reach. Looking on Him as He hung suspended there, they felt Him to be wholly at their mercy. And then the flood of blasphemy and mockery pours forth, wagging of heads and jeer on jeer, taunt and scoff shaping themselves out of fears but just now dead: "He saved others; Himself He cannot save. If He be the king of Israel, let Him now come down from the cross, and we will believe Him."

It is a strange and almost appalling fact, when you come to reflect upon it, how, sometimes, the deepest expressions of the deepest truths have come from the lips of godless and wicked men. We are led to see that the Almighty does not limit Himself to His own chosen servants, but often employs instrumentalities which we should not have suspected for the declaration of eternal principles and the manifestations of His will. Men, consciously or unconsciously, are made to fill a place and take a part in that purpose which runs through all the ages. It is not only the hardened heart of the Egyptian king that has been raised up to be a blind and unwilling servitor of the Lord; nor only the avaricious Assyrian prophet that has been constrained to speak words deeper and truer and more far-reaching than he knew. All history, in this sense, is but the repetition and confirmation of these Hebrew records, and men come upon the stage and pass away with no thought that they have said or done anything not altogether of their own volition, and yet after-ages have detected in their actions or their speech something behind the mere words and deeds,—that Providence which guides and controls and penetrates them all. Thus, as we look back, perhaps the deepest expressions of the sacrifice of Christ have come to us from the lips of His enemies. There are two instances of this, each, in its way, most significant and remarkable,—instances where the utterance from the standpoint of the speakers was partial, unrighteous, and untrue; but from our standpoint, the standpoint of Christian faith, contained the very sum and substance of the truth. The earlier of these is the judgment of Caiaphas, the Sadducean high priest; when urging the death of Jesus, he declared that it was "expedient that one man should die for the people, and that the whole nation perish not." As he meant it, it was a cruel, wicked, and indefensible sentiment. His opinion was, that as Jesus might possibly become the innocent occasion of a collision between the Jews and the Romans, it would be better to murder Him than run any risk of such a catastrophe. We need not argue now the immorality of that judgment. We are all agreed, in theory at least, that it is never expedient to do wrong; never expedient to commit an act of flagrant injustice. Yet there is a sense in which it *was* expedient that one man should die for the people—that sense in which the Heavenly Father could give up the only-begotten Son, and the only-begotten Son could give up Himself to die, that all mankind should not perish. And St. John, recalling that expression years afterwards, could find in it so deep a statement of the sacrifice of Christ that he could say of Caiaphas, remembering his office, that "he prophesied!" The other instance is this taunt of these priests and scribes and elders at the cross: "He saved others; Himself He cannot save." How false was that, as they understood it! How great the delusion that could suppose that the same power that rebuked the winds and bade the waves be still; that made the blind see, and the deaf hear, and the dumb speak; that restored to the widow of Nain her son, and raised up Lazarus from the dead,—could not, indeed, come down from the cross! Did they imagine that the nail had been wrought, or the cord woven, that could hold Him there,—Him whose slightest word, as they stood by in their fancied security, would have brought down fire upon their heads from heaven, or at whose call legions of angels would have rushed to sweep away that paltry guard? Him in answer to whose dying cry the earth shuddered and the sun itself grew dark? The might of omnipotence still trembled on His word. We know that He could have saved Himself at any moment if He would. He declares, distinctly, "No man taketh my life from me; I lay it down of myself." He says to Pilate, "Thou couldst have no power against me except it were given thee from above." Even in the hour of His arrest He healed an assailant's wound. On the cross itself He could open the gates of paradise to a penitent. How, then, could He not come down? Still, there, too, His revilers prophesied better than they knew. He could not, in very truth, come down. "He saved others; Himself He could not save." The constraint of love, the moral necessity involved in His character and mission, kept Him there. The condition of the salvation which He brought to man was the sacrifice of Himself. *Because* "he saved others," therefore "Himself He cannot save." That is the law of redemption always; that is the meaning, the principle, the eternal necessity of the Cross of Christ.

The work of Christ as the mediator may be considered under two distinct aspects : namely, the reconciliation of man to God, and the reconciliation of God to man; and in each of these the cross was equally a necessity.

Thus in the first it was essential for the removal of the hostility, enmity, and alienation which ever since his fall had turned the heart of man against his Maker. St. Paul, in an expression which seems to cover the whole ground, has given us this statement of it: " You, that were sometime alienated and enemies in your mind by wicked works, yet now hath He reconciled in the body of His flesh through death." The representation seems to be—and all our deepest experience is in accordance with it—that by evil-doing we become in our own minds alienated, estranged from God, and at last even His enemies. As we recall the hints that are given us in Scripture of man's original condition, and contemplate the nobilities which even in his degradation remain to him, we gain the conception of a being who was in very truth the moral likeness of his Creator, and can well believe the assertion of the apostle that a man " is the image and the glory of God." Then, in that pure, fresh, primeval time, when sin as yet was not, the relation between the human and the divine must have been that of most true and perfect harmony. The phrase which represents the man as walking in sweet companionship with his Maker seems not so much a figure as a reality. No cloud, no suspicion, no estrangement was between them then. As long as obedience was unbroken, man never doubted God, never misinterpreted, never misunderstood Him. There was no let or hindrance to his love. But with the first transgression all this was changed. The consciousness of guilt led the man to hide himself; to alienate his affections from God, to be afraid of Him, to distrust Him, almost to hate Him. We know how true that is even in our own experience with each other. You cannot sin against an earthly father, and not thereby in your own mind put a constraint upon the freedom of your communion with him, dim your knowledge of him, and estrange your affections from him; it is so with husband and wife, friend with friend. And this grows with the frequency and the depth of the transgression. Thus it has been with man and God. Not only the Bible, but all history, shows how soon and how far the human race wandered from its first estate. Out of his own fear, distrust, suspicion, all the evil imaginings of his heart, man created for himself a God of his own; not the God of Adam, but his debased and degraded counterfeit; not a father, a companion, a friend, but a taskmaster, a tyrant, yes, even an enemy. The revelations of Himself, which God from time to time still gave, had only a partial and restricted influence. Even the special education of a chosen people for more than a thousand years could not win them back to see Him as He is, to know and love Him. The suspicion, the distrust, had become so inveterate that it seemed as if no instrumentality, no resource, nothing human or divine could remove it. And so in the "fulness of time" came the last appeal. *God was manifested in the flesh.*

The life of Jesus Christ was the new and completed revelation of the nature and character and life of God. Yet that, too, could only avail as it should demonstrate beyond even the possibility of cavil the infinite tenderness of the Infinite Love. For this men must see God in sacrifice, must be astounded and overwhelmed by the exhibition of the fact that sacrifice—"to give rather than to receive," mysterious and incredible as it may seem—is the eternal law of His Being. And therefore, in His perfect revelation of the character and life of God, in His disclosure of Him as He really is, the cross of Christ, the sacrifice of Himself, became a moral necessity; He could reconcile us, who sometime had been alienated in our minds, in no other way than "in the body of His flesh through death."

But Christ, as the mediator, must also reconcile God to man. I do not propose to enter here upon any of those aspects of the Atonement which are so dim and dark, and hard to understand. There is at least one sense, perfectly comprehensible, in which this reconciliation was effected. God must be reconciled to man, and who of us can doubt, looking in upon himself and sadly conscious of all the evil that is in him,—who, I say, can doubt that such reconciliation is needed? God, by necessity of His own inherent holiness and purity, can never be satisfied with man, can never be reconciled to him until he sees him being or becoming what, in the beginning, He created him to become and be. But man, fallen as he is, can, of himself, never rise to that. He has offered many sacrifices to God, but conscious always that they were imperfect—that they could never take away his sin. And therefore Christ, as the mediator, comes as his representative to offer the one perfect sacrifice for him—to stand, as it were, in his stead, and be and do what God would have him be and do. Now what is that which God would have and see in man to make him acceptable before him? Nothing less than the reflection of His own character, conformity to His own spirit, absolute, implicit obedience to His will. And that was realized in Jesus Christ. His life was the pattern of God's perfections, His spirit was the answering spirit to that which is in heaven, His obedience had that absoluteness which had been prophesied as the meaning of His life. "Lo! I come. In the volume of the book it is written of Me to do Thy *will*, O God!" But the doing of that will involved faithfulness unto death. That alone could be the perfect vindication of His utter self-abnegation, and attest the worth of that absolute sacrifice of His own will which He should render. And so the cross was "set before Him." What its acceptance cost Him we read in all the closing chapters of His ministry, and more especially in the record of His passion. Whatever else may be uncertain, this, at least, is sure: that sacrifice was no semblance, no unreality, no make-believe. He shrank from death with a strange and terrible recoil. As its prospect grows nearer every day, His soul becomes " exceeding sorrowful." In the garden there are "strong cryings and tears," the almost passionate entreaty, "O, My Father! If it be possible, let this cup pass from Me." But when He becomes satisfied that it is inevitable, that it is a moral necessity in the great work of redemption, that only thus can He offer in behalf of man a perfect and sufficient sacrifice to God, there is the meek acquiescence: "Nevertheless, not Mine, but Thy will be done!" The last struggle is over, and He has given up Himself to die. And thus the sacrifice which had been found to be a principle in the nature of God is made now and forever the highest law of humanity. *We save others; ourselves we cannot save.*

For, let us realize and believe, on this day above all others, that just as surely as we are participants, alas! in that guilt which nailed Jesus to His cross, through the sinfulness common to us and the priests, scribes, elders, people gathered there; so, too, we may have, nay, must have, if we are to be accepted, our part in the sacrifice of Jesus Christ. What He did perfectly we must do over again in our imperfect way, surrendering up ourselves to the will of God as completely and unreservedly as we can. Here, too, the Lord has left us " an example that we should follow His steps." If He is to be in very truth our Representative, our Advocate, our Redemption, our Satisfaction with the Father, we must take up and repeat, in our degree and measure, the lesson of His cross. And how better can we show our love and gratitude for all that He has done and suffered for us than by giving entrance to His spirit in our hearts, to let it mould and shape and inspire our own lives? "He saved others; Himself He cannot save." That is the motto of the cross of Christ; and the reversal of that—we save ourselves, others we cannot save—is to "crucify the Lord afresh, and put Him" again to "open shame."

XIII.

THE CREDIBILITY OF THE RESURRECTION.

[KINGSBRIDGE, 1876.]

"Why should it be thought a thing incredible with you, that God should raise the dead?"—ACTS xxvi. 8.

WITH the return of Easter we give expression again to our immortal hopes. We commemorate a divine event on which these hopes are upbuilt. We look back over nineteen centuries to an open sepulchre, a vacant tomb, some "folded linen clothes," "the shining angels," and the glorified Presence which "appeared unto many." This fact has confirmed and fortified the deepest instinct of our nature; it has given a new impulse to "those thoughts that wander through eternity;" it has reinspired man's heart; it has translated the hesitating conclusion of his reason into the firm assurance of his faith. We feel and know, now, that we are immortal; and for witness to it we point to the Resurrection from the dead. We say that, "as in Adam all die, even so in Christ shall all be made alive." We say that, as we are "planted together in the likeness of His death, we shall be also in the likeness of His Resurrection." We will suffer no doubts, no misgivings, to rob us of this our great Christian heritage. For it *is* our great Christian heritage: this high, hopeful, on-looking assurance into which we all are born. It has become the birthright of the world; although, unlike other birthrights, it may, by the world, be little valued. Yet is the hope of immortality something which a man—simply because he is a man—should never suffer himself, under any stress of adverse argument or appearances, to part with. It brings with it "the power of an endless life;" and, without that power, life is, and can be, only "vanity and vexation of spirit."

But however it may be with a distrustful world, however it may be with gathering numbers here and there, the Church's heart stands firm. Men may have abandoned their own hope, and sought to prove hers an illusion, but with every returning Resurrection Day she lifts her voice again in adoration and thanksgiving. Wherever in this wide world she hath a habitation and a name, there her praise bursts forth, and her joy rolls on, in carols and anthems and the Easter hymn. Flowers typify, as only such fair symbols can, the gladness that is in her. For her high assurance is this: Death hath now "no more dominion" over us. We have been "begotten again unto a lively hope, by the Resurrection of Jesus Christ from the dead!"

Immortality, we read, hath been "brought to light" in the revelation of Jesus Christ. It was, as it were, in the twilight before—a dim, obscure, shadowy kind of hope—something that was apt to fade and melt away upon any close inspection of it. Always an instinct of our nature, it was hardly ever more than an instinct, and grew, as instincts grow, only fitfully and slowly, into a rational conviction; and even as a conviction of the reason, so uncertain was the ground, it was generally weak and inoperative. A speculation rather than a belief, a dream of the imagination rather than an assurance of the intellect—this alone is the witness to its essential feebleness. Sometimes, indeed, as in the Eastern religions, it was exalted into an article of faith; but it mostly assumed a vague, pantheistic form, and so emptied itself of all moral power. Egypt, perhaps, is the only exception to this; but there the doctrine of immortality became the antagonist rather than the stay of ethical conceptions; insomuch that some scholars think that Moses designedly thrust it into the background lest Israel should be corrupted by the superstitions which, in their Egyptian experience, had been inseparably connected with it. Greek thought, it is true, had found many noble arguments and beautiful analogies in support of a life beyond the grave; but the analogies failed before any rigorous criticism, and the arguments rose and fell in the changing fortunes of debate. Body and soul, moreover, seem to be inseparable, not only in fact, but in our conceptions of them; and therefore, in the almost universal separation of them, the personal immortality of the individual hardly ever advanced in definiteness and reality beyond the old idea of the Homeric shade.

There was, indeed, a remedy for this; but, as we know, when the Greek first heard of the Resurrection from the dead, he "mocked." Among the Jews, too, the cultivated and sceptical Sadducees denied it. Perhaps the most that we can say on a review of ancient thought is this: that this deep instinct of our nature had been slowly growing until it was prepared to pass into a *spiritual conviction* when once immortality, in the revelation of Christ, should be brought to light. Sure it is that it first became this " spiritual conviction" on Easter Day. No mere instinct, no mere argument henceforth, but an inspiration of the mind and heart, which should change the whole course of human history and transform the world.

Perhaps we shall realize best our great " Christian heritage,"—what cause we have to-day for adoration and thanksgiving,—if we contrast two ever-memorable scenes, far apart in space and time, yet having a kindred significance, and a real relation to each other,—occasions on which the credibility of man's immortality was the question asked and answered. The one is the very noblest scene in all pagan literature; the other, one of the most inspiring incidents of early Christian history.

Some hundred years before the Advent there was a little band of brilliant men assembled in a prison at Athens. They had come together to take a last farewell of one who was very near and dear to them. For the master, of whom these men were the disciples, was condemned to die. It was early morning now, but he was to drink the deadly hemlock as the first shades of evening fell. With the closing day he should look his last upon the bright city and the fair earth and the genial sun. He had been a "witness to the truth," and his fate was the doom with which men so often reward that witness. And standing thus face to face with death, on the very threshold of eternity, the question of all questions with him is this question of the credibility of man's immortality. Once again, in the way of reassurance, he will go over the great argument. He fears, however, that his personal interest in the matter may be too deep to permit him to be impartial, and therefore entreats his friends to refute him should his reasonings fail; not to suffer him to delude himself or them with fallacies, and thus, like the bee, "leave his sting" in them before he dies. Two doubters of an opposing school are present on this occasion, and they readily agree to perform the part required of them. And so through a long summer's day the great argument—logical, ethical, metaphysical—rises and goes on. At first, triumphantly, the goal appears in sight, and the conclusion clear. But as the controversy deepens, suddenly there comes a check, nay, a reverse, swiftly passing into disaster, and to all appearance irretrievable defeat. For a time the contending voices are hushed in silence, depression comes upon the spectators, a kind of despair seizes them, and they say, bitterly, that they will never trust to arguments more. The master alone is undismayed. His favorite disciple is seated at his feet; he puts his hand upon his head, and says: "To-morrow, Phædo, I suppose that these fair locks of yours will be severed."

"I suppose so."

"Not so, if you will take my advice."

"What shall I do, then?"

"To-day, Phædo, and not to-morrow, if this argument dies and cannot be brought to life again, you and I will both shave our heads; and if I were you, and could not maintain my ground against these men, I would take an oath, like the Argives, not to wear hair any more until I had renewed the conflict and defeated them."

And thereupon the inquiry is taken up again, and the argument proceeds uninterruptedly on to its triumphant end. But, after all, it has led only to a hesitating conclusion, and the disputants concede to it only such qualified approval as is consistent with the weakness of our human faculties. Socrates dies in the hope of immortality, but neither the argument nor the hope could altogether silence his friends' fears; for "there is a child within us," as one of them expressed it, "to whom death is a kind of hobgoblin, and who will not be persuaded not to be afraid when he is alone with him in the dark."

Pass now to the other scene; it is at Cæsarea Philippi, a city some distance from Jerusalem; the time about midway in the first Christian century. Here, too, the chief speaker is a prisoner, a man "in bonds." *His* course, also, is drawing to its close. He is to be sent in chains to "Cæsar's judgment seat," and then, in a little while, all will be over. About him now are gathered a brilliant company—a king, a queen, a governor, and various other noble lookers-on. They, too, would hear the great argument of man's immortality. For here, also, this is the subject of inquiry. The prisoner says: "I stand and am judged for the hope of the promise made of God unto our fathers: for which hope's sake, King Agrippa, I am accused of the Jews. Why," he goes on, "why should it be thought a thing incredible with you, that God should raise the dead?" He, too, will set forth this great credibility; but with him it is not a speculation, but a revelation; not an array of reasons, but an array of facts; and what an array it is! "I verily thought with myself, that I ought to do many things contrary to the name of Jesus of Nazareth. Which thing I also did in Jerusalem: and many of the saints did I shut up in prison, and being exceedingly mad against them, I persecuted them even unto strange cities. Whereupon, as I went to Damascus, at mid-day, O king, I saw in the way a light from heaven, above the brightness of the sun, shining round about me and them which journeyed with me. And when we were all fallen to the earth, I heard a voice speaking unto me, and saying in the Hebrew tongue, Saul, Saul, why persecutest thou me? And I said, Who art thou, Lord? And he said, I am Jesus whom thou persecutest. But rise, and stand upon thy feet: for I have appeared unto thee to make thee a minister and a witness of those things which thou hast seen. Whereupon, O King Agrippa, I was not disobedient unto the heavenly vision: but continue unto this day, witnessing both to small and great, saying none other things than the prophets did say should come: that Christ should suffer, and that he should be the first that should rise from the dead." But here the governor, with loud voice, breaks in: "Paul, thou art beside thyself; much learning doth make thee mad." And the prisoner answers, with pathetic courtesy, "I am not mad, most noble Festus, but speak forth the words of truth and soberness." Yea, "words of truth and soberness," but what a great " spiritual conviction " was in those words! No hesitating conclusion, no qualified approval of frail arguments here, but, in one heart at least, a mighty, irresistible faith. The king himself is " almost persuaded " to be a Christian.

For the moment that brilliant company is hushed and overawed before the revelation of spiritual power. The prisoner goes to " Cæsar's judgment seat," but his faith makes converts even " in Cæsar's household." Everywhere it inspires the hearts and minds of men. It becomes a world-belief. The issue of it is a Christendom.

St. Paul's testimony was "with power," because, as the scriptures say, he had " the witness in himself." It became inseparable, indistinguishable from his inmost consciousness. He did not rest his assurance of immortality upon a mere speculative logic, nor yet upon the mere external evidence of fact. With him it had passed beyond these things into the revelation of the spirit. Now and always it was *a spiritual conviction.* That heavenly vision was indeed a reality—an outward fact; and it is thus that he brings it forward in the great argument of the Corinthians as his own personal testimony to the Resurrection of Christ: " Seen of others, and, last of all, seen of me also, as of one born out of due time." But again, as in the Galatians, it is the spiritual revelation that is uppermost in his mind. "I certify you, brethren," he says, "I certify you, that this gospel is not after man, neither received I it of man, neither was I taught it, but by the revelation of Jesus Christ." "Ye have heard how in time past I persecuted the Church, but it pleased God to reveal His Son in me." "Reveal His Son in me!" Christ "revealed" *in* him, "formed" *in* him, "risen" *in* him—this, and this alone, made a literal Resurrection not incredible. The apostle himself was, as it were, a man "alive from the dead." The past had fallen all away, and he had come forth into a new and divine life. His Lord had given him the victory. He felt now that "death had no more dominion over him," and could say that it had lost "its sting."

Our hopes, indeed, are inseparably bound up with the great fact which we commemorate; but only as God translates that fact for us into a spiritual experience, only as it pleases Him to "reveal His Son" in *us also*, do we reach the high assurance of faith. Arguments may fail, facts may be disputed, but the soul knows "in whom" it has believed. The Spiritual Resurrection here and now, the Resurrection of our own dead selves—this, and this alone, can make the resurrection of all other dead things credible.

But then all other resurrections *do* become credible. Then is the fulfilment of the Lord's word, and "all things" become "possible to him that believeth." In that possibility life itself is glorified and transfigured. A sovereign joy wells up in the midst of the world's tribulation. What are jailors and dungeon walls and Cæsar's seat to a man who stands in this apocalypse? His own life becomes the paradox of which he speaks: "Dying, and behold we live; sorrowful, yet always rejoicing; having nothing, and yet possessing all things." To him belong the lessons of the past, the meanings of the present, the prophecies of the future. He is an heir of Christ. Hope, imperishable hope, and all its divine illuminations, are his heritage. And so this prisoner of the Lord can turn, in the splendid magnificence of his great humility, to that almost persuaded king, and say, "I would to God, that not only thou, but also all who hear me this day, were both almost, and altogether such as I am, except these bonds." Ah! how blessed should we be could we only rise up to and abide in this high spiritual exaltation of St. Paul! Then, indeed, should we hear a divine voice, saying, "Behold, I make all things new." And what reassurance for ourselves and for the world would that voice bring us! How these clouds of gloom, despondency, despair, would all break and pass away! For with the apostle the Resurrection did not mean simply man's personal immortality. It meant more, much more than that. It meant "the restitution of all things," the life again of hopes which had seemed to die. It meant the victory of truth, the triumph of virtue, the persistence of the good. It was the witness that nothing worthy is, or can be, "holden of death." It was the assurance that no man's work is vain "in the Lord."

It was his gospel of hope. Christianity rose upon his vision with smiles in her eyes, and sunlight on her brow. To him the Resurrection of Christ was the revelation of the divine, the universal law—the law of life, everywhere and in everything victorious over the law of sin and death. His whole mind was, as it were, dazzled with that brightness of the mid-day heaven. For in that light, that divine light, history could no longer be to him the dreary funereal pageant which men make it; the sad, continuous procession of vanishing forms—forms which are seen a moment, only to sink into oblivion. Men, institutions, nations, do indeed die; but the essential life in them reappears again, and is immortal. The history of his own lost people, his "brethren according to the flesh," was not yet told. The "remnant" lived, and in the remnant, as he says, should "all Israel be saved." Everywhere about him was a dying pagan world, but everywhere about him, too, were pagan converts in these pagan cities—men who, in a figure, had come forth out of their graves, and at the word of the Master had been "loosed" and "let go." Nay, nature herself should share in this great Resurrection, which her own fair symbols typified; for in his divinely illumined eyes the whole creation, the visible earth and heavens, was expectant of the hour—waiting for "the manifestation of the sons of God."

"Why, then, should it be thought a thing incredible" with us "that God should raise the dead?" Let it be our Easter service to think it not incredible. Let us rather find our joy and peace in believing. The frowning face of circumstance may be set against us, our feet may be in the mire where no ground is, our hopes may be broken, and our hearts have failed us. The more need, then, to take home to ourselves the comfort of this Easter Day; the more need, then, to realize the divine law of life which works in us and in all things—the law of renewal, revival, Resurrection; the law which is mighty, and which must and will prevail.

XIV.

THE POWER OF THE RESURRECTION.

[KINGSBRIDGE, 1877.]

"That I may know . . . the power of his resurrection."—
PHIL. iii. 10.

IN the services of the Christian Year, the life of our Lord has been brought before us in its historic reality. The solemn hours of Advent, with their waiting expectation, were followed by the hymn of the Nativity. At the Baptism we went with the Redeemer to the work of His earthly ministry; and thence, step by step, we passed in the progress of the story through all the scenes of His great humility—through the lonely temptation, and the sorrowful farewell, up to the bitter cross itself, on which the great sacrifice should be completed; and then we saw the body, bruised and broken, laid away in the guarded sepulchre. It was the seeming triumph of the powers of Darkness. Death was apparently the victor, and its captivity still remained, in outward seeming, with the grave. But it was only in appearance. For from the grave and death and hell the Redeemer was to rise again—to rise in the might of an eternal conquest. "*He is risen.*" And therefore the sorrow of the Passion is transfigured in the joy that fills the Easter hymns. "Old things have passed away; behold, all things are become new." Henceforth death has lost "its sting," and "the victory" is no longer with the grave. For "now is Christ risen from the dead, and become the first-fruits of them that slept."

The transition of feeling which marks the passage from Holy Week to Easter is prophetic of that other transition to which the Church shall pass when, no longer militant, she shall be at last triumphant. The joy which this high festival brings us is an intimation and an earnest of that other and more abiding joy which shall be ours when the dispensation of grace shall be closed in the dispensation of glory. The principle of sacrifice is that which still meets us now. The cross is still the law of each disciple's way. The humiliation of the Master must be repeated in all the Master's followers. For us, too, there must be temptation and passion, and death and burial. For we live here, in the expression of St. Paul, filling up "the measure of the sufferings of Christ." We have to pass through the baptism that He was baptized with, and to drink, however unwillingly, of His cup. And therefore in the Christian life, however hopeful it may be, there is, and must always be, something of sadness. It is because of this life-long companionship, this necessary school of obedience, as has been often pointed out, that Christianity so exalts—nay almost enthrones—sorrow. And yet through all the humiliation of earth there runs a deep undertone of joy. In that sad record of the passion which we so lately read, were we not conscious of a reserved assurance which made the reading of it possible?

Could we have borne to dwell on all the details of the crucifixion of the Lord Jesus, had not our thought anticipated "the third day," when He should "rise again"? Even so, in all the travail of the world, our thought goes on before this "light affliction which is but for a moment," to the "far more exceeding and eternal weight of glory." We read of our Saviour that, for the joy that was set before Him, He "endured the cross, despising the shame;" and it is written that because He became "obedient even unto death," "therefore God hath also highly exalted Him." The same joy, the same exaltation, are set before us. "For this cause we faint not." Nay, may we not say in the spirit and in the words of the apostle, "I count all things but loss for the excellency of the knowledge of Christ Jesus my Lord," "that I may know Him, and the power of His resurrection, and the fellowship of His sufferings, being made conformable unto His death; if by any means I might attain unto the Resurrection of the dead"?

The pledge of that attainment, for himself and for us, he found in the fact which we commemorate. Well may we come with flowers and hymns and uplifted hearts to welcome Easter. Let children sing the Resurrection carols, and let all the earth be glad. Our highest efforts cannot reach the full measure of the benediction which the season holds. No human thought can compass all the issues that are involved in it. God placed of old His bow of promise in the clouds, but in the Resurrection of the Christ we have a fact before which all earthly hues grow dim. The very life core of Christianity, as has been truly said of it, is in one simple picture which the gospels give, —the broken tomb, the risen Christ, "the shining angels," and, apart and away by themselves, "the folded linen clothes." For so shall the corruptible accidents of our mortal bodies be all laid aside, and we— we ourselves—be "clothed upon with our house which is from heaven." But blot out that picture, and our faith is vain. A dead Christ cannot be a quickening spirit. Because He lives, therefore "we shall live also." That is the Christian ground of the Christian hope. For He in whom our "life is hid," and with whom all our immortal fortunes are bound up, was "declared," as the apostle says, "to be the Son of God, with power by His Resurrection from the dead."

But while we accept the Resurrection as a fact, and commemorate it as an historic event, we shall be led also and more especially, if we enter into the thought of St. Paul, to realize it as a power, or spiritual principle, operative in nature and the life of humanity. He speaks of the *power* of Christ's Resurrection. The word translated "power" has been defined as the original of our word "dynamic," denoting a certain impetus, a causative force which is cumulative, growing stronger and more impelling as it goes. Thus it stands for an active, living, efficient spiritual principle. It is not a mere fact, nor is it the mere influence of a fact, that is brought before us; it is the eternal law, rather, of which the fact is only an expression. Over against "the law" of Death the Scriptures disclose "the law" of the Resurrection. "As in Adam all die, so in Christ all are made alive." In us, but not of us, there is a vital spiritual force which can quicken our mortal bodies, inspire our thoughts, and transform our lives. It is something which will become for us, if we will let it, a vital energy operating in our hearts, —the seed within us, as it were, of a new and regenerate life. It is the renewing, the restorative, the re-creative influence of heavenly things. It is the quickening inspiration of God's breath. It is the principle that makes all things new. And therefore St. Paul prays that he may feel and know in his own soul this divine power, this spiritual life-giving principle, which had its highest manifestation in the Resurrection of the Christ. For the " power" which " raised up Jesus from the dead," which made it impossible that He should be " holden of death," is declared to be the selfsame power, the selfsame principle, which must quicken us also at the last day, and raise us now out of deadness in sins to " newness of life."

That was the great inspiring gospel of St. Paul. From land to land he went, preaching everywhere Jesus and the Resurrection. He proclaimed not only that the literal fact itself was the only foundation on which men must rest their belief in the reality of a future existence; but also, and more especially, that the power, the spiritual principle, the operative quickening grace of God, which had its highest and most wonderful expression in that fact, is and must be the cause of the new birth, the new life, the spiritual resurrection of the believer. And the results justified this gospel which he preached. The Resurrection and its principle, proclaimed to the world, became a power in the world. It broke the long night in which for so many ages it had lain ; it stirred men's hearts and consciences as the renewed life of Nature stirs all her forms again in spring; society, which was morally dying or dead, gave signs of returning vitality ; the dry bones came together and revived ; and the utter spiritual dearth of the Empire was transformed into the zeal and energy, the faith and hope and charity of the Catholic Church. Then was seen everywhere a moral and spiritual parallel to what St. Matthew says happened at Jerusalem on the occasion of the Resurrection. The bodies of some that slept, he tells us, came forth, and "went into the holy city, and appeared unto many." Throughout the whole world men arose, as it were, from their graves. For a voice had sounded in each man's ear : "Awake thou that sleepest, and arise from the dead, and Christ shall give thee light."

It is, then, the power of the Resurrection as manifested in our own lives—the fact of *a spiritual resurrection in us*—that St. Paul more especially insists on, and continually seeks in one way or another to bring before us. He tells us that we are "risen with Christ," and bids us "set our affections" upon those heavenly things which alone are worthy of new-born and regenerate men. He declares that we have been ransomed from Satan and the grave ; that the vocation of holiness has been opened to all ; that the lusts of the flesh, the servitude of sin, the seductions of the world, have, or should have, no more dominion over us. He exhorts us to be worthy of our high calling, to bear in mind the spiritual estate to which we have come, of which we are now made heirs and inheritors; to remember in all this, our sojourning on the earth, that we are citizens of an eternal kingdom. Thus the Resurrection in his thought is connected, and connected inseparably, with the practice of virtue, with growth in holiness, with the simple, homely, common moralities of our every-day life. He will not suffer us to give it a merely speculative instead of a practical interest. Only once does he sum up the evidence in its favor, and ask, triumphantly, "Why should it be thought a thing incredible with you that God should raise the dead?" In the Corinthians he has made, as everybody knows, one great argument from it in support of man's immortality; but with the conclusion of that he passes to the more spiritual view of the matter, and the reiteration again of his own favorite theme. He will not even linger long over those visions of glory, those beatitudes of heaven, those unspeakable things, for which the opening of this mysterious gate of death might have prepared us. He seeks rather to impress upon us, with all his own wealth and energy of expression, that there is a *spiritual resurrection*, a literal "dying unto sin and living again unto righteousness," a veritable "rising from the dead," possible for each and all of us here and now. We are called to believe and realize that all the great realities in our Lord's experience may become to us—nay, should become to us—even while we wear this mortal flesh, equal realities in our own; that we may be "baptized into Christ's death;" that by "continually mortifying our corrupt affections" we may be "buried with him;" that the very self-same power which quickened and raised the Lord's body may quicken and raise a soul "dead in trespasses and sins;" that as Christ came forth from His sepulchre " alive for evermore," so we may come forth from the graves of " our dead selves " to higher and better things; that as He ascended in visible presence to " the right hand of the Father," so we, also, though our feet still linger on the earth, " in heart and mind may thither ascend, and with Him continually dwell."

The spiritual resurrection, then, according to St. Paul, is no figure of speech, no rhetorical analogy, no fanciful conceit, no dream of a mystical or disordered mind. Perhaps to some of us it may seem so, for we are fallen upon evil times; our lot is in an age whose boast is in its shallow logic, and which delights to honor a pretentious and vainglorious science. We are affected more than we know by the intellectual atmosphere we live in, and the drift of thought to-day is largely in the direction of a vulgar, self-confident materialism. There are no longer any mysteries, as it would seem, for some of our foremost minds. The multiplication-table and the rule of three, these things, and such things as these, are the only criterion of positive knowledge. All else is guess and fancy and dream. What science cannot tell you is not worth knowing, and what logic cannot prove is unworthy of your belief. No analysis has discovered the secret of life, and therefore it is concluded by some, wise in their own conceits, that there is no secret to discover. There are names—and distinguished names—of men who discredit the existence of the human soul, for no better reason, when you state it plainly, than because the dissecting knife cannot detect it. This strange, mysterious something within us, which holds the vision of invisible and the secret of unutterable things, which looks round on the earth, and sun, and stars of heaven, and yet seems humbly conscious of its own superior greatness, which whispers so persistently in our ear suggestions of its own immortality, which aspires and soars and beats against its earthly tenement sometimes as against prison bars—this strange, mysterious inner man, with all his divine hopes and all his divine fears, he is nothing but a myth, a fraud, an unreality to the mere anatomist. And to such an order of mind, to such a habit of thought, what is this fact of a Resurrection which we commemorate to-day worth? It is worth nothing, because he thinks the evidence for it inconclusive and insufficient. But suppose that evidence could be made overwhelming? Suppose it could amount to a mathematical demonstration, what then would the Resurrection of Christ to such a man be worth? It would be worth this, and only this: He would see in it presumptive proof that the human soul is immortal, that there is another life beyond the grave. But to St. Paul this was only a part, and I think only a secondary part, of the witness of the Resurrection. To him the Resurrection was the pledge, not only of man's future immortality, but of his present perfectibility, of his capacity to rise out of his lower self into a higher and nobler being. It was the witness not only that he would rise, but that he had already risen. For with Christ, and in Christ, according to St. Paul, a new, divine, creative, regenerating power entered into the world; the literal Resurrection of the Christ had its counterpart and its completion in *the spiritual Resurrection of humanity*.

The Christian conception, as it is given by one of its foremost modern expositors, is this: Humanity is re-constituted in Christ. Of the new man He is the ideal and the archetype. The spirit in Him which manifested its life-giving power in raising Him from the dead is no more limited to His individuality than flesh and blood were the attributes of Adam only. It spreads to the whole family of which He is the Head, springing up into His kindred; it flows into them as they look up to Him, and repeats in them the fruits which it produced in Him, making His Resurrection but the first pulsation of an act which next proceeds to theirs. Thus in the Christian thought Christ is not merely an historic individual, but a generic nature, the archetype of a spiritual humanity, sharing his attributes and repeating His experience. And therefore for believers the Resurrection Day is indeed the new birthday of the world. Henceforth man is to count himself as dead unto sin, but alive unto God. He is to claim the condition of one redeemed; of one declared to be *under the law of the Resurrection*.

Wherever we look back to apostles and confessors and martyrs, to noble-minded Christian men and women, to those humbler servants, too, who in their several ways have done the work appointed them faithfully and well, there we may see working in and through them this same life-giving and life-renewing power. Wherever there have been resurrections of nations and communities, wherever after long periods of decay and seeming dissolution they have started into a new growth, and passed from dreary winter to a joyous spring, there has been the manifestation of the law, the power, the spirit principle of Christ's Resurrection. It is the same power, too, which stirs in *us* desires which reach to heavenly things, desires which lift us out of and above ourselves. They are not earth-born; theirs is no mortal source. He who "raised up Jesus from the dead" is the same who inspires us to yield to love, to follow truth, to be worthier and nobler and better men. In every life there are Resurrection hours—and may these Easter hours be numbered with them—hours when we yearn for a freer, fuller, diviner life, and feel and know ourselves amid all the transitoriness of earth to be yet citizens of an eternal kingdom.

The great fact, therefore, which most concerns us, the great truth to which this day should bear its chiefest witness, is the spiritual resurrection which is here and now. For the essential life of heaven, the very life of Christ Himself, first breaks upon us when we rise from sin and self to go forth with purified vision and unworldly mien to do His will; when we know for what we live, and life is opened to us in its divine meaning and in its blessed and triumphant end.

"That I may know the power of His Resurrection"—"that I may know the power of His Resurrection"—yes, let that be our Easter prayer on Easter Day!

For what else do we so much need as this, that the principle of the Lord's Resurrection may find in this present life some sure and true manifestation in us; that these cold, torpid, hardened hearts of ours may be inspired with the enthusiasm of a divine love; that these wasted years may be redeemed by the nobler energies and worthier aims which shall inform those that still remain to us; that we may consecrate ourselves in very deed and truth to God; that all evil habits and desires may die and fall away; that we may take on the similitude of Christ; that we may rise out of the grave of a sad and ignoble past to live more worthily and unselfishly for the future? That is St. Paul's conception of a risen and regenerate man—when the liar becomes truthful, when the robber becomes the giver, when the foul and filthy speaker utters gracious and healthful words. *And that is the one miracle in human experience.* Is there any one here who "thinks it incredible that God should raise the dead;" any one who doubts that bone may come to bone again, and the sinews be re-embroidered on it; who conceives it to be impossible that the dead and buried body should ever rise up again and live? Well, there has been within his own observation or experience, unless both have been singularly contracted and impoverished,—there has been, I say, within his own observation or experience, a moral miracle no less astounding than that. For have we not known—has not every one known—at least one instance of a *spiritual resurrection?* If ever you have seen a man such as the Scripture would describe as "dead in trespasses and sins," irreligious and depraved, given over to evil courses and evil associates, leading a mere animal existence, living out his years "without God in the world;" and if ever you have seen such an one under the mysterious quickening of divine grace rise, whether slowly or suddenly it does not matter, rise to his true and better self, and become pure and noble, and simple and good,— then you have seen that "power of the Resurrection," in comparison with which the literal raising of a dead form to life again is an inferior thing. For the resurrection begun in us is the assurance that the resurrection shall be completed. Let me only rise in heart and mind with Christ, and I need no argument to convince me that my body shall not lie forever in the sepulchre, but shall be rehabilitated and fashioned after the glorious similitude of His own. The great question for you and me and all of us is not whether we shall rise hereafter, but whether we are risen now, whether we may yet arise, before that "night" shall overtake us "in which no man can work."

May we know, O Lord Jesus, the "power" of Thy Resurrection! May we put our unworthy past behind us, and go forth in the might of Thy divine conquest to be truer disciples, more faithful servants, and better men! "Restore to us the years which the locusts have eaten." Let wasted opportunities be redeemed by others more zealously improved. Let the enfeebled will take on new strength, the failing energy find fresh inspiration, and the cold heart glow with rekindled fire. Thou "knowest," Lord, "our necessities before we ask, and our ignorance in asking;" but on this day, at least, we come before Thee with no unworthy or misguided prayer, that we may rise here and now with Thee, content in assurance that thus shall we rise and reign with Thee hereafter!

XV.

THE ASCENSION.

[KINGSBRIDGE, 1869.]

"And while they beheld, He was taken up; and a cloud received Him out of their sight."—ACTS i. 9.

THE last fact recorded in the Scriptures of the person of Christ is His Ascension from Olivet. The strictly biographical narrative terminates with this event, and it is here that the Gospels bring the wonderful history of Jesus to its triumphant close. We shut the book: and the sojourn—the visible life— of the Son of man on earth has ended. That life, indeed, in another and a larger sense had not ceased; and, as we pass on to the history of the Church, we shall find everywhere, in the minds of men, the consciousness of His spiritual presence; everywhere, in the progress of truth, the manifestation and the witness of His unseen continuance in the world. But in visible and earthly guise He no longer exists. With that last journey to Bethany the tale of His journeyings was ended. The places that "knew Him" should henceforth "know Him no more." Men should not seek Him at Nazareth or Capernaum or Jerusalem. That presence should not be seen again on the hill-sides nor in the streets. That voice should be lifted no more in synagogue or temple. No longer should the favored disciples look upon His face or sit at His feet, listening reverently to the wisdom of His words. Here, on the mount, they had looked and listened, even now, for the last time ; and as they looked, and while the echo of His words yet lingered, " He was parted from them ; and a cloud received Him out of their sight." The visible companionship in which they had walked with Him so long was finally interrupted. *They* still remained upon the earth, but their *Lord* had ascended into the heavens.

It cannot fail to excite some surprise, when we come to think of it, that the fact of the Ascension, holding the place in the Gospel which it does, should receive from us comparatively such little attention. It seems, in a measure, to have been lost and swallowed up in greater memories. One might be led to suppose that it held an inferior significance to the other facts of Christian commemoration, or, unlike them, had no practical relation to the Christian life. We are not unmindful of the Nativity and the Crucifixion and the Resurrection, and come to their observance with feelings more and more deeply stirred with each returning year. But beyond the Resurrection from the dead our interest does not often seem to go. Here we leave our Christ, and the fact which follows finds but a vague and uncertain recognition in our thoughts. Yet this is neither the teaching of Scripture, nor the experience of the early or the middle ages of Christianity. The account of the Ascension in the Gospels is indeed brief; but the fact scarcely admitted of a detailed description, with writers who so invariably confined themselves to the most simple and brief narration. It was hopelessly beyond the power of any rhetoric to display; no words could set forth its dignity and grandeur to the eye of men, and the most unpretentious statement of it seemed to be the most fitting. Yet it was a fact scarcely inferior to any other in its influence with the first Christians in the inspiration of its memory and the significance of its teaching. The author of the Book of the Acts makes it the starting-point in his history of the Christian Church, and there is a continually recurring reference to it throughout the Pauline epistles. How large a place it originally held, and for many ages continued to hold, in the thought of Christendom, is seen in the frequent use of it by the great Christian painters. They delighted to lavish upon it all the resources of their art, all the wealth of their genius, and, indeed, never before nor since have art and genius been furnished with such a transcendent theme. But we seem rather to miss its meaning, either from a growing incredulity as to its actual occurrence, or a failure to appreciate the truths of which it is the special and conclusive witness.

It must be acknowledged that the mental habit of our age is somewhat sceptical; that in very many minds there is a deep-seated prejudice against anything that savors of the miraculous and supernatural. This position, of course, if it be consciously assumed and consistently adhered to, necessarily rules out all revealed religion whatsoever. The man who will not admit the possibility of miracles, who will accord to no event a supernatural character, has no place in his recognition for historic Christianity. It is and it must be to him something essentially and altogether different from what, on its face, it so manifestly claims to be. He may do homage to the moralities of the gospel; he may honor its spirit; he may confess that its teaching has been, on the whole, advantageous to mankind; he may even concede that the general outline of its story is grounded on an actual occurrence: but he denies, and on his principles he must deny, every fact which is not capable of a purely natural and rational interpretation. It is evident that the whole body of Christian evidence is thrown away on him; that between such an one and a believer there can be no compromise, no common ground whatever, for he starts out with a proposition which makes it simply impossible for Christianity to vindicate its claim to a divine and authoritative character. Settle it with yourself that a miracle never has occurred and never can; bind your God down, whatever your conception of Him may be, to a strict and invariable conformity with nature's phenomena and laws; make it inconsistent with the divine character that He should for any cause or on any occasion transcend them, and the dogma of a supernatural revelation becomes simply preposterous; you have no alternative but to disallow at once and peremptorily every fact upon which Christendom is upbuilt. It is not, of course, to be supposed that this position should be consciously assumed by an avowedly Christian man, yet the influence of those who do assume it may be traced often enough in modern Christian thought. The influence, indeed, is not altogether bad, for it acts as a check against undue credulity, which not infrequently degenerates into vain and idle superstitions; it makes us cautious in investing with a supernatural character facts and events which admit of a natural explanation. Nevertheless, in the main, it is unquestionably an influence for ill. Some of us are dimly conscious of a certain uneasiness, a vague trouble in our thought, when we are brought face to face with facts which must be either admitted as indisputably supernatural, or else resolved into a mere legend or myth. Such facts, for instance, as the Incarnation, the Resurrection, and the Ascension, admit of no compromise; they cannot be toned down to the level even of extraordinary things; it is impossible to receive them in any sense, and at the same time explain more or less of their miraculous character away. They must be accepted or rejected without equivocation. Yet these facts are so tremendous, both in their nature and their consequences, the demand which they make upon our faith is so enormous, that it is scarcely to be wondered at if even the avowed believer should pause sometimes and half re-open the question of their credibility. The first two, indeed, have a witness in our own hearts more and not less conclusive than any outside testimony. We feel that the Saviour, as he is presented to us in the gospels, must have been divine; that such a character, unlike any other that we have known or read of, did, in very truth, proceed and come from God. And so, too, when we have seen Him slain by His enemies, and His body laid away in the sepulchre, we have within us an almost instinctive conviction that such a life did not and could not die; and the tidings of the Resurrection come, as it were, in answer to the spontaneous hope of our own thought. But when we pass on to the Ascension, it would seem that we are not equally constrained to meet the assertion of it half-way. Here we seem to realize more the marvellous and supernatural character of the event recorded, and at the same time to realize less our own concern in that event and its relations to Christian thought and life. It is something astounding to look back over the centuries and believe that some eighteen hundred years ago a man ascended bodily into the heavens, and is standing now in human guise at the right hand of the Father. Yet, even if we credit it, some of us, perhaps, may fail to see what particular significance is involved in it.

Now, the fact of the Ascension stands on precisely the same ground as the Nativity, the Resurrection, and every other fact of historic Christianity. They are all equally credible or incredible, according to the position from which you look at them. If you assume that the ordinary course of nature and the common experience of men must be the sole and invariable test of what is true and what is not, then all these facts are alike discredited. The supernatural is simply inadmissible, and the story of the Gospels becomes nothing more than a beautiful invention or myth. But if you believe that when God made His world He did not limit Himself forever to what are recognized by us as the laws of His ordinary providence, but left Himself room for special and extraordinary manifestations, then every fact in the Christian creed may claim our unhesitating belief, and the Ascension no less than the rest. It has the same testimony, the same witness of the same men, who attested in their own blood the depth and the sincerity of their convictions as to the truth of what they said. And they have recorded the fact, of which they claim to have been eye-witnesses, that the Lord, after His Resurrection, having tarried with the disciples forty days upon the earth, "was parted from them and received up into heaven."

Before speaking of the significance of this fact, it may be well to say a word in reference to its position in the Gospels. It is the last fact recorded of the person of Christ, and it is worthy to be the last. It is in every respect the fitting and beautiful termination of His earthly career. The deep propriety of it is something which vindicates itself more and more as we think of it. How nobly sustained, even in a merely artistic point of view, is the unity of that wondrous story! What more impressive or appropriate close could have been given to the narrative of the Evangelists' than the Ascension from Olivet! If that narrative is to be accounted, as some would account it, a mythical one, then most certainly it is unique and unparalleled in all imaginative literature. The world has nothing that it can place beside it in the way of lofty conception and sustained power.

And the conclusion to which we must come is this: that some rude and unlettered peasants of Galilee have immeasurably surpassed the sublimest works of genius, not only of their own, but of any previous or succeeding age. That is the simple absurdity to which one is brought when he seeks to deny the literal verity of the facts of the New Testament. For those facts cannot fail to impress us with the divine unity that pervades them, and their essential consistency one with another. Each has its fitting and appointed and necessary place. What, for instance, could have been more grand and noble than the Ascension as the last chapter in the biography of Christ? What could have brought His sojourn on the earth to such a sublime and peaceful close? We read the narrative of the Crucifixion, and our hearts are stirred, as nothing else can stir them, in the portrayal of that great agony. Then follows the Resurrection with its unspeakable joy, and it seems for the time as if no other word could or should be told. What could come after that which would not be poor and pitiful; which would not seem a reaction and a fall from the height to which we had been lifted? Nevertheless there was still one word to say, one other fact still remained to be recorded. The Resurrection gave the Lord the victory over death, but it left Him still upon the earth. There was needed the visible fact of the Ascension to testify to His serene and triumphant entrance into heaven. And that fact, in the simple dignity of its expression, does not fall below its predecessor, but is, and is felt to be, the crown and the consummation of the Gospel.

"He was received up into heaven and sat down on the right hand of God."

The significance of the Ascension in its relations to Christian thought and life is too varied and manifold to be brought within the compass of a single discourse. I simply propose on the present occasion to refer briefly to some two or three points which may illustrate its practical worth to the first disciples and to us.

1. And first, it witnesses, as no other fact could do, to the continued existence of Christ. How important this truth is no words can tell. All energy is from a living source, all growth must be fed from living springs. If the cross which was on Calvary eighteen hundred years ago still wins us, it must be because He who hung upon it still lives. If the words spoken so far away in Judæa comfort and inspire us, it must be because we feel that they come from a living and not from a dead man's lips. If Christianity is to be a power to-day, it must ally itself with the present as truly as with the past. Christ must be felt and realized as living now. He must hold the same relation to us which in the days of His earthly ministry He held to others. Yet, without the fact of the Ascension, this truth would have only an uncertain tenure in our thoughts. The tendency to think of Him simply as one who had been would be too strong for our feeble faith. Even His immediate disciples, had it not been for that scene on Olivet, would have come sooner or later, notwithstanding the assurance of His continual presence, to

associate Him exclusively with their past. Suppose, for instance, that the Lord had withdrawn himself from their visible companionship in some other way? We read that during the forty days after His Resurrection He did not abide and walk with them as of old, but was accustomed to appear suddenly among them, and then as suddenly to vanish away. Suppose that after one of these disappearances He had reappeared among them no more? Would they not have been left in doubt as to whither He had gone, and what might be His fate? Might they not even have suspected that His resurrection, like that of Lazarus, was only for a time, and that He had died again? As far as we can see, reading their characters by the facts which they themselves have given us, that would have been their almost inevitable conclusion. And it would also have been ours. They would have lived on their recollections of Christ, and transmitted them in turn for us to live on. But it would have been sad for them, and far sadder still for us. They, perhaps, might have followed feebly on, in the footprints graven so deep in their memory, but in the course of ages a merely historical influence would have passed away. The changes of the world would obliterate it. Time conquers all things, and recollections which go back over centuries are faint and dim. The Christ of history would be for us to all intents and purposes a dead Christ, one separated from us by some two thousand years. But the mode of the Lord's departure from earth was such as to make indubitable the conviction of His continued existence. The manner of His going would be proof and demonstration that He still lived. When our friends die, despite our assurance of their immortality, we know how often we practically think of them as having ceased to be. But if they had been received up visibly before our eyes into the heavens, they would simply seem to us as having passed into another country or another clime; we should have no question of their continued life. And such was the Ascension of the Lord from Olivet. He rose, all instinct with power and vitality. He rose slowly, fading from the disciples' sight, and not returning to earth again. Yet now at last there remained in their minds no vestige of their old doubts. These had gone forever. The men of Galilee, when the Master was laid in the sepulchre, said that He was dead. But not so when He ascended. Then they stood gazing upward toward the parted clouds, until their thoughts were called back again to earth by the admonition of the angel. And we, if we receive their testimony, may rest our conviction of the Lord's continued existence not on faith only, but also, as it were, on sight.

2. Again, the Ascension and the manner of it witness to the fact that Christ not only lives, but that He lives essentially the same as the disciples knew Him, and as they have represented Him to us while on earth. The Lord whom we shall be "caught up to meet," as the apostle says, "in the air," will not be another Lord, but in all respects the same Lord over whose picture we have lingered in the Gospels. When we realize this, we can understand how the friends of his earthly ministry should look forward so

eagerly to the future, how they should count joyfully on the hour of their release, and say that to "depart and be with Christ" was " far better." We are sometimes troubled, in thinking of the friends that are gone, by a fear lest they should change and lose their human sympathies. We cannot bear to entertain the thought that in their larger sphere they may outgrow the old associations; that we shall find them other than those whom we have loved—and different. Yet such a thought must have come to the disciples sometimes when thinking of the departure of their Master. Would He not be changed in the assumption of that glory of which He so often spoke, and be removed beyond the possibility of the old familiar and affectionate intercourse? The Ascension was to them the evidence that He would not. It was, moreover, the only evidence which would have sufficed for this conviction. There were other ways, perhaps, in which they might have been assured that He still lived. A voice from heaven might have come to them, as it came to Saul of Tarsus, converting on the instant the persecutor into the disciple. But that dazzling brightness, outshining the midday sun, would have seemed to the men of Galilee something altogether different from the Jesus whom they had known. They, too, would have " fallen to the earth," blinded at His presence. To them, henceforth, He would not be and He could not be the same. All that would seem to them to have been lost in mysterious changes. But in the Ascension they saw Him go into heaven the same, and no other, that they of old had walked with. It is noticeable, in the account which they give of it, that there is no indication of any change; no trace of that halo which art has thrown around it; no hint, even, of a transfiguration such as on the Mount had before dazzled and overpowered the three favored apostles. They simply say that as He talked with them "He was parted from them, and a cloud received him out of their sight." He ascended, indeed, in His resurrection body, but that body was the medium and not the bar to the old intimate communion. It linked Him indissolubly to their past and common experience. Whatever change had passed upon it, it still bore in itself, as we know, the evidence of His suffering and humiliation. From the brief glimpses that we have of those forty days after the Resurrection it would seem that the disciples, when the first affright at His sudden and unexpected reappearance had passed, held the same unconstrained intercourse with Him as they were wont to hold. And it was in this guise, and no other, that He finally disappeared from their view. To the last it was the same form that had walked with the wondering disciples to Emmaus, the same that Peter and John had discerned through the glimmering morning's dawn by the Lake of Gennesareth. It was the pledge that He who lived and loved was, and would be still, the same; that "neither life nor death, nor things present, nor things to come, should separate them" from the sympathy and fellowship of Christ. And the Ascension may be to us all that it was to them. If we, too, have been drawn to the Master by the attractiveness of His spirit, by His meek and lowly mind, by His holy devotion and self-sacrifice, then for us, also, this fact so full of human elements will strengthen all those ties. We, too, may look on to the reunion that awaits us as to a meeting with the same and no other who has already won our hearts.

3. And still again, the Ascension witnesses to the exaltation of our common humanity in the person of the man Christ Jesus. This common nature which we wear was visibly lifted up on high before the eyes of men. It was given to mortal vision to behold the enthronement, as it were, of our human, no less than our divine, representative. As God, He could receive, indeed, no addition to His essential glory. No higher place than He already held could have been bestowed upon Him. And in that, whatever it might be, we could have had no share. But in the Ascension, the humanity which the Son assumed was forever glorified. It was the fulfillment of the promise that "all things should be put under His feet." It was the assurance that God had "highly exalted Him, and given Him a name which is above every name: that at the name of Jesus every knee should bow, of things in heaven, and things in earth, and things under the earth; and that every tongue should confess that Jesus Christ is Lord, to the glory of God the Father." It was the great and final triumph of the Son of Man. He came in lowly guise, and His cradle was the manger. He wandered on the earth, not having where to lay His head. He was spitefully entreated of men, and put to a shameful and ignominious death. But the same eyes that

had seen His humiliation should also look upon His glory. They who had mocked at the Crucified One should now be told of His exaltation, that He had gone "into heaven," and was "on the right hand of God, angels and authorities and powers being made subject unto Him." Yet in that exaltation we, too, if we will, may have our share. The very fact that Christ ascended in the same body in which He had died and risen from the dead is the evidence that our common humanity has been and will be glorified in Him. It is the assurance and the proof that our common nature, banished once and driven out from God's immediate presence, has been reinstated in His favor and exalted to His right hand. There the Redeemer stands forever as our eternal representative. Thus the fact of the Ascension is made the ground of the highest and most far-reaching hopes. How much gladder and brighter does the thought of our future become! With what unspeakable glories is man's inheritance invested! How transcendent the vision thus opened before him! For now "our conversation is in heaven," and when we are bidden to lift up our hearts, it is to an ascended and glorified Lord.

Let us strive, then, in this season which specially commemorates the Ascension, to realize that Christ lives; that He lives always essentially the same, and that in His exaltation all may share. Let it be our comfort to believe and know that we may have with Him a human companionship which cannot be interrupted, which no time can lessen, and no distance take away. Let it be our endeavor to enter ever more deeply into that divine communion, and to make always our chief prayer this: That "like as we do believe our Lord to have ascended into the heavens, so we may also in heart and mind thither ascend, and with Him continually dwell."

XIX.

THE CHURCH A UNIVERSAL AND IMMORTAL FAMILY.

[KINGSBRIDGE, 1870.]

"*The Father of our Lord Jesus Christ, of whom the whole family in heaven and earth is named.*"—EPH. iii. 14, 15.

"THE Father of our Lord Jesus Christ, of whom the whole family in heaven and earth is named." The expression is a somewhat peculiar one, and may not at first, perhaps, have for us any clear and satisfactory significance. It occurs here in a kind of parenthesis, and for the determination of its meaning it will be necessary to trace back the connection of the thought, and consider also in what sense this peculiar phraseology, at the time it was employed, would have been understood.

The apostle, in the preceding chapter, had been assuring the Gentiles that they were no longer "aliens from the commonwealth of Israel, and strangers from the covenants of promise," but, through Christ, had equal access to the Father. He called them "fellow-citizens with the saints," and told them that they, too, were "of the household of God." These words —"commonwealth," "citizenship," "household"— all implied one and the same fact; namely, that there was a divine society, communion, or church, into which the Gentile, no less than the Jew, had been admitted. The apostle had gone on to elaborate and illustrate the conception of the Christian Church under the figure of a temple, fitly framed, of which "Jesus Christ Himself was the chief corner-stone," built for the indwelling of the Most High. Now in the passage which we have taken for our text, he recurs to this thought, but at the same time expands it and varies the expression of it. The figure of a temple is dropped, and "the household of God" is conceived under the closer analogy of "a family." A living human relationship is substituted for the material representation. The thought naturally gains by the substitution; for the moral relation which is involved in the family offers a deeper and truer analogy to God's Church, or household, than can be found in the purely material combination of different stones in the same building. But the thought gains also in another way. The temple stands for unity, but the family stands for catholic unity. God's household is not only one, but one under all circumstances and conditions. The apostle calls it "the whole family of heaven and earth." He may even mean to include, and probably he does include, angelic as well as human beings in this great universal family. The Jews were accustomed to speak of the family above and the family below, meaning thereby the angels of heaven and the Israel of earth. But without pressing this inference now, we may say that the phrase does undoubtedly include in one communion, church, or household, all the faithful upon earth and all the spirits of just men made perfect in heaven.

The other expression, " of whom the whole family is named," is an obsolete form of speech, and was a Hebrew mode of saying what we should express in a very different way. With the Jews, and indeed with all ancient peoples, names had a much deeper and more real significance than they retain with us. The name of a thing expressed its nature, character, and qualities. It was a kind of portraiture, or word-painting, a representation of the thing itself. Thus when Adam named all the beasts that " the Lord God had made," his names were no unmeaning appellations, as if, with the mere purpose of distinguishing one from another, he had ticketed the several animals with their respective numbers. They were literal descriptions, and expressed the essential characteristics of each. So again in respect to persons, names in Biblical usage often, if not always, were a kind of summary of each one's special work, mission, or character. Thus: Abraham means "father of multitudes ;" Jacob, " supplanter ;" David, "beloved ;" Elijah, " Jehovah is God ;" Isaiah, " God's salvation ;" Jesus, " saviour ;" Peter, " a rock." In these and many other instances to know the name of a person was equivalent to knowing what that person was, what was his distinguishing characteristic, and what he was intended to do. Now, when we bear in mind the close connection in Hebrew usage between the name of a thing and the substance of it, it becomes evident that to say how anything was named was only another way of saying how it was constituted, how its character and qualities were determined. Thus when the apostle says that "the family of heaven and earth" is "named of the Father," he means that this family derives its family character from God; that it is He who makes it a family; that the family relationship inheres in Him, depends on Him, and in Him eternally subsists. It is the same as if he had said: "This whole family I speak of has been constituted a family and remains a family in virtue of something in the nature and character of God." And not of God the Father simply, but of God "the Father of our Lord Jesus Christ." The fatherhood of God, not as a figure of speech, but as a literal reality in the revelation of His only begotten Son, is made the ground or foundation of the family of earth and heaven. How the Church derives its family character from the Father of our Lord Jesus Christ, or, what is the same thing, how it becomes a family, and a universal family, in virtue of the essential principles of Christianity, will appear more clearly as we consider in their order the different points which the analogy involves.

We have reached, then, as preliminary to that, this general exposition to begin with: "The whole family of heaven and earth" is another expression for the Christian Church in the largest and most catholic conception of it, and this Church is said to be "named of the Father of our Lord Jesus Christ;" that is, its family qualities are said to proceed from and depend on Him, because it is constituted in accordance with the fatherhood of God, as that fatherhood is revealed to us in the gospel.

1. The Church, then, is set forth under the analogy of a family, and the first fact involved in this analogy is this: The relation that binds men together in one Christian communion or fellowship is not an artificial but a natural relationship. It is not a contrivance of man; it is not, if one may so speak, an after-thought of God, but inheres from the beginning in the original constitution of our nature. Man did not invent this relation for himself, nor did God at some late stage in human history invent it for him; it was a relation inherent in us from the very first. This, I say, is the most obvious inference of the analogy under which the Christian Church is set forth. For, however it may be with other things, the family relation will be universally admitted to be a natural one. It is not an expedient which we may have devised, it is not an artificial arrangement, it is not a result of civilization or culture. It lies back of all civilizations, all arrangements, every kind of culture. Knowledge may ennoble our conception of it, but the reality of the relation itself is something quite independent of our moral or intellectual advancement. The family is the integral element of society, the indivisible unit beyond which no analysis can go. It does not come within the power of our art. We do not make it, we are born into it. It is the earliest recognition of our awakening intelligence. The first fact in a man's life is this: he is a child; he has a mother, a father, perhaps brothers and sisters, too. His relation to these is something which he feels with more or less intensity, but whatever the measure of his feeling be, it is something that he can

never adequately express. The tie that binds him and them together is mysterious, incomprehensible, and the more he considers it the more mysterious and incomprehensible does it become. It seems simple enough at first sight, but upon second thought we begin to suspect that there is something in it which is inscrutable. This common blood flowing in different veins—how should that have such uniting force, and why should it bind the various members of a family so indissolubly together? Why should it constitute such a sacred bond that the instinctive and universal feeling of mankind accounts anyone monstrous who can disown and divest himself of it altogether? All we can say is, that it does, and we can give no further account of the matter. We accept the family in the same way that we accept any axiom, any first principle, any ultimate fact. That is, we accept it because it is impossible not to accept it. Any attempt at explanation, however, meets with the same mishap that befalls all explanations of self-evident truths. That is, it obscures the subject instead of making it more plain. The family relationship is a natural relationship. We are born into it and constituted in it, and when we have said that, we have said the deepest thing that we can say of it.

Now the Church is a family because the relation which it involves is natural, too; because all that can be said of the one applies with equal force to the other. Perhaps we may not think so, and certainly it is not in this light that it is generally regarded. The ordinary conception of the Church does not go beyond the outward formal organism, and our connection with that is referred back to some definite transaction, in which we acted for ourselves or in which others acted for us. There is, of course, a certain relative truth in this representation, but not the whole truth, nor the deepest part of it. For the Church, in the absolute conception of it, is the expression not of formal, but of spiritual unity, and our relation to it inheres in our spiritual nature. The tie of blood is not more independent of our art or volition than is the spiritual affinity that underlies and is the ground of all ecclesiastical society. Every one who admits that he has a soul, must admit also that there is something in his being, as it was originally constituted, which implies and involves this relationship. It is no exaggeration, but the literal truth, therefore, to call this relation a natural one, since it is grounded in our nature, and is coeval and coextensive with it. Nor let it be thought that we are pursuing here a merely verbal or fanciful analogy. The analogy is lost rather in the identity of things. It can never be asserted too emphatically that man's spiritual relationships are not the less natural because they are spiritual, and that the Church which is founded in his religious nature calls for no less instinctive reverence than the family which is founded in his domestic. Indeed, it is the larger and the higher nature to which we are untrue when we withhold it. For though we may practically ignore and repudiate the relationship, though we may refuse or neglect to give it any outward expression, still we cannot make it unreal. It inheres in the original constitution of our being. And if men account it monstrous to disown the tie of blood, how monstrous must it be accounted by a wise and loving Intelligence to disown the relationship of souls!

This relationship, in the recognition of every Christian man, at least, has a foundation which is absolute and incontrovertible. It is laid in the divine nature. For the Gospel assures him that he is God's child, and that in no merely figurative sense, but in the deepest application that the expression can bear. When the Lord taught us to say "our Father," He was not putting into our mouths an empty metaphor. God *is* our Father, really and truly our Father, though that fatherhood is a mystery which we can but dimly understand. We are infinitely more to Him than all the creatures which He has made. The relationship is of that kind which involves a kindred character. There is indeed one only-begotten Son, but through our union with that Son, through our spiritual identification with Him, we too are God's children. And this relationship of man to Christ, through which man has relationship also with the Father, is not an artificial but a natural relationship; that is, it is involved in the very nature of things. In some deep way the Son is from all eternity our Elder Brother. The incarnation did not make Him one with us, it was the consequence rather of His being already one; for, as the writer in the Epistle to the Hebrews says: "Forasmuch then," "Forasmuch then, as the children were partakers of flesh and blood, He also Himself likewise took part of the same." Thus man is God's child because there is something in the divine nature, as well as in the human, which involves that relationship. But it follows that if men are children, they must also be brethren. The Church, therefore, is a family; that is, the spiritual bond which unites its members is a natural bond, because it has its primal origin in God, " the Father of our Lord Jesus Christ."

2. Another inference from the analogy is the universal character which the Church should bear. The apostle calls it " the whole family of earth." In his conception it is to become at last coextensive with our earthly humanity. It is to be the largest, the widest, the most comprehensive of all human relationships. The nations themselves are to be merged in it. All separative conditions are to lose their separative power here. Even racial distinctions in its uniting bonds are to pass ultimately away. For " there is neither Jew nor Greek, there is neither bond nor free, there is neither male nor female: for ye are all one in Christ Jesus." Thus the Church, in the analogy of the family, is to be the realization not only of unity, but of catholic unity. And perhaps there is no other analogy that could set forth with equal force this great and essential characteristic. All mere associations and combinations of men, all organizations which are the work of a human craftsman, are necessarily restrictive. They are not, and cannot be, universal societies. Their exclusions must begin somewhere. They do not permit the widest differences, and such differences as they do permit interfere with and weaken the integrity of the organization. But the family in its own little world is the very impersonation of a true catholicity. It has a place for every possible diversity. There are found

in it oftentimes the very greatest dissimilarities, not only in habits and aims, but in character and convictions. And these differences, so far from being irreconcilable with the unity of the family, do not even detract from it. The kindred bond is something quite independent of those sympathies which in the outer world generally bring men together. You may have nothing in common with your brother but the blood that is coursing in the veins of both, but despite all other differences, that one uniting fact binds you two together indissolubly. Even the grossest moral turpitude cannot absolutely separate you. You may be tempted sometimes to think otherwise; you may reason yourself into the conviction that it ought and can; but how often will a word, a look, an old association—seemingly some slight and trivial thing—put in Nature's hand an irrefutable vindication of her claim against you! No, this family bond is something that cannot be utterly and irrevocably broken. Our lives may lie far apart from those who were once in the same household with us, but we bear in our own veins the witness that there is something left which unites us still.

And is not this, too, the conviction that lives on through all the divisions of Christendom? The external unity of the Church is, indeed, broken; and to speak of it now, in any such reference, as "the whole family of earth," would be not a characterization, but a satire. But the common relationship to Christ, the spiritual kinship with Him, that is something which has not passed, and cannot pass away. And may not that be the ground of a real though invisible unity—a unity not of form, but of spirit? Having a common Lord, must we not all in some deep way be at unity with each other? Must we not constitute in some true sense that universal Christian society in which every form of Christian goodness is included? Nay, may not goodness that is not consciously Christian be included too? May not those who, without the knowledge of the Master, are, nevertheless, according to the light they have, doing the Master's work, be counted also among His disciples? On one occasion Christ is recorded to have said: "He that is not against us is on our part." And when He Himself defines His Church, may it not be larger than the most catholic of us have suspected? The denominations now stand apart and work apart, for in the present diversity of Christian development any other course appears to involve either unseemly collisions or an equally unseemly sacrifice of principle. But this merely formal separation does not, or should not, lessen our conviction of an inner and substantial unity. That remains, and will doubtless take on the outward form prepared for it when the time is ripe. The day when Christendom was externally one has long gone by, and if it is ever to be externally one again, as so many everywhere hope and pray and believe that it will be, that reunion must find its fulfilment in a churchly organization which shall be, like the family, natural enough to give birth to every phase of Christian thought and character, and catholic enough to tolerate it.

3. But in the representation of the apostle, the Church is more comprehensive even than this. It is

not only the whole family of earth, but the whole family of earth and heaven. All the good of the human race, and perhaps other intelligences also, are included in one universal household of God. The living and the dead, spirits here and spirits there, are united still by the same kindred bond. Death involves a change in our locality and condition, but no change in our essential relationship. The unity of that is something which is not and cannot be broken or interrupted. It lives on, and makes of one communion, still, those who have left the world and those who are in it. We must all admit the singular force, the personal appeal, as it were, of the illustration which the apostle employs. For in our several family circles we do not strike out the name of the one who has lately died. We speak of that one as brother or sister still, and could not bear to think that together with that form which we had laid away in the ground " we had buried the reality of kinship" too. We are convinced that the relationship survives, and our instinctive thought is that of Wordsworth's little maid, who persisted, even in the churchyard where her brothers lay, in affirming : " We are seven." And when that conviction extends, as in the apostle's conception extend it must, to the universal Church of God, what an inspiring and consoling truth is thus presented to us! The spiritual affinity that binds men together here, binds them together here and there, as well. The tie is of that kind which can never die. Those who have gone before—the good of all ages—are *our contemporaries.* They and we together constitute one family—"the family of earth and heaven." In passing from the world they have not lost their relation to it, but are as truly one with us as before. And this relationship survives as all else survives in and through our Lord Jesus Christ. He is no longer with us in the flesh, He has ascended into the heavens, but He has told us that He is always with us in the spirit, and therefore we may know that every spiritual relationship is an imperishable one—is something which neither time nor distance nor death itself can break or interrupt. The dead have not really died, but are "the great cloud of witnesses" that now "encompass us about." They have true though unseen fellowship with us still. Our hopes, our aims, our destinations are the same. The essential unity of God's household is unbroken. The only difference is, they have gone before, and we are following after.

> "One army of the living God,
>   To His command we bow;
> Part of His host have crossed the flood,
>   And part are crossing now."

"The whole family of heaven and earth" is a reality which may not often come into our thought, but it finds a solemn and significant expression in one act at least of our Christian worship. Before the Master was visibly separated from His disciples He enjoined upon them an observance which should keep Him in their perpetual remembrance, and help them to realize their continued though unseen fellowship with Him, and consequently with each other. I refer of course to the sacrament of the Lord's Supper. The Church calls it the Holy Communion, indicating thereby the divine mystery which it was intended to express. And it does express it as nothing else could. No one, even though he had never heard the name of Christ, can go into a Christian congregation and see men and women gathered about the same board, eating of the same bread, and drinking of the same cup, and not recognize instinctively that they symbolize in that impressive act some solemn bond of unity among themselves. And if he should observe, moreover, that all classes and conditions, without distinction, partook of this common meal; and, as he went from church to church, and land to land, should see men of different nations and kindreds and tongues partaking of it too, he would begin to suspect that this Christian society was a universal one, something which disowned all limitations of place and time, and sought to extend itself over the whole earth. And if, thereupon, he should inquire what this bond of union was, and find it to consist in a common relation to a common Lord, and that Lord not an earthly but a heavenly one; that the act he witnessed testified to the reality of an invisible but unbroken fellowship; he would conclude that the membership of this society, whether in earth or heaven, was unbroken too. For all this, and more than this, is what the great Christian sacrament does in very truth express. It renews and keeps alive in us the conviction of the essential unity of "the whole family of heaven and earth." It reminds us, with every recurring celebration, that we may claim kindred and have intercourse even with the skies.

For the Holy Communion is the symbol of that universal and divine society which has been nobly described as "the new Jerusalem," a society of which "God and Christ are members," in whose ranks "death makes no vacancy," but at whose 'banquet table the perfected spirits of just men, with an innumerable company of angels, sit down beside those who have not yet surrendered their bodies to the grave."

XVII.

THE SUFFERANCE OF THE TARES.

[KINGSBRIDGE, 1870.]

"Let both grow together until the harvest."—ST. MATT. xiii. 30

THE mixed character of the Christian Church, that is to say, the co-existence in her membership of good and evil men, is one of the plainest facts of history and of individual observation and experience. The proofs of this fact, no matter what age or condition of Christianity may be selected as an example, are so conclusive and overwhelming that no one ever dreams of disputing it. The recognition of it is simply universal, and one would as soon think of verifying any other self-evident proposition, as of seriously attempting its demonstration. Ecclesiastical history itself, at the very outset of its testimony, is fatal to any theory or dream we may be disposed to cherish in respect even to an original, though long-gone, purity as a general, still less an invariable, characteristic of Church membership. We learn from the New Testament Scriptures that many of these members, as far back as the apostolic age, were thoroughly unworthy ones; that in the infant organization of the Church there existed almost every form of evil that may justly be considered inconsistent with the sincere profession of discipleship. And when we leave those Scriptures and pass to the ecclesiastical records, following the course of the Christian society down through the successive centuries, the intermixture of good and evil men, the association in the same body of false brethren and true, becomes more and more extended and apparent. So general and self-evident, indeed, has this intermixture been, that it has seemed sometimes as though the great warfare against Satan, sin, and death were waged not so much outside of this organization as within it; as if the contest for supremacy lay not so much between the Church and the world, as between the good and evil members of the Church itself. Nor, despite the recurring reformations whose results we have inherited, does the Church of our own day present in this respect any different spectacle from that which it has always presented. The membership of the Christian society now, no less than in the past, is of a very mixed and miscellaneous character. The good and the bad, the false and the true, the worthy and the unworthy, in ever-varying proportions, continue to have part in it.

This is not a fact which needs any special testimony, for each one may verify it for himself in his own observation and experience. It is practically acted on and taken for granted by all. The name of a disciple, in and by itself, is seldom or never accepted as a sufficient guarantee of character. Any attempt to trade upon it, to bring it forward as the equivalent of that, is looked upon with suspicion.

For it is nothing more or less than the proffer of what everybody knows to be a very doubtful kind of security. It is the advancement of a claim which is neither warranted by facts, nor conceded in the recognition of society. Perhaps it will generally be admitted that the distinctively Christian portion of any community is on the whole the better portion; but in any special individual instance the mere assertion of Church membership by no means satisfies us as to a man's purity or integrity. He may be a disciple, but that is nothing until we know what kind of a disciple he is. We all agree that his profession ought to be the index of his character, but we all agree, also, in the admission that "quite as likely as otherwise it is not."

Now this state of things, in one who seriously ponders it, may very naturally excite a sad and deep surprise. The surprise will not be lessened when he recalls and tells over to himself the numberless passages of Scripture which ascribe to the Church a sacred, holy, and divine character; which unfold the grandeur and magnitude of her mission, and foreshadow the unspeakable glories which are to be her ultimate and triumphant end. How is this noble portraiture to be reconciled with the comparatively pitiful reality? Is this organization, numbering indeed many pure and exalted characters, yet also tolerating in its membership many confessedly unworthy ones, so that the Christian name simply in itself often has little if any discriminating value, is this organization the veritable society which the Master instituted, and of which He predicted such great things?

Has there not been some terrible mistake in its constitution or administration, some guilty and inexcusable omission of the severity of discipline, some strange and fatal departure from the policy enjoined upon it in its inauguration? And if not, is this then to be accepted as the legitimate result, the later counterpart of that original Christian community which Christ established? We might resort to the convenient theory of modern degeneration, but history reveals the same mixed character in the Church of the past that we recognize in the Church of the present. Our doubts and questionings, whatever they are, are concerned, therefore, not only with our own age, nor can they stop at any intermediate stage; it is evident that they must be carried back to the very fountain head.

And if these doubts and questionings are stumbling-blocks in the way of some devout minds, some who belong to and believe in the Church, what must they be to those who are indifferent or antagonistic to her? We know as a matter of fact that the practically miscellaneous character of her communion is often adduced as the *argumentum ad hominem* in repudiating the reality of any distinction between the Church and the world. The distinction is disposed of as an arbitrary and artificial one, with no foundation or correspondence in life. This is an assertion more often than not thrown out simply in the way of an evasion of duty; a plea put forth to justify one's self in standing aloof and declining to make any formal profession of discipleship. But sometimes the statement is consciously pushed to its ultimate consequences, and this same fact of an indiscriminate membership, a mixed and miscellaneous communion, is urged as an unanswerable argument against the Church's divine origin and character and mission. Such an one might say, and indeed practically does say: the Master Himself was a visionary, an enthusiast. His own heart was full of noble thoughts and exalted aspirations. The world without took tone and color from the world within. He dreamed that fair dream of human perfectibility. He conceived it possible to inaugurate and perpetuate on earth a society which in its own immaculate purity and righteousness should be as leaven, leavening the whole lump. He proposed by imparting to it the propulsion of His will, and by bequeathing to it the legacy of His character, to endow it as it were with supernatural powers. The society was established, and while not denying in any way the vast good that it has accomplished, what nevertheless when tried by its own tests has been the result of the experiment? One of the original band proved himself a traitor. Some of the others lived to bear ample testimony to the corruption and insincerity of many of their converts. The succeeding centuries disclose in monotonous repetition the same contrasts of light and shadow. And when at length we reach the Church of to-day, is there any need to say how Christ's dream of human perfectibility has been dissipated, and how His expectations of the Christian society have been disappointed?

The sufficient answer to all this is in the fact that Christ never dreamed that dream, and never entertained those expectations. Whatever great things He predicted of his Church (and it would be hard to overstate them), there is nothing in anything that He said which is necessarily inconsistent with this very state of things which has always been more or less a subject of scandal and reproach. We must avoid confounding in our minds the ultimate ideal of the Church, that which in its glorified and future state it shall finally become, with the necessarily imperfect character which it meanwhile presents under its temporary and earthly conditions. The time indeed will come when it shall be wholly purged of "the uncircumcised and the unclean;" when it shall be, in very deed and truth, "holy and without blemish," having "neither spot, nor wrinkle, nor any such thing." But that time will be the consummation of all things, when the opposing powers, which are suffered to prevent it now, shall have fallen and passed away. Our Lord nowhere intimates that He expected an approximation even to any such result meanwhile. On the contrary, He distinctly foresaw and distinctly foretold this very intermixture of good and evil in the membership of the Church, which is urged as an argument against her divine origin and character. Not to speak of various intimations to this effect, there are at least two clear delineations of it especially striking and significant. It was the custom of the Master to picture out and portray the different conditions and aspects of His Church, "the kingdom of heaven," as He called it, under certain figurative representations which are known to us by the name of parables. In one of these he described it as a field sown with wheat, but which an enemy's hand had subsequently oversown with tares, so that the wheat and tares were intermixed, and sprang and grew up together. In another He represented it as a draw-net let down into the sea, which gathered fish of every kind, both good and bad. These illustrations must make it sufficiently evident that, whatever Christ expected of His Church on earth, He certainly did not expect that its communion would be invariably or even generally pure and irreproachable. And any argument, therefore, which would impugn the divine origin and character of the Christian Church by asserting that it has disappointed the expectations of its Founder, and so by implication impugning the divine authority of that Founder Himself, becomes utterly untenable. For assuredly no just inference can be drawn against the supernatural mission of Christ, or the supernatural mission of the society which He instituted, from the fact that this same society, in every age, and as we see it now with our own eyes, presents that very spectacle of a mixed and miscellaneous communion which He foresaw and foretold in respect to it.

But one of the parables goes much farther than this. It tells us not only that Christ foresaw and foretold this state of things, but that He expressly forbade any rash and summary attempts to have it otherwise. For when the servants of the householder, on the discovery of the tares, came to him with the inquiry, "Wilt thou then that we go and gather them up?" he said: "Nay; let both grow together until the harvest." Here, unquestionably, the plain inference is, that the Church is to resort to no precipitate and coercive measures to rid herself of unworthy members. Notwithstanding the scandal, they are to remain within the pale of her communion, upon sufferance. Whatever evils may come from the association, they are nevertheless to be tolerated and endured. Of course the distinction is not to be lost sight of between what Christ simply foresees and permits, and what on the other hand He designs and purposes. He could not be the exalted character that we acknowledge Him to be, had it been His desire or intention that His Church should present to the world this spectacle of mingled good and evil. As far as His will and agency are concerned, it is of a pure and unmixed character. Every influence He exerts upon it is for good, and for good only. He sows no tares, He inspires no noxious growths, yet none the less does He foresee that under the circumstances it is inevitable that tares will be sown. He accordingly accepts the fact, and provides for it. Why He does so will appear hereafter. But this much, at least, we may already determine on: that just as His prediction of the unworthy membership in the Church, a scandal and reproach as it so often is, shows that that membership is not necessarily inconsistent with her divine origin and character, so His permission of it shows that this state of things, despite the evils that attend upon it, is not necessarily inconsistent with her sacred mission. The tares would have been rooted out at once, had they been absolutely fatal to the fair fruitage of the field.

The reason which the householder assigns for refusing to permit his servants to resort to this summary process indicates the true nature and significance of that toleration of evil which the Church is constrained to show. He will not suffer the tares to be gathered up, lest while they "gather up the tares," they "root up also the wheat with them." Now this answer in the application amounts evidently to this: Unworthy membership in the Church, unnatural and pernicious and offensive as it is, must nevertheless be tolerated, because any coercive and premature attempts at its extinction are likely to result in far greater evils than those which they seek to overcome. Nay, it is even intimated that these attempts would be, what the scandal confessedly is not, wholly irreconcilable with the leading use and purpose of the Christian society. They would be fatal to its controlling and distinguishing characteristic. The one consideration to which all others are to be made subordinate would practically disappear, and be lost sight of; for the expulsion of any number of disreputable members is not worth the sacrifice of some sincere and genuine ones. To have one's field cleared of tares would poorly compensate for having it cleared also, in the process, of more or less of the wheat. In the divine economy, at least, the value of a single soul is incalculable. Any policy, therefore, that might involve, however accidentally, such a loss, is wholly inconsistent with the fundamental idea of the kingdom of heaven.

We come, then, to this fundamental idea. We put the question: What, among the different characteristics of the Church on earth, is to be its leading and controlling one? Beyond all doubt it is to be not holiness, not separation from evil, but catholicity, universality. The Christian society is not simply, nor even chiefly, an association of holy persons gathered out of the world, banded together, and carefully fenced off as far as possible from any contact with unrighteousness. In its future and triumphant state it will be, indeed, in the strictest sense, a "communion of saints," an assemblage of "spirits of just men made perfect." But that exclusiveness is not and cannot be the prominent feature of it now. Its object is not so much the collection and concentration of holiness as the development and perfection of holiness. It exists to make the bad good, and the good better. It is, as it were, a vast training school to do the best it can with every variety of material that is gathered into it. It was instituted, primarily, for the regeneration of mankind. No lesser aim can consist with the injunction of its divine commission. Our Lord says expressly, "The field is the world." The bidding was to "preach the Gospel to every creature." The Church, therefore, admits within her pale, and tolerates within it, all who by complying with the very simplest conditions may manifest any disposition to enter. She pushes her catholicity to the very verge of indiscrimination. The Lord, indeed, laid down conditions and exacted them; but as a practical test, it must be admitted that they were not of the most rigid kind. A profession of faith in Him, a proffer of service: that was all that was required to entitle one, outwardly at least, to the recognition of a disciple. Even this faith might be of a vague and indefinite character, and there was no previous probation to test the sincerity of the proffered service.

And His Church, on the whole, has been faithful to His behests in this matter. Whenever she has departed from them, she has exchanged the spirit of a Church for the spirit of a sect, which is exclusiveness both in faith and practice. Departures there have indeed been, and probably there is no occasion to enumerate those instances which have become famous in history for their folly and disaster. It is the tendency of human nature to be exclusive, to cut off and pare away with no sparing hand. But notwithstanding this, the Church, all things considered, has been to a certain extent mindful of the prohibition of the Master. When she has violated it, it has generally been in the heat of theological excitement; and that it has not been done with a settled, deliberate purpose is shown in the fact that her excisions have been for misbelief rather than misconduct. She has at least always professed to be Catholic, to be universal, and in her constitution certainly has realized more or less of that character. For the one thing which the Church cannot long forget is that her field is co-extensive with the world, that she is not to be a kind of close communion, but the very largest and freest that is consistent with any positive teaching and definite existence. That is the justification of her being, the primary reason why she is. God can protect, and, as it were, fence off, His elect in other ways. His Church exists as an organized power to influence, and finally absorb into herself, the life of humanity. You may come within her pale on the simplest conditions, and once within it there is no earthly power that can rightfully expel you. You may be censured, you may be put under discipline, you may be even excommunicated from certain sacred privileges; but you cannot be, here on earth, absolutely and irrevocably cut off.

1. We see, then, the reason for the prohibition of the householder. The rooting up of the tares is forbidden, because, in the first place, that process would be fatal to the fundamental idea of the Church. It would be inconsistent with her catholic and universal character. Even on the presumption of supernatural wisdom, as well as zeal, on the part of the servants, the excision of objectionable members would be undesirable. As the world and human nature are constituted, it would inevitably circumscribe the influence of the Church within narrow and ever narrower limits; it would dwarf her organization into that of a sect; and, if the process of excision were persisted in, the organization itself would sooner or later pass away.

2. But aside from that, even were this excision of members desirable, there are none who could be safely intrusted with its execution. Our Lord indicates the insuperable difficulty here when He says, "lest ye root up also the wheat with them." When we remember the imperfection of our human nature and the strength of our human prejudice, what probability is there that the unworthy, and only the un-

worthy, would be expelled or excluded? With the best intentions, men can see but a little way. Yet to discriminate justly, the farthest-reaching glance into the connection of cause and consequence, the most exhaustive knowledge of all the circumstances involved, the nicest delicacy in disentangling the false from the true, would be absolutely indispensable. Who, in such a momentous matter as expelling and irrevocably shutting out a member from the Church, would take the responsibility of that? And if one *were* rash enough to take it, would not the result more often than not be the retention of the hypocrite and the exclusion of others, who, despite some irregularities of faith and practice, might nevertheless have "the root of the matter" in them?

3. Moreover, however it may be in the physical world, there is no impassable barrier between different moral and spiritual conditions. A man's state, his character, whatever it be, is never fixed and unalterable. Here, indeed, the reality outruns the illustration. For tares are always tares; they will never become wheat, no matter how long they may be suffered to remain. But bad men, even insensibly to themselves, change their dispositions and become better than they were. False brethren, through the influences that are brought to bear upon them, may after a while be made true. The unworthy members of the Christian society, by very reason of its sufferance of them and their continuance in it, may be led to a life of more consistent discipleship. There is a fearful reality in the loosing or binding power of any community. Stamp a man with infamy, and he re-

mains infamous; shut him out from all communion with the good, and you wed him indissolubly to evil. And that, at least, is not the work which the Christian Church was sent into the world to do.

4. And still, again this office of excision is forbidden her, because Christ has reserved it to Himself. The prerogative of judgment is His alone. He only is sufficient, impartial, and all-wise; and, therefore, He only can judge in every instance, not according to the appearance, but according to the truth. From His doom and sentence there is and will be no appeal. If He can tolerate the evil meanwhile, His servants, it is to be presumed, can tolerate it too. The purity of His glorified Church shall be vindicated, and the searching discrimination between the good and bad in her communion shall be made at last. For He says "Let both grow together until the harvest: and in the time of harvest I will say to the reapers, Gather ye together first the tares, and bind them in bundles to burn them; but gather the wheat into my barn."

From all that has been said, there follow three practical deductions which we should take away with us. Let us remember, then, in the first place, that the mixed character of the Church, the association of good and evil persons in her membership, this scandal and reproach that we hear so much of, is no argument at all against her divine origin or mission. On the contrary, it is a positive confirmation of it. It was clearly foreseen at the outset, and distinctly foretold and provided for. It is tolerated, not because Christ or His Church is indifferent to moral distinc tions; not because there is any laxity in the code of either; but because only on the condition of this toleration can the greatest good eventually come. We might as well doubt that God was the creator of the world because, as it is constituted, evil seems to be, if not a necessary, at least an unmistakable, ingredient in it; as doubt that He is the author of the Church because so many of her recognized members seem to be leading lives, and seem to be tolerated in leading lives, utterly inconsistent with their professions.

2. The second inference is, that this state of things in the Christian society can justify no one in standing aloof from any definite connection with it. If the distinction between the Church and the world seems to you an unreal one because you detect the same differences in moral character within as outside of her communion, you have to remember that Christ foresaw these differences, and yet did not account the distinction unreal. With the clearest foreknowledge of the tares, He imposes upon each and all, without exception, and not a whit the less imperatively, the obligation of a pronounced discipleship. You are to assume the Christian name, you are to enroll yourself in the Christian ranks, you are to march under the Christian flag, no matter how much defection and disloyalty you may see about you. If you urge this plea merely in the way of an evasion, holding a kind of sophistical argument with yourself in order to avoid a duty, be sure it will avail you nothing, and you yourself, sooner or later, will be forced to confess its unworthiness. If you urge it sincerely, is it not a

sad instance of unreason? For if others seem to you unfaithful to the cause which they are pledged to serve, and yet that cause you must concede the very noblest one, is not the obligation, if anything, the more imperative upon you to bring whatever integrity of purpose you may have, as your contribution to that organized power, which, more than any other, at least, is battling with the sin and evil of the world?

3. Our final reflection is a brief word of warning. We are admonished, in the close of the parable, not to presume that because the toleration of evil, for prudential reasons, is enjoined here, it will or can be permitted hereafter. Because our irregularities, our derelictions of duty, are, perhaps, overlooked by the Church, we are not to suppose that they will be overlooked by the Judge. That we have not been cast out by the earthly society is no presumption that we will not be cast out by the heavenly one. The temptation with us, sometimes, is to think so; to look upon our membership in the Church militant as a kind of pledge of our membership in the Church triumphant. But that is an issue which must abide a very different kind of test. For, in the interpretation of His parable, our Lord's words are, if possible, still stronger and more emphatic. "The Son of man," He says, "shall send forth his angels, and they shall gather out of his kingdom all things that offend, and them which do iniquity; and shall cast them into a furnace of fire: there shall be wailing and gnashing of teeth."

XVIII.

ST. PETER'S DISCOVERY.

[KINGSBRIDGE, 1868.]

" Then Peter opened his mouth, and said, Of a truth I perceive that God is no respecter of persons: but in every nation he that feareth him, and worketh righteousness, is accepted with him."—ACTS x. 34, 35.

THERE are few things so rare and wonderful in human life as sudden radical revolutions in thought and character. Such transformations are sometimes described as moral miracles, and the more we reflect upon them the less are we inclined to dispute the accuracy of the description. That there is a miraculous element—something beyond, and, indeed in opposition to the ordinary course of nature—in every such sudden, radical, inward change, is a conviction that grows upon us just in proportion as we recognize and appreciate the strength and universality of those laws which control the development of man's mental and moral being. They find a popular expression in the phrase we use of them, "the force of habit," and every one knows, sooner or later, what is involved in that. The sure tendency of any habit of a man is to become that man's law, and it is no ordinary occurrence or influence that can dethrone its tyranny and restore to him his freedom. The moral constraint that is put upon him comes in time to be equivalent almost to a physical necessity, and scarcely more can he change his opinions and desires than can the leopard his spots, or the Ethiop his skin. Thus, as a general thing, men, after they reach the full period of maturity, either do not change at all, or their changes are very gradual and imperfect. A certain petrifaction, as it were, of thought and character, is a fact borne out by our common observation and experience. Middle age and old age are proverbially unsusceptible and unimpressionable. The mass of converts of any kind are the young. The character then, whatever impress may have been put upon it, is not yet fully formed, and it is possible to mould and modify it as in later years one can seldom or never do. In the history of religion it is rare, indeed, to find the hoary head reënacting the parable of the Prodigal Son. And what is true of man's heart and conscience is true also of his mind. All find it difficult, and some well-nigh impossible, to change their thoughts and opinions; to abandon or modify the convictions of a life-time. Innumerable influences, too subtle for analysis, combine to keep us in the old ways, to wed us indissolubly to the ideas and traditions of our past. It involves a kind of moral convulsion, almost the rending of one's self in twain, to break away from them. That innate something which we call prejudice grows with the years, and strengthens every day. It fortifies the old convictions with that obstinate unreason which is simply invincible because it is impenetrable to light, and blind and deaf to knowledge.

Thus the multitude of men—the vast majority of the human race—live and die in the creeds and convictions, religious, political, or social, into which they were born. It would seem often as if nothing human could dislodge an idea when it has once gained a mature and conscious recognition. It is only youth, which takes up opinions hastily and as hastily abandons them, that offers much encouragement for proselyting. To attempt age or manhood is, generally, altogether hopeless. And, therefore, when we hear of one in the maturity of years not only undergoing a radical and sudden transformation of character, but abandoning at once, and on the instant, prejudices and convictions which have grown with his growth and strengthened with his strength until they have become, as it were, a part of his very nature, it is a spectacle not impossible indeed, but a spectacle, to say the least, most unusual and extraordinary.

This is the spectacle, the moral miracle, that is presented to us in the tenth chapter of the book of the Acts of the Apostles. The central figure there is one that appears often in the Gospel narratives, and his character, as we have read it, is that of a man earnest and impassioned, but singularly tenacious of his opinions, and with a certain intellectual narrowness which made it peculiarly difficult for him to emancipate himself from his prejudices. With him, too, that impressionable period of life in which emancipation is most easily won had passed. St.

Peter is said to have been the eldest of the apostles, and he was now probably in the full maturity of middle age. He came moreover from those simple, but rude and untutored classes of the community whose bigotry and intolerance are generally quite commensurate with their simplicity.

Ignorance is ever the favored handmaid of superstition and fanaticism. Thus the fables of paganism continued to be reverenced by the illiterate long after they had been discredited by the philosophers and the men of culture; and Jewish prejudice had its citadel not more in the schools of the Rabbis and the sect of the Pharisees than in the simple bigotry of the fishermen of Galilee and the populace of Jerusalem. St. Paul, referring back to his own misguided zeal, speaks of himself as a Hebrew of the Hebrews, but it may be doubted whether the cultivated disciple of Gamaliel ever shared to the full in all the prejudices of his more ignorant countrymen; and certainly there was that in his scholastic training, in the largeness of his nature, and in the breadth and comprehensiveness of his intellect, which fitted him to be what he afterwards became, the great apostle of a universal faith. But with St. Peter the case was different. By nature intellectually narrow, perhaps all his early surroundings, illiterate and superstitious associates, would incline to confirm him in his narrowness. A bigoted and intolerant Jew, his natural tendency would be to be equally bigoted and intolerant as a Christian. With him the Gospel would be only Judaism over again, with a new name, and in another form. No vision of the universal Church would dawn upon his eyes—the great multitude out of every tribe and nation and people and tongue. Even after the resurrection of Jesus his chief concern was and would still be this: " Lord, wilt thou at this time restore the kingdom to Israel?" Still to him would the Gentile be an alien and accursed, one common and unclean. And even when that inveterate prejudice had at last been overmastered, enough of it would yet linger to lead him on one occasion, at least, to act with such glaring inconsistency as to constrain an associate apostle " to withstand him to the face, because he was to be blamed."

Yet it was necessary that this man, naturally so narrow and exclusive, should be brought to recognize the universality of the Gospel. St. Peter, whether from seniority, the indomitable energy of his character, or some still deeper reason, had been called to a kind of primacy among the apostles. Humanly speaking the future of Christianity would depend largely upon his conception of it. It could not be permitted, therefore, that his prejudices should stand in the way of its normal and true development. They were to be swept away at once and forever. He had learnt many things since that vain boast of his at the Supper; he was now to learn something more surprising than all. He had come to know already that the Gospel was to be preached to every creature; he was now to know, and rejoice in knowing, not that humanity should be gathered into Israel, but that Israel should be absorbed into humanity; that the door of the Church should be thrown open wide to the Gentile, not upon the condition of his becoming a Jew or a Jewish proselyte, but to the Gentile as such; that the uncircumcised heathen also were to take possession of the kingdom of God. That was the truth, new and astounding as it then was, which was to dawn upon his mind and heart. And, therefore, to St. Peter, praying by the sea at Joppa, there came one day a great discovery.

The ceremonial law of his fathers prohibited the eating of certain flesh under certain circumstances as involving a ceremonial defilement. But in a trance he saw a great sheet let down from heaven, wherein were all manner of beasts and creeping things, and heard a voice commanding: " Rise, Peter, kill and eat." But the dreamer, true to the instinct that was in him, objected: " Not so, Lord, for I have never eaten anything that is common or unclean." And then came that significant reply, thrice repeated, reply doubtless strange enough and unexpected and overwhelming to him: " What God hath cleansed that call not thou common." And he was left to meditate and ponder on those words, and question with himself what the vision could mean. But that was only the beginning of his discovery, a mere hint at the deeper truth which it involved. The meaning of the vision became clear and plain, when in the house of Cornelius the centurion he heard how the prayers and alms of an uncircumcised man had gone up for a memorial before God. Here, indeed, was the interpretation of his dream, the open secret of the voice that sometimes speaks in dreams.

St. Peter had made a great discovery, and now he announces it in ever memorable words: "Of a truth I perceive that God is no respecter of persons: but in every nation he that feareth him, and worketh righteousness, is accepted with him."

What a grand utterance was that to come from a Galilean fisherman, a bigoted, ignorant, and intolerant Jew! How it puts to shame our pretentious liberality, sounding out, in its lofty supremacy, far above all the prejudices and narrownesses and limitations of the systems of men! We speak sometimes of teaching which we have come up to, and passed beyond, and outgrown. Shall we ever come up to, or pass beyond, or outgrow this? Shall we ever fathom or exhaust it? Will the practice of our charity, our Christian toleration, ever look back to it and say, "All this have I done. What lack I yet?" Do we not feel, rather, that there is in it a meaning which sweeps beyond our grasp, something which transcends the immediate occasion of its announcement—a truth which, with all these added years, the Christendom of to-day is just beginning to appropriate and teach?

This declaration of St. Peter is an affirmation of the absolute fairness and impartiality of God. That is a proposition which every one will readily assent to. There is something in us which responds to it, and we do not at first take in all the consequences to which it commits us. There is a certain vagueness about generalities which not infrequently is deceptive and illusive. We enthusiastically re-affirm them, and are surprised and indignant that any should question them, so self-evident at first they seem; and yet the moment we try to reduce them to practice, and apply them to particulars, we are astonished to find that we ourselves virtually repudiate them. The absolute fairness and impartiality of God—is that, in very truth, a self-evident proposition? Let us, then, reduce it to its constituents, and see more clearly the inferences that are connected with it.

1. And first it implies the entire equality of all nations before God—"every nation," "no respecter of persons." In reply to that, the Jew could point significantly to his own election and calling. And, indeed, if we take up our Bibles and begin at the beginning, we shall not go very far before we are led to suspect God of favoritism and partiality. We see a people supernaturally guided and guarded, marching on to the promised land, driving out its inhabitants before them, and finally settling down and taking possession of it. Nor does it avail to close the book and turn from that marvellous story to the pages of secular history. Here, again, the suspicion reappears. Two or three nations soon emerge into prominence above the rest, and the history of mankind becomes the record of their superior greatness and progress. It wouldseem, often, as if the world itself existed only as the theatre on which their drama should be enacted; as if the welfare of all other peoples were held by the mysterious power behind the scenes as always subservient and subordinate to theirs. Is God, then, in reality impartial? Can His fairness be reconciled with these facts as

they come before us? Must it be vindicated by a kind of pious atheism which shall empty history of its Providence, and the Scriptures of their Jehovah? Shall we say of Him that He sitteth afar "in the circle of the heavens," and "takes no thought" of the fortunes of His world? That were a poor escape from the enigmas of the divine providence, which should lead to a practical denial of the divine existence, which should leave mankind without a disposer of events, without an arbiter and a guide. We cannot give up our faith in God; neither can we give up, when once we have grasped it, the conviction of His equity. There must be some way in which the seemingly contradictory facts of history may be reconciled with that. And the riddle is in the way of a solution when we are led to the perception of the truth, of which the whole Old Testament itself, from its opening to its close, is the witness, that the history of every people is ordered by that Providence which shapes it in accordance with, and in relation to, the true welfare and the highest good of all.

The Jew had indeed been set apart and chosen, but set apart and chosen for what? Not, as he himself came in time to answer it, that he might be the recipient of special favors; not that he might have to himself the exclusive appropriation of Jehovah; but that he might be the custodian of the oracles of God, the conservator of truths that were not meant to die, the witness of the divine unity and goodness and holiness to all the nations of the earth. The ground of his election was in the purpose that made him a minister, a servitor of the highest interests of humanity, and the moment he ceased to be that, he was thrown aside as a broken and useless thing. Is not this too the history of the foremost nations of the pagan world? Was not the Greek inspired to be the teacher of wisdom to mankind? Did not the Roman achieve his dominion that he might bequeath to the world the priceless legacy of law? Were not these, too, though they knew it not, the servants and servitors of the great family of which they were members?

And if this be so, may we not believe, despite all the seeming contradictions of it, in the righteous equity of God? May we not believe that the uncircumcised Philistine whom the Jew contemned, the outside barbarian at whom the Greek scoffed, and the oppressed tributary whom the Roman bowed beneath his yoke, were equally dear and cared for, with one and the other, in the thought of Him with whom is "no respect of persons?" And is not this the truth which even in our own day we have so often to emphasize and repeat before we can get it believed? Though the abstract statement of it seems so inspiring and attractive, do we not find ourselves halting and stumbling woefully when occasionally we are called to reduce it to practice and particulars? Are we not conscious of a certain humiliation in the thought that the most degraded peoples of the earth, races with whom we can scarcely bring ourselves to acknowledge a common origin or a common destiny, should nevertheless stand side by side with us in the sight and in the providences of God? Yet that is one of the truths involved in St. Peter's discovery.

"God," he says, "hath shewed me that I should not call any man common or unclean."

2. Another truth was this: Salvation is limited neither to Jew nor Gentile, *to no visible institution or church among men.* He was led to see that though a religion may be undoubtedly divine in its origin, it does not therefore follow that there can be no truth or worth or acceptableness in any other. We should scarcely expect such an admission from a bigoted and intolerant Jew, one who had been long accustomed to look upon the heathen as destined to perdition. But is the admission even now a universally Christian one? Is every one who bears that name prepared to affirm without jot or tittle of abatement, to echo in all its length and breadth, St. Peter's assertion: "In every nation he that feareth him and worketh righteousness is accepted with him"? The Jew thought that the Gentile could not serve God acceptably unless he first became a proselyte to his ancient faith. It is not so long ago since no inconsiderable number of Christian people felt themselves constrained to believe in the eternal loss of those to whom the knowledge of Christ never came. And even those who involuntarily shrank from such a thought, had yet no better hope for them than to consign them in doubtful phrase to God's "uncovenanted mercies." Men were made bigoted and intolerant by the glosses which they or their fathers had put upon the Gospel. The conviction of the necessity of Christ's redemption, the assurance that "there is none other name given under heaven whereby we can be saved," this great

truth was made the foundation of a system which, built up step by step with a remorseless logic, necessarily excluded from eternal life every one who had not heard of, and consciously professed his faith in, his Saviour. True it is that Christ's redemption is necessary to salvation; but that salvation was made for all mankind. True it is that "there is none other name given whereby we may be saved;" but that name avails, even though it has never been, and in this world shall never be, on many, many lips. If it be true that Christ is indeed that Light which "lighteth every man that cometh into the world," then all purity and goodness, in whatever age or clime, must be an emanation from Him, and therefore has been, and is, and will be accepted with Him. We may believe that the pure and the wise, the good and the true of all ages, though separated often apparently so hopelessly, and with lives set outwardly so far apart, are yet gathered into a noble communion, an invisible fellowship, larger than our poor thoughts can reach. We may believe, and rejoice in believing, that they "who have not the law, yet who do by nature the things contained in the law, are a law unto themselves"; that God accepteth a man, in St. Paul's expression of it, "according to what he hath, and not according to what he hath not." And with the recognition of this truth, in all the length and breadth of it may come that charity, that toleration, which the Jew once denied the Gentile, and which now in turn the Gentile seems often to deny the Jew; that Christian toleration which shall extend to all religions, and recognize in them whatever there may be of truth and worth; which shall acknowledge, and be glad in the acknowledgment, that however false and in themselves insufficient they may be, it is yet possible for a benighted soul to "fear God, and work righteousness," and be "accepted with him."

3. The final truth involved in St. Peter's discovery, and that of which we have, perhaps, the greatest need, is his recognition of the fact that intellectual error is not incompatible with moral goodness. A simple proposition, is it not? and yet it may be doubted whether you can find a man who in his actual practice, his every-day experience of men, yields an unhesitating assent to it. Some of us, perhaps, have not found it very hard to believe that those heathen have been accepted to whom the knowledge of the truth never came. But is our belief equally ready in respect to those to whom the truth has come, but who from previous education, the force of circumstances, or some constitutional peculiarity, have found themselves incapable of receiving it? Is it not a first and strong temptation to explain all such incapability under the head of wilfulness or obstinacy or perversity, or, to use a more scriptural expression, a "hardening of the heart"? The prejudice seems to be inveterate which leads us so generally to associate intellectual with moral obliquity. There is in the one, indeed, a tendency to produce the other, and that is not a remote connection which exists between a true thought and a true life. But sometimes, shall we not say often, the life is true according to its knowl-

edge, while yet the man's creed is sadly astray? Can we not conceive that the reception of many truths which we deem, and rightly deem, vital and essential, is, for some men, to all intents and purposes, practically impossible? We cannot reconcile this, perhaps, with other convictions which we have, but it seems to be a fact, nevertheless. We are slow to admit it, because it is just in connection with those truths which we most earnestly believe in, that we are, as it were, irresistibly impelled to visit with moral condemnation all who oppose them. It is difficult to believe that what we consider a bad creed is not held by a bad man. But do we not meet many who we feel are altogether wrong, far and far astray, denying much that seems to us unspeakably sacred, and who yet force upon us the conviction of their sincerity—who seem to be living in the fear of God, and working righteousness according to the light they have? Would it be a satisfaction, or an occasion of perplexity, to think of them as not accepted? Is it not rather a comfort, an occasion of adoration and thanksgiving, to be told, as was Peter, their " prayers and alms have gone up for a memorial before God;" and to be able to say with Paul: "O the depth of the riches both of the wisdom and knowledge of God! How unsearchable are his judgments, and his ways past finding out!"

XIX.

THE WIDOW WOMAN AND ELIJAH.

[KINGSBRIDGE, 1869.]

"The barrel of meal wasted not, neither did the cruse of oil fail according to the word of the Lord, which he spake by Elijah."—
1 KINGS xvii. 16.

AMONG the grand and imposing figures in the prophetic history of the Old Testament, Elijah is, in some respects, the grandest and most imposing of all. No other prophet makes a profounder impression on his countrymen, and with no other were such hopes and long-continued expectations associated. There had been something awful and mysterious in his whole life and character and mission. He appears on the scene of Jewish history at a period of great national degeneracy, when he, and, apparently, he alone, remained to vindicate and do battle for the faith of his fathers. The circumstances of his position, and the character of the work that had been assigned him, combined to make his course a stormy and terrible one. He had to oppose himself in bitter struggle against an apostate king, and be the mouthpiece of vengeance on an apostate land. Persecuted from city to city, the terrible manifestations of his prophetic power made his own name a name of fear and dread. He dwells apart in an impenetrable solitude, girt round, it would seem, by fire from heaven, or appears a moment before the eyes of men, to disappear again as suddenly. When he comes before them, he comes as a stern, upbraiding, and destroying presence. John the Baptist, his later likeness, was immeasurably milder and less awe-inspiring than he. John was the prophet of " wrath to come," but Elijah was the prophet of an immediate and visible vengeance. When we think of him, we seem to see him standing before Ahab, and declaring that "there shall be no dew or rain upon the earth all these years;" or slaying the false prophets of Baal at " the brook Kishon;" or sitting on his hill in the wilderness, and the "captains and their fifties" consumed to ashes at his feet. No wonder that this stern, wild, hairy man, with "the leathern girdle about his loins," became the most awful and mysterious figure in Jewish history; no wonder his record was indelible in the remembrance of his people; no wonder that in times of special apostasy and degeneracy, times of national degradation and servitude, they looked to see one come "in the spirit and power of Elias," to rebuke kings and people, and to be, mayhap, the solitary yet sufficient champion of right and truth. He had not died as other men die, but his stormy course had had its own stormful and triumphant close. He had "gone up," they said, "by a whirlwind into heaven." And they looked to see him come again in the "whirlwind," to sweep and cleanse and purify the earth.

Yet in this troubled record we come upon one

gentle and tranquil page. In this life so stern and far apart from ordinary human sympathies, there is one passage of singular and touching tenderness. Among all these miracles of wrath and vengeance there is one miracle of mercy and beneficence. The drought which the prophet had predicted came to pass, and its long continuance was followed, as in the East it always is, by famine. The fair fields of Palestine were dried up and withered, and misery and death stalked hand in hand over the whole land. Elijah himself was not without his share of the common suffering. We see him first by the brook Cherith, dependent, for his scanty and seemingly precarious subsistence, on the ravens which frequented that one green spot—the morsels of "bread and flesh" which they laid night and morning at his feet. But the drought continued, the brook dried up, and the birds had no more "bread and flesh" to bring. The prophet is bidden to arise and go to Zarephath, into the coast of Zidon, with the dubious assurance that "a widow woman there" had been "commanded to sustain him." It was far that he had to go, beyond the borders of Israel, into the maritime plain of the Mediterranean. But here also the drought had extended, and here also the sad spectacle of famine confronted him. As he stands before the city gates he sees "a widow woman gathering sticks," to prepare, as she thought, a last meal "for herself and for her son." Worn with hunger and thirst and travel, he prays her to "fetch him a little water in a vessel, that he may drink." Unmindful, apparently, of her own misery; unmindful, too, of the fact that the person who addressed her was a stranger and of a hostile tribe; mindful only, it would seem, of the instincts of humanity, she turns silently to fetch it. But as she goes he prays her again to bring him "a morsel of bread" in her hand. And then at length her own tale of want and wretchedness is told: "As the Lord thy God liveth, I have but a handful of meal in a barrel, and a little oil in a cruse; and, behold, I am gathering two sticks, that I may go in and dress it for me and my son, that we may eat it, and die." But the prophet reassured her with the promise of Divine provision, and bade her "make first" a little cake for him, and "afterward" for her and her son. She obeyed, partly, doubtless, through the humane instinct which we have seen already working in her; partly, too, through the faith which his words had excited, and thus saved in him her own deliverer. For "the barrel of meal wasted not, neither did the cruse of oil fail," but "she, and he, and her house, did eat many days." And afterwards, when her son sickened and died, he was restored to life again at the prayer of Elijah. Thus there waited upon that woman's act of charity, as has been fitly said of it, "a rebound of unexpected benefits, such as sometimes, even in the prose of common life, equals the poetic justice of an ideal world." And if we see in the fact of the prophet's individual sufferings, in his hunger and thirst and weariness, a witness to the truth that God makes the instruments of his wrath, however personally guiltless they may be, to participate in and bear their share of the woes which they have been called to denounce against others, lest they should stand apart and be separated in common experience and fellow-feeling from their kind, may we not also see in the blessings which his sojourn brought upon that widow's house, a kind of compensation, as it were, made to him and the human heart within him, for that terrible chastisement and bloody vengeance which it was so often his lot and part in life to speak and execute? The home at Zarephath, and the deliverance and joy which followed on his presence there, must have been a consoling episode in the otherwise unvarying experience of the awful and dread Elijah.

That incident—the preservation of the widow and her house—is, on the face of it, a miraculous occurrence. It is so presented to us in the sacred narrative, and that is the only possible light in which it can be regarded. There is no natural explanation of "the barrel of meal" that "wasted not," and the "cruse of oil" that "did not fail." It takes its place as a miraculous incident in a miraculous history, and must be accepted in that character, or discarded altogether. And, accordingly, those who halt and stumble at the supernatural whenever and wherever they may come upon it, will class this story with others of its kind, under the head of myths and legends, beautiful, indeed, and not without a certain value in its moral sentiment, but utterly worthless as any solid foundation of faith and practice. The mere materialism of their creed discredits any truth or witness that may lie beyond it. But we, who have no foregone conclusion of that sort to disturb us, we who believe in a God who can and does work in ways which transcend the ordinary experience of men and processes of nature, are confronted by a difficulty of an exactly opposite kind. We do not halt and stumble before the fact of the supernatural, but we do halt and stumble before the fact of its apparent infrequency. We are not surprised that the little store of this widow was miraculously replenished, but we are surprised that other little stores, under similar and analogous circumstances, are not oftener replenished too. One such instance seems to necessitate that there should be many more. Our difficulty is not in the fact that once upon a time God went out of His way, as it were, to preserve a faithful and dutiful servant, but in the attempt to reconcile His omnipotence and goodness with the fact that He so seldom, if ever, as far as we can see, goes out of His way to preserve *others* who are faithful and dutiful. The religious mind is half-expectant of the miraculous always and everywhere. It is rather impatient than otherwise of uniform law and the natural sequence of events. It looks to see a ghostly hand thrust forth from out the darkness, to put straight the things that have gone awry. It listens with an ill grace to any argument of necessity—the sure relation between cause and effect. It is scarce content to wait and carry on into a future world the solution of the whole matter. It wants some open, visible interference now. If God be omnipotent and good, why is there so often a color for the sceptic's sneer that He is on the side of the strongest battalions? Why does a righteous cause go down so often before its iniquitous oppressor? Why does the "only son of his mother" die, and she "a widow," and no voice avail to bring him back to life again? Why does the meal waste and the oil fail, and leave, alas! many a devout and trusting heart to perish? Are miracles simply things of the past? And if so, why are they recorded to raise expectations which are doomed to be disappointed in our own experience?

Now it is just at this point that we have need to distinguish. It is one thing to believe in the supernatural, it is another thing to dictate the forms and the manifestations of it. There is one sense in which this story which we have read is purely exceptional, standing altogether apart from ordinary human experience; and there is another sense in which it is not exceptional, but the expression, rather, of a universal fact. There is no reason to disbelieve, indeed it would be a kind of atheism to disbelieve, that God is equally present and directive in the concerns of life now as of old. He is no more prohibited from interference by natural laws now than He was then. He does interfere, but in subtler and less discernible ways—ways which shade off imperceptibly into and are scarcely distinguishable from natural causes.

There is a kind of grossness, if one may say so, in the Bible miracles. I mean that they are so plain and unmistakable, they confront us so squarely, and thrust their evidence so directly in our face, that they scarcely leave us room for the exercise of a perceptive faith. To see was to believe, and the only way to discredit the fact was to act upon the principle that if you shut your eyes to a thing you will not see it. Our Lord Himself often seems to weary of this kind of demonstration, and sometimes turns half contemptuously from it, as if the faith which it excited He did not value very highly. Yet there was a time in the education of the world when such plain, palpable, and, to use the expression again, "gross" evidence was needed. Once for all it had to be demonstrated, beyond all possibility of cavil, that God is not bound up in the inexorable laws of nature, but that He transcends them; that He can and does act *immediately* and *supernaturally* in the affairs of human life. Of this truth the Scriptural miracles are the perpetual and incontrovertible witness. They stand as the memorials, the landmarks, of an advance, a progress, a position gained, in religious history. They are exceptional therefore in this sense, that their work having been done, and done effectually, we have no reason whatever to look for or count upon their literal repetition. And yet in another sense they are not exceptional, because the fact to which they witness, namely, God's immanence in human life, is not an occasional but a universal fact —a fact as true in our day as it was in the day of Christ and in the day of Elijah. Be sure the substantial reality of the miracle is about us everywhere. It may not be wrought in such open and unmistakable ways, but still there are times when the devout heart can feel, if it cannot trace it. The believer insists, and insists rightly, that there ought to be, that there must be, that there is, such a thing as a "special providence." Some whose experience has been blessed will join with some whose experience has been bitter, in repelling, as the mere idle and unregarded wind, any argument that you can bring against it. All this jargon of law, all these postulates of a materialistic philosophy, they heed not. They know—and what argument can avail against knowing—they know that their lives have been disentangled, though only for a moment, from the web of circumstance; that laws, aye, laws, have been turned aside or transcended for them, and that the hand of God has been laid on them directly and immediately, either in chastisement or blessing. And that assurance will not be lightly disavowed when supported by the confirmatory witness of the story which we read to-day—a story which does not, indeed, give us any reason to count on its literal repetition within our own experience, but which is none the less, therefore, a witness to the fact that God always and invariably, either in natural or supernatural ways, *enables us to do, and blesses the doing of the duty which He imposes.*

Let us look a moment at this "duty" that is brought before us, for at first sight it is certainly a remarkable and extraordinary one. A widow woman, in a time of drought and dearth and famine, is commanded to sustain Elijah out of her scanty, nay, all but exhausted, store. The prophet presents himself before her and asks for food at the very moment when she is preparing, as she thinks, to eat her last meal. In other words, she is expected to do what to human sight must have seemed impossible. The doing, then, of *the apparently impossible*, is the special duty which her story teaches. And let us remember that this is no mere paradox, but a veritable reality. The duty is none the less a duty because we may have found, perhaps, no place for it in our vaunted Christian code, nor ever even seriously considered it

There are some things which we have considered, and which have been accorded an almost universal recognition. Such, for instance, is the duty of wealth, of large opportunity, of conceded ability of whatever kind. Such gifts are looked upon as trusts, to which there is attached a sure and solemn responsibility. The Gospel has sufficiently set forth this view of the matter, and it is backed up and enforced now by an enlightened and Christian public sentiment. The man of means, of influence, of position, who meets with suffering and does not relieve it, who meets with wrong and makes no effort to redress it, who meets with need of any sort and has no corresponding response, must stand in his own eyes self-condemned. Or, if he be not self-condemned, it must be because he is a kind of moral monstrosity, one who is utterly out of relation with the moral tone and consciousness of his age. Public opinion condemns him, whether expressed or unexpressed; be sure of that. Society ascends into the judgment-seat and passes sentence, not in the sense prohibited by Christ, but in the fulfilment of His law that the Christian community shall "bind" or "loose on earth" what is "bound" or "loosed in heaven." There is no need to argue of duties which have this universal confirmation and witness in the minds of men.

Nor, again, is there any special need to demonstrate the duty, whatever our circumstances or position, of doing whatever good we can. We have learned, in some measure at least, we trust, the obligation and the worth attaching to even the feeblest discipleship, the most insignificant influence, the mere "cup of cold water" given "in the name" of Christ. The Master's comment, "She hath done what she could," is an incentive and encouragement which cannot help but linger in our ears. Service, and service the most acceptable, is not reserved exclusively for the favored and the great. The poor man as well as the rich, the most humble as well as the most exalted, has his duties, and duties, too, of equal worth. We know, whatever our lot in life may be, that that something which we can do, that good which we are consciously capable of, is imperative, and obligatory upon us.

But beyond this we seldom or never go. Yet there are occasions when we seem to be summoned beyond it. It will happen sometimes that we refuse to take up the burden to which we are called because we are more than doubtful of our ability to bear it. Or we put aside some behest which seems waiting at our hands, because it confronts us with an apparently impossible requirement. We dismiss the matter, more or less summarily, upon the plea, often genuine and sincere enough, of utter inability. We decline, not, indeed, without a strange and unaccountable twinge of conscience, to consider such things in the light of duties at all. There must have been experiences of this sort in all our lives, and we, each of us, perhaps, can furnish a pertinent instance and application. Is the apparently impossible, then, to be put aside at once as something with which we can have nothing to do? Let us go back again to our story for the answer. This widow woman of Zarephath, would she have been justified in refusing to share with the prophet that last meal which she was preparing for herself and her son? She was famishing with hunger, utterly wretched and miserable; and misery can seldom see beyond itself. There seems to have been no communication of God's purpose made to her beyond the evident necessity of Elijah. He was a stranger, an alien, one hitherto unknown. As for his assurance of a miraculously replenished barrel and cruse, she had nothing more than his simple word to go upon. Would she not have been justified in turning him off on others, and bidding him leave her and hers to enjoy alone the poor luxury of that last meal? No, not justified. Excusable, perhaps. No one, certainly, would have the heart to blame her. It would have been very natural. But still she would not have been justified. Had her story read thus, we should accord her pity, and not reverence. In her circumstances, doubtless, we would have turned him off too, but that fact does not dim the clearness of our moral perception as long as we do not happen to be actually concerned. Her story then would not have touched or ennobled or inspired us. It would have been one of those common tales, too common to have been recorded. Or, to look at the matter in another way, suppose no miracle had been promised or wrought, and sharing that scanty meal with the prophet it had, indeed, been her last, who does not feel that her noble humanity would have been something imperishable, something to fire and kindle and glorify his thought? There would have been nothing of that vague, undefined dissatisfaction which is at once suggested by the other hypothesis. And besides all this, we who stand, as it were, behind the scenes, know that this scarcely possible thing came to that poor woman in the shape of a duty; that in her hour of bitter agony it was the great burden which God had given her to take up and bear. Nobly did she stand the test, and nobly were her humanity and her faith requited. One such instance is worth many arguments and many words. Perhaps in the reading we have been led to see that many things which we have summarily put aside as impossible were in very truth duties, and were actually required of us. If such occasions have not come already, be sure they will. Some time or other we shall have to decide whether the call which seems to us so preposterous, and which yet cannot be dismissed without a vague feeling of uneasiness, is, indeed, preposterous, or to be dismissed at all. God, remember, does not condition His behests upon our own conscious and clearly recognized ability. The measure of our responsibility is not the grace we have, but the grace we may have; not our present means of meeting it, but the means which God will open to us. To do our whole duty here in life we must sometimes attempt even the seemingly impossible. If the call is one which with a clear conscience and a quiet heart we cannot altogether put aside, we must be content to take it upon trust, to make a venture of faith. We cannot tell, there is no way of telling, what in any given instance we may be, naturally or supernaturally, enabled to do, until we have honestly and sincerely tried.

For the impossible becomes possible when we have once seriously set ourselves to undertake it. The obstacles which at a distance seemed insurmountable begin to melt away as we approach them. The road opens for us, we know not how, and the waves recede for us, on either hand, as we go forward. Our purpose, our work, our mission here, is wrought out, sometimes in the even tenor of events, sometimes in strange surprises and combinations. Our life, the more deeply we ponder it, is seen to be girt all round with mystery. Where the natural ends and the supernatural begins we cannot say. We only know that in a very deep and true analogy there is or may be, that in every life which corresponds to "the barrel of meal that wasted not," and "the cruse of oil that did not fail." The grace to do what has been given us to do comes with its exercise, and the more abundantly the more implicitly we rely upon it. It will be sufficient, we may be sure, for every duty that is really ours, and will verify the promise that "as our years," as our behests, as our trials are, "so shall our strength be."

XX.

SAMUEL'S CHALLENGE.

[KINGSBRIDGE, 1876.]

"And he said unto them, The Lord is witness against you, and his anointed is witness this day, that ye have not found aught in my hand. And they answered, He is witness."—I SAM. xii. 5.

THESE words, which are taken from the first lesson of this morning's service, bring before us one of the most impressive scenes in the earlier history of Israel. It is a great state occasion, when the last of the judges lays down his trust, and asks and receives from the nation its witness to the integrity of his administration. The picture is a simple and primitive one; it takes us back to a kind of golden age, when, in the recognition both of the magistrate and of the community, character was still the one inestimable thing. It is the anticipation of many a later political ideal, and forewarns us, as indeed all Scripture forewarns, that the righteous ruler can only come from, and is only possible to, the righteous people. This is the moral of the incident, and our discourse will be the assertion of it.

There is no word more often on the lips of this generation than the word "progress." It represents an idea which in greater or less measure we all believe in. The belief that the world moves, and moves on —that the life of man is advancing through higher physical, social, governmental conditions—is the conviction of all but a few pessimist philosophers. To think otherwise, to suppose that the course of human history can be more than momentarily a stationary or a downward one, involves as its ultimate logical result utter disbelief in God and utter disbelief in man. Our self-congratulations may be often vain and boastful; nay, in the temporary retrogressions of the individual and of society, they may become a sad satire on our hopes, yet these hopes are not without a substantial justification. It is not, therefore, in regard to the fact of progress, still less in regard to the idea of it, or the possibility of it, that the difference between Christian and unchristian thought begins. It begins when we ask whence does this progress come, and what are the conditions of its continuance? Here, indeed, the divergence becomes wide, and apparently hopeless.

The Christian position may be given in the words of the ancient Book: "There is a spirit in man, and the inspiration of the Almighty giveth him understanding." The Church asserts, therefore, that true progress is possible only in the lines of revealed truth. These postulates, however, the world is disposed to ignore or deny. It affirms that all man's advances are due to himself—to the unaided, inherent force of his own mind. The assumption that there is "a spirit in him"—something which makes him capable of inspiration—is mere foolishness in the eyes of our dominant materialistic philosophy. Man has no spirit, no inspiration, it says, and he needs not any. His reason is his strength and stay; let him trust to that, and that alone, and his progress is secure. In this view, of course, the common judgments of mankind must be all reversed. For the influence of Revelation in human history on this supposition either goes for nothing, or appears only as an obstructive superstition. This, indeed, seems to be the last word of our modern materialism, since one of its foremost exponents can allow himself to speak of Christianity as " that awful plague which has already destroyed two civilizations, and threatens now to extinguish whatever hope of good is still left in man." But the wild criticism of these wild words had best, perhaps, be left to the somewhat disdainful comment of one who is himself an unbeliever, but who thinks it hardly worth our while to concern ourselves with the mad utterances of one who can " stand on the shore of the mighty sea of time, and instead of listening to the solemn boom of its waves, prefer to raise the echo to his own whoopings."

The Christian position, as was said before, is simply this: All true progress must be in the lines of revealed truth. In other words, it must be a development of the principles of the Bible. For the Scriptures are the source whence we get our ideals; they, and they alone, contain the germs out of which must come the fruition of our hopes. The recognition of the principles of the Bible, therefore, and the acceptance of those principles, are the conditions, and the essential conditions, of any true advancement. Following them, we shall always be on the right road; but whenever we lose sight of them, we stray away into error.

Now the vindication of the Christian position is found in connection with all the foremost questions of our modern world. Take, for instance, the relation of the sexes, the place which woman is to fill in the civilization of the future. The Bible indicates this at the very outset when it calls her the helpmeet for the man. For the expression implies that she is to be his companion, counsellor, comforter, and friend. To be all this she must be his equal. What Mr. Mill calls the subjection of woman has no recognition in the Scripture. Her relationship as outlined there involves subordination, indeed, but no inferiority. Consequently every real advance in her position has been a legitimate outcome of the Biblical conception. All other theories have either wilfully degraded her, or, exalting by unsexing, have degraded her no less. It is quite as fatal to her progress to make her man's rival as it is to make her his plaything or his slave.

So, too, in regard to the all-important question of education, that is another of our watchwords. But here also the Bible anticipates us by holding up the ideal of a man ever growing in the divine knowledge. Whether education with us shall advance or go back must depend upon what we educate; whether we keep "turning the eye of the soul toward the light," educating the moral and spiritual nature, or whether we simply concern ourselves with the accumulation of facts, and the sharpening of our mental faculties.

The latter process at the best can only make us clever men, and very possibly clever knaves.

The physical science of our age has opened to us many splendid visions, but here again the Bible is still before us. One of Mr. Buckle's famous generalizations is, that the Oriental nations crouch before nature, while the Western nations defy her. Yet in the literature of at least one Oriental people there is found something better and higher even than defiance, the calm assertion of an ever-increasing mastery. In the Scripture man is incited and bidden to assert his dominion over nature, to "replenish the earth and subdue it." And what triumph of science can ever more than fulfil the prophecy of the Christ: "Behold, I give you power to tread on serpents and scorpions, and over all the power of the enemy; and nothing shall by any means hurt you"?

It is in the domain of political science, however, that our age seems most inclined to deny its obligations to the Bible, to repudiate the influence and authority of revelation. Here, if anywhere, man is supposed to be capable of working out theories for himself. And yet in two respects, if in no more, this self-same Bible will always be every wise statesman's great political text-book.

1. For, first, it sets forth on many a page, both by precept and example, the true condition of all real national greatness. "Righteousness," it affirms over and over again, righteousness "exalteth a nation." This is the true flourishing of a land; where this is, other things follow as the shadow does the substance. And although to teach thus may seem, as Milton

says, "mere pulpitry" to politicians, yet it is a teaching which is vindicated in the pages of the secular no less than of the sacred historian. The people who account this lesson of Scripture obsolete have entered upon that downward way from which there is no returning.

2. Again, it is to the Scripture that we must go to learn the true source and character of all political authority. The Bible, indeed, in the apprehension of many, is the stronghold of political superstitions. To them it appears the last bulwark of decaying tyrannies, the very citadel of ancient wrong. What a strange misreading of the Book which, so far as human rights are concerned, is more radical and revolutionary than any other! For the "powers that be," in the Biblical account of them, never appear in their origin in connection with the ideas of heritage, right, prerogative, privilege, dignity, or honor. In Scripture these words represent only relative and secondary conceptions—accommodations, as it were, to the infirmities of human thought. The primary and the absolute conception is always that of responsibility. Every office is conceived of as a trust from God—a stewardship—something which involves, directly or indirectly, a divine call and a divine appointment. According to Holy Writ, no man bears rule for his own pleasure or honor or emolument. He is the servant, rather, on whom the weighty responsibility is laid. When Israel goes up out of Egypt, Moses assumes the leadership, not eagerly, as if to exalt himself; but reluctantly, in obedience to a divine command, almost a divine men-

ace. The long period of the judges who succeed him—Jephthah, Gideon, Barak, Samuel—all these names are the names of men whom the exigencies of the time, in one way or another, constrained into the acceptance of the trust. The kings who follow are the answer to a growing political necessity—the necessity of a more stable and permanent authority. Yet the last of the judges did not inaugurate the first of the kings without most serious misgivings. He feared that the hereditary character of the monarchy might lead to a misapprehension of the royal office; that the trust might be degraded into mere privilege and prerogative. He said to the people: "This will be the manner of the king that shall reign over you: He will take your sons, and appoint them for himself, for his chariots, and to be his horsemen; and some shall run before his chariots. And he will take your daughters to be confectionaries, and to be cooks, and to be bakers. And he will take your fields, and your vineyards, and your oliveyards, even the best of them, and give them to his servants. He will take your goodliest young men, and put them to his work. He will take the tenth of all you have, and ye shall be his servants." This gloomy anticipation was realized. All this that king did, and all this for the most part other kings have done. The sense of trust, of responsibility, soon passed away, and was succeeded by assertions of prerogative instead. The growth of the divine right in most nations is veiled in obscurity, but in the case of Israel it is an open page. Here we may read the analogy of all other usurpations, whether in Oriental despotisms or Western tyrannies. And despite the ancient witness of the Bible against it, the misconception has lived on almost to the modern time. It is only in the later stages of man's history that he has won his emancipation from this political superstition.

It is no advance, however, no progress, to get rid of the superstition of divine right merely to fall into that barren rationalism which makes rulers the mere creatures of the people—the favorites whom in one way or another they may delight to honor; for here, under another guise, the misconception is still the same. Here, too, there is no sense of trust, no sense of responsibility; but office is regarded as a kind of prize, whose chief work consists in the emolument or the dignity which it brings to him who fills it. This view is more mischievous, because more degrading, than the other. It leads to mere place-men, mere self-seekers, vain or mercenary candidates for official station. No reverence can wait on such a conception; no solemnity fill the thought of executive, legislator, magistrate, or people.

Political progress, like all other progress, must be in the lines of revealed truth. Both rulers and people, in accordance with the conception of the Scripture, must look upon office as a trust, a responsibility. Every one who ventures to accept public station should be conscious of an inherent or acquired fitness for it; in other words, he should be conscious of a call—a call that will come to him in the spontaneous recognition of others, for such a consciousness as this always goes hand in hand with modesty. It will wait, it will bide its time, until its summons comes. These are the leaders who guide a people wisely and well, who truly interpret and adequately express its spirit. And these are the leaders that we want: not scheming, intriguing candidates, not weak, mediocre men—men who start from the ground, like the dragon's teeth, at the mere mention of office, eager and clamorous to fill it.

But there can be no sense of responsibility in the ruler, unless there be also a corresponding sense of responsibility in the people. The Bible nowhere leads us to suppose that we ourselves are the ultimate source of political power. It is a stewardship —something which we have received, and for which we are accountable. Indeed, the theory of self-government implies the greatest responsibility of all. It is a trust which we can delegate only with reverent carefulness. If we make it the prize of mere cleverness—of ambition, vanity, intrigue—we must expect the "evil tree" to "bring forth evil fruit." Only as we believe what the Scriptures say, that "the powers that be are ordained of God," that is, that they have a divine call and consecration; only as we believe that and act on that, will rulers recognize and obey the divine law which applies to Church and State alike: "He that will be chief among you, let him be your servant."

Every ruler's sense of the responsibility of his office will have its practical witness in the purity and integrity of its administration. Let him have a true conception of the trust, let it be clothed in his eyes with its proper reverence, and the faithful exercise of it will infallibly follow. He will have no thought of self-aggrandizement, no dream of turning public station to selfish use, but will be chiefly solicitous to discharge its duties with a conscience void of offence. Personal interests will be put aside; no ambition will tempt him to play an unworthy part; still less will the illegitimate emoluments of office find any recognition with him. He will be as sensitive to any imputation on his integrity as a woman is sensitive to any breath against her honor. For his reward he will look on to the vindication of God and man. And when his work is done, he will come down from his high place with unclouded brow and unsullied name.

Look at Samuel's surrender of his trust, this last of the judges, worthy, indeed, to be the last in that great roll of famous names! With him station was a trust, a responsibility, and it was filled in accordance with that conception. When the time comes for him to give place to his successor, he can do so with a noble challenge on his lips. There is no slinking from the reach of a tardy justice, but a proud vindication of integrity before all the people. What a noble scene it is! The world has not framed and hung it up in her great historic gallery, but methinks no annals and no people can furnish another picture worthy to be compared with that.

It is the assemblage of the Hebrew tribes. Their first king is to be inaugurated. Their last judge lays down his trust, and, as he lays it down, he stands forth full and fair to public view, and says: "I am old and gray-headed; and I have walked before you from my childhood unto this day. Behold, here I am: witness against me before the Lord, and before His anointed : whose ox have I taken? or whose ass have I taken? or whom have I defrauded? whom have I oppressed? or of whose hand have I received any bribe to blind mine eyes therewith? and I will restore it you. And they said, Thou hast not defrauded us, nor oppressed us, neither hast thou taken aught of any man's hand. And he said unto them, The Lord is witness against you, and His anointed is witness this day, that ye have not found aught in my hand. And they answered, He is witness."

Any comment would mar the touching simplicity of this speaking occasion. But why does it stand almost alone in history, solitary and exceptional? The world is sufficiently familiar with inaugurals— vain, boastful, pretentious promises. Virtue would be enthroned could we accept them as faithful portraitures. But with Samuel's noble challenge on his retirement from office the world is not so familiar. And yet it ought to be. For office of which that is not the last word, be it spoken or unspoken—office of which that is not the last word is not honor, but infamy.

And yet here again the trouble is mainly with ourselves. Water cannot rise higher than its source. Rulers cannot be better than the people whom they rule; representatives will express truly the constituents whom they represent. In these modern days the air is darkened on all sides with charges of corruption. Hardly any well-known name escapes the imputation. Those in high place, and those who aspire to it, are equally attacked. Here and there individuals may be innocent, but there is little doubt that the many are guilty. And how should it be otherwise where the nation itself is guilty? The righteous ruler is possible only for the righteous people. Why should we expect our public men to be incorruptible, when we ourselves are not incorrupt? Is the charge false? Is it a libel on this nation and this age? Must we go over all the weary counts in the indictment? Perhaps, in view of the scandalous disclosures which every day are spread before our eyes, a mere reference will be sufficient.

Is it a fact, or is it not a fact, that with us commercial morality is becoming more and more a mere tradition, that our successful business men, not all, but many of them, are becoming more and more men of sharp practices—men, as the expression goes, of the "steel-trap" order, just escaping legal dishonesty, and sometimes not escaping that?

Is it a fact, or is it not a fact, that maladministration, breach of trust, defalcation, violated pledge follow one upon the other now with appalling frequency? Let the innumerable savings-banks that have gone down, the endless life insurance companies that are bankrupt, the legion of railroads whose capital is obliterated, the guarantees here and there and everywhere repudiated by corporations and communities, meet and answer that. Why, when I think of all the money that has been stolen within the last decade, and when I consider that the burden of all these frauds comes, and must ultimately come, upon the labor of the land, I wonder not,

I wonder not, that now and then it lifts its head in insurrection.

What shall we say of our well-to-do people, these gentlemen and ladies who go pleasuring abroad, and, returning with the spoil of foreign parts, make their first act on reaching home an act of bribery, seducing their country's officers to betray their trust and falsify their word? With what face can our dainty tourist declaim against corruption in high places, when in low places his gold and his silver have done their utmost to corrupt? And that they have done so, let the recent manifestoes of the department witness!

But worse than all is the comparative indifference of citizens, reputable themselves, to dishonesty in others. There seems to be no social ostracism now for the man who retains his wealth, no matter how he may have acquired it. Disreputable millionnaires occupy the foreground in every picture. They receive the foreign prince, and the dusky embassy from Ind. The Church, too, has bowed her forehead to the ground, and makes them pillars, and delights to honor them. She has no excommunication for wealthy knaves. If, indeed, one of these come to some mishap; if his riches melt away and leave him weak and impotent; if he lie at last on a sick-bed, a ruined, disgraced, impoverished man, then, perhaps, she will bend on him the "awful and majestic wrinkles" of her brow, and cast him out of her synagogues. But let him retain his wealth, ill-gotten though it be, and even a bishop will come half-way across the continent to do honor to his burial.

May it not, then, be said to us: "Physician, heal thyself"? Must we not look for a regeneration in ourselves before we can look for it in our rulers? It will not come till then, but then it *will* come. Righteous officers must come forth from the rightous people, for "the good tree cannot produce evil fruit." When we ourselves believe, and act upon the belief, that public station is a divine trust, a sacred responsibility; that "righteousness," and not wealth, "exalteth a nation;" then, and not till then, may we expect that our rulers will be as incorruptible as Samuel was, ruling in the fear of God, and laying down their trust at last with clear conscience and clean hands.

XXI.

THE REBELLION OF KORAH.

[KINGSBRIDGE, 1875.]

"And they gathered themselves together against Moses and against Aaron, and said unto them, Ye take too much upon you, seeing all the congregation are holy, every one of them, and the Lord is among them: wherefore then lift ye up yourselves above the congregation of the Lord?"—NUM. xvi. 3.

THE story of the rebellion of Korah and his company, naturally enough, produces very different impressions upon different minds. The tone or habit of thought which is characteristic of men will largely influence their respective conceptions of it. To many of us, perhaps, it brings with it in the reading, a certain confusion of thought, certain moral bewilderments, doubts that come and go, a vague uneasiness—something that leads us to turn from this story, with a sigh of relief, to other and less perplexing things. Thus, we may have heard or read it many times, and yet never once subjected the story or its moral to a clear, searching examination; content, rather, to pass it by as lightly as possible, vaguely conscious that any closer consideration of it might involve for us difficulties of a serious, and even fatal, character. But meanwhile the story itself comes round again, year after year, in the table of the Lessons; again and again we are constrained reluctantly to read or reluctantly to listen to the awful visitation that befell these rebels who asserted, as they claimed, the rights and holiness of the congregation against the exclusive rights and holiness of the priesthood; to be reminded yet once more how the pit opened her mouth, and Dathan and Abiram and their wives and their little children went down into it; how fire came forth from the Lord and consumed Korah and the two hundred and fifty men that offered incense. Whether we will or no, the narrative continually returns upon us; and our vague uneasiness in regard to it, the mingled attraction and repulsion which it excites in us, all the uncertain questions upon which we come, are as continually repeated.

There are two orders or classes of minds, however, to whom this narrative occasions no trouble and no perplexity, who draw the moral of it with no uncertain hand, whose inferences and deductions from it to themselves, at least, are perfectly clear, logical, and satisfactory. They both interpret the story in the same way; but starting with the same interpretation as a premise, the conclusions are diametrically opposed to which they come. For these two classes stand at the very antipodes of thought and feeling. The poles themselves are not wider asunder than they. Thus they have nothing common in this narrative beyond the assumed meaning of it. The one sympathizes, and sympathizes deeply, with the moral which they each acknowledge, while the other abhors and repudiates it. The one would exalt this moral into an authority for all time; the other would make this self-same moral a conclusive argument against the authority of the sacred record which is supposed to contain it. The one is the bigot of a false conservatism, the narrow-minded superstitious defender of exclusive dignity and privilege; the other is the radical of a false liberalism, the self-confident, rationalistic asserter of human equality and rights.

In the apprehension of both, notwithstanding their mutual antagonism, the moral itself, as was said, is the same; and that moral, briefly stated, is this: Venture not, in the name of humanity, or on the ground of essential human equality, to disturb men or orders in the exclusive possession of their peculiar dignities and privileges. You are impious and rebellious if you do. They are the divine investiture. To raise hand or voice against them is to incur the wrath of God. The rights of privileged persons and privileged classes must be respected. Men are not equal; they are essentially unequal. Some, and not others, have an inherent or a traditionary right to teach, to sacrifice, to rule. Your duty is to be taught, to be atoned for, to be governed. Accept the situation, therefore, without gainsaying. For all the congregation are not holy; only Aaron and the Aaronic family have the sanctity which entitles them of right to the priesthood. You have the proof and the illustration of that in this historic record. The rebellion of Korah and his company was a popular insurrection against the civil and ecclesiastical authorities. Moses, they said, had come to be a prince over them: his brother Aaron was in exclusive possession of the priestly power. The uprising against them was in the name of the people. The rallying cry was the delusive watchword of equality—"All the congregation are holy, every one of them"—and the answer to that was then, and in some form will always be, the yawning pit and the consuming fire.

Now to the defender of exclusive right, rank, prerogative, dignity, privilege, no moral could be more useful or satisfactory than this. It disposes summarily of all those insurrectionary tendencies which, in its fancied progress, in the vain imaginings of its upward and onward way, have marked the course of the human mind. In church and state alike it lays the axe at the very root of many evil trees. Indeed, it is a word to conjure by, and accordingly has not been suffered to fall into disuse. Here, from age to age, believers in divine, exclusive, inalienable prerogatives have found an argument which has been to them a tower of strength. Behind it, as behind an impregnable wall, privileged persons and privileged classes, whether civil or ecclesiastical, have been intrenched. The logic of ultra conservatism has always been short, historic, keen: "The leadership, the ennobled name, the priesthood, belong to others; they are not for you. Stand back far from their sacred circles; intrude not within them lest you be, in the language of the Scripture: 'As Korah and his company,' as Dathan and as Abiram."

To the radical, rationalistic champion of popular rights and equality this moral, as might be supposed, is sufficiently distasteful. So little is he inclined to submit to its authority, that he rejects the whole story itself as an imposture. He adduces it as one among other evidences, that the sacred record was compiled in the interest of priests; that its origin was a sacerdotal one; that here and there and everywhere facts have been distorted or tampered with. The priesthood, he says, in all ages and in all lands, has been noted for its ambitious, arrogant, self-assertive character. It has always guarded its exclusive prerogatives most jealously and tenaciously, and, when endangered by popular questioning, has never scrupled to save itself by working on the superstitious fears of men. Here, far back in the Mosaic history, is a signal illustration of this. For, what was Korah's crime but the same crime which has been charged upon the upholders of the rights and equality of the people against exclusive orders and privileged classes in all ages? To modern, enlightened, scientific criticism, he assures us, the mythical character of the whole narrative is patent on the face of it. But in ancient times, as also in the dark, superstitious, mediæval age, the story was a convenient story to tell; and the memorial, no doubt, answered well enough the purpose for which it was designed, when the priest could point, either in fact or fancy, to the legendary plates covering the altar, made up, as men supposed, of the census of those "sinners against their own souls," who "perished in the rebellion of Korah."

I have sketched, as I think, fairly, the respective positions which two antagonistic orders of mind occupy in relation to this narrative—the one making what it assumes to be the moral of the story an authoritative, permanent principle; the other bringing forward this very moral as a proof that the sacred record is not all sacred, but in places, at least, bears marks of the invention and craft of man. Are we constrained, then, to choose between these alternatives? and if so, where shall our choice lie? Not, surely, with that impatient, sceptical liberalism which would impugn the integrity or authority of Holy Writ; which hesitates not to stigmatize as an imposture and fraud any portion of it whose assumed meaning it may chance to dislike, or which may seem to clash with its preconceived opinions, with its favorite watchword and party cry. That were to enter upon the sad, weary way which ends, and can only end, in self-will and the repudiation of all authority whatsoever. But, as we turn from that, are we content with ultra-traditional conservatism; to admit a principle which is, and always has been, fatal to human progress; which raises up barriers of essential, inherent difference between man and man; which separates them by distinctions of dignity, privilege, prerogative, not to be overpassed; which makes the maintenance of these distinctions a great duty, any protest against them a great sin? We had thought the Bible the great charter of civil and religious liberty; the ground, indeed, of social order, but the ground also of reform, if need be of revolution, too; the supreme vindication of the equal worth and equal rights of all. Is it, then, the stronghold of a priestly or any other caste? Are only Aaron and his family holy? not "all the congregation," not "every one of them"? Have certain individuals and classes a traditionary and exclusive right to the regal, the prophetic, the sacrificial offices of humanity? We have heard of fortune's favorites; are we to learn that God has favorites too? Or, if this conclusion seems to us scarcely more satisfactory than the other, have we no resource but to refuse to choose, and relapse again into the vague uneasiness of indecision?

We are reduced to no such necessity. We may put both these alternatives aside as no proper alternatives for us, for the moral which they go upon is a false moral, not the true moral of the story. The bigot and the radical have alike misread this narrative, and have missed alike the real meaning of it. Their common premise being false, their respective conclusions, therefore, are equally inconclusive. It is assumed by both that the moral is the sacredness of exclusive rights and privileges; on the contrary, the real moral is the sacredness of definite trusts and responsibilities. The issue is not an issue between privileged and unprivileged men, between the rights of one class and the opposing claims of another. The judgment involved is not a determination of essential differences between man and man, or the validity of their respective pretensions. The decision does not decide whether all the congregation are or are not holy; whether in this respect, or in any other, men are or are not equal. True, Korah, Dathan, and Abiram raised this very question of equality. They sought to make the issue one of right and privilege, but unwittingly they came upon a far deeper issue than that; for the real question was not whether this man is or is not holier than others, whether Aaron has or has not a superior right to the priesthood, but *to whom has this trust been committed? on whom has this responsibility been laid?* They are confronted with duties and obligations when they had been thinking only of dignities and immunities. To make the purpose of this narrative, therefore, the vindication of special prerogatives, is to misread and miss the great principle of which it is indeed a most tragic assertion. That principle is the inviolable character of a trust, the sacredness of a responsibility; a principle which may involve, nay, does involve, in some secondary sense, the question of rights, but from which the question of rights as rights is necessarily excluded.

This distinction in the moral between privileges and trusts, between rights and responsibilities, may seem, at first, a mere verbal distinction. It may even appear, perhaps, an unworthy attempt to evade a difficulty, instead of furnishing any genuine solution of it. But we need not be told that any such attempt would be as vain as it would be dishonest. Evasions are always futile; the spectres they seem to lay are sure to return again to plague us. And as for verbal distinctions, we may remember that distinctions apparently verbal sometimes hold worldwide differences. The greatest conflict in relation to the person of Christ which the Church has ever known, was made to turn upon the seemingly verbal distinction between the "homoousios" and the "homoiousios"—of the "same substance," and of "like substance,"—words differing only in a single letter, indistinguishable almost in sound, and yet the issue led away on one side into Arianism, Socinianism, and, in later days, into mere humanitarianism and utter unbelief; and on the other led up to the great verities which constitute the catholic faith. Scarcely less vital is the distinction we make whenever we conceive of any office, place, rank, position, as a privilege or as a trust, as a right or as a responsibility. The vindication of privileges is in itself a gage of battle, for it involves self-assertion on the one hand, dissent and jealousy on the other. Any adequate recognition of trust, on the contrary, implies that humble sense of obligation which gives no offence and takes none. Whenever the Aarons and their families are chiefly concerned in vindicating their rights to the priesthood, we may be sure those rights will be questioned and opposed, often justly questioned and justly opposed; but when, in a meeker spirit, they are content simply to acknowledge the *responsibilities* into which, in the providence of God, they have come, then they stand upon a ground which has no proper place for self-assertion, and any intrusion of jealousy there is sin.

Now, in the Bible, all offices, whether civil or ecclesiastical, are viewed as trusts, as responsibilities. That is the primary conception. The idea of privileges, of prerogatives, does not appear at all, or appears only as a subordinate and secondary consideration; something which may have a conventional, a relative, but not an absolute, propriety. Indeed, the only rights which the Bible knows are the rights which belong to man as man. Personality, for instance, is such a right—the right of every man to be considered a person and not a thing; and, accordingly, in Scripture, personality and its kindred rights find abundant assertion. But when we pass from what is common to men to the differences between them, we come not upon rights, but upon trusts, upon responsibilities. No man has a right to rule over his fellows; no man has a right to exercise the prophetic office of the teacher; no man has a right to sacrifice at God's altar. It is a right, moreover, which he cannot acquire, and which cannot be given him. For, strictly speaking, the word "right" is inapplicable as applied to these things. They are not, and cannot be, any man's possession. Nay, the very acquisitions of his own hand are not his property, but his stewardship. The distinctions which men covet most, when seen truly, are seen to be distinctions not of privilege, but of obligation. From the very structure of society after the analogy of the body, differences of office and station must and will exist. The respective trusts and responsibilities which grow out of them are necessarily exclusive, but they have their purpose, and consequently their justification, not in the exaltation of an individual or of a class, but in the well-being of all. The very idea, therefore, of a trust, the very conception of a responsibility, precludes all self-assertion. Humility is the condition of its bestowal and continuance. It has its ground in the Master's law: "He that will be great among you, let him be your servant." For, the moment the idea of privilege intrudes into the trust, the trust is on the wane; when once the claim of right has succeeded to the sense of responsibility, the responsibility itself has passed away.

We have an illustration of this, on a grand and tragic scale, in the whole course of Hebrew history itself. They were a consecrated family, a royal nation, "a peculiar people," chosen and set apart—but chosen and set apart for what? To receive privileges, to enjoy immunities, to exercise prerogatives, to be, in short, in the invidious sense of the expression, a kind of spiritual aristocracy on the earth? They came in time to think so, but then the final catastrophe was near. In the earlier and the better days, their calling was recognized as a trust, a responsibility—something which was to make them a blessing to others. While that conviction lived in them, how noble and fruitful was their history! And that it might live in them, how often were they reminded that they were nothing in themselves; that Jacob was "a worm," and Israel "a bondman in the land of Egypt"! To keep them humble, how often were they bidden to "look to the rock whence they were hewn, and to the hole of the pit whence they were digged"! But at last the proud boast came, prouder than any other, for no pride of place or lineage ever reached up so high as theirs: "We be Abraham's children." They took their stand upon their ancestral dignity, upon their exclusive rights and privileges, and then was fulfilled the word of Hosea: "God shall cast them away, and make them wanderers among the nations."

And what was true of the people as a people, was true also of the respective orders within it. For when an order lost its sense of responsibility, when it asserted claims and prerogatives instead, then the order degenerated into a caste; and when it became a caste, its use was gone, its mission ended. How fair and stately was the ideal of the Hebrew king, how exalted his regal seat, how awful the majesty of the Lord's anointed! Yet when royalty had failed of its kingly trust, it became at last a childish royalty, none of "its seed sitting on the throne of David, or ruling any more in Judah." This earth has seen nothing so noble as the prophetic order, but when the prophets came to pride themselves upon their gifts, the divine voice within them died away, and there was "no open vision"—a silence and dimness of four hundred years, from Malachi to John the Baptist. And as for this Aaronic priesthood, with its splendid lineage, its long ancestral line, that too passed away when in its arrogance and self-assertion, the very idea of a priest, as of one "who is himself also compassed with infirmity," had been forgotten. What a reversal of the mere surface meaning of this story! What a lesson may we not read in the fact that despite the vindication of that priesthood's sacred, exclusive trust, despite this memorial of broad plates set up to perpetuate that judgment forever, "strangers" now, "not of the seed of Aaron," come before the Lord to offer incense at His altar!

Are we not justified, then, in the position that only trusts, only responsibilities, are sacred? that what we call rights, privileges, prerogatives, instead of being sacred in themselves, detract from the integrity of the trust, from the sanctity of the responsibility, just so far as they intrude into it? God will vindicate His own distinctions, but He will not vindicate ours. Korah rebelled, not against exclusive privileges, as he thought, but against the divine call, and the inviolable commissions involved in it. For in those days the priesthood was not a caste, but an order, filled with that sense of obligation wherein its life consisted. Aaron and his family were inspired by the spirit of Moses, and the Scripture tells us that the man Moses was "very meek." So far was he from being the ambitious aspirant for honors, one who would have made himself a prince over them, as Dathan and Abiram charged, that he shrank at first with an almost abject humility from the place and work to which he was called, so that the anger of the Lord was kindled against him. Afterward, in the wilderness, again and again his spirit well-nigh fails under the weight of his obligations. "Wherefore," he complains unto his God, "have I not found favor in thy sight, that thou layest the burden of all this people upon me? Have I conceived all this people? have I begotten them, that thou shouldest say unto me, Carry them in thy bosom, as a nursing father beareth the sucking child?" "If thou deal thus with me, kill me, I pray thee, out of hand," "and let me not see my wretchedness." The complaint may not have been altogether noble, but it bears witness, in the heart of Moses, to that awful, overpowering sense of obligation and responsibility, which, in every age and in every land, has forced at times some such cry from every true leader and ruler of his people. And it was against this trust, maintained in the spirit of a trust, that the standard of revolt was raised. God punished that revolt fearfully, dreadfully, as He has always punished it, and as most assuredly He always will.

For the Scripture itself gives us the "conclusion of the whole matter" when it defines the sin of these rebels as a sin "against their own souls." The more you look into that sin, the deeper and the darker does it become. For who was Korah? A Levite, himself a member of the consecrated tribe. Who were Dathan and Abiram, and all their company? Princes of the assembly, famous in the congregation, men of renown. They themselves had been called to fill high place and station. That fact itself, interpreted in the light of their revolt, is proof that they had failed to realize their own trusts, failed to appreciate their own responsibilities, and thereby came, as was natural enough, to intrude upon trusts and responsibilities which were not theirs. The sin of omission ends in the sin of commission. Before that rebellion was possible, these nobles of Israel must have come to consider all offices as dignities and privileges, to repudiate the very idea of obligation, to look upon all these things as prizes to be scrambled for and fought over. Nay, more than that, they prostituted a great truth to the service of their mean ambition. They seduced the people with the watchword of equality. They led them to mis-read the purpose and the meaning of their consecration. For though "all the congregation were holy, every one of them," yet the trust of ruler or priest had not been committed to all, nor was it upon every one that the responsibility was laid. The equality which knows no subordination would have been anarchy then, as it is anarchy always. Nothing is so dangerous, so fatal, as truths which are misapplied. It was a question whether the nation itself should live or perish. Yet Korah dared to play the demagogue, the worst demagogue, namely, he who steps down from a high place, to incite the people, with a perverted truth, against others whose station is more exalted than his own. And still more than this, he made the issue on his right to sacrifice; that is, he sought in the sacrificial offering the occasion for the assertion of that self-seeking principle which is itself the denial and the repudiation of sacrifice.

This was blasphemy, this was a darkening of his inward light, this was a sin "against his own soul." Shall we wonder that it was so fearfully visited? Can we scarce believe that the divine judgment was really as dreadful as it is represented? Are there then no parallels to it both in and out of the sacred record? Wherever the sin of Korah and his company has reappeared, and it has reappeared in many ages and in many lands, has not this same decree of doom gone forth? There may have been no yawning pit, no consuming fire, but have not the moral earthquakes, the social convulsions, the long agony and sword and flame of war, been more dreadful and more ruthless still? All history has been lurid with these divine judgments; it may be lurid with them for ages yet to come, for the law is written, and you cannot reverse it: "Whosoever exalteth himself shall be abased, and he that humbleth himself shall be exalted."

XXII.

THE INDICTMENT OF JUDAH.

[KINGSBRIDGE, 1874.]

"For the vineyard of the Lord of hosts is the house of Israel, and the men of Judah his pleasant plant: and he looked for judgment, but behold oppression; for righteousness, but behold a cry."—ISA. v. 7.

IN the reading of the Scripture no one can have failed to notice the oft-recurring expression of "the Day of the Lord." We meet with it again and again in the prophetic writings of the Old Testament, and it passes into familiar usage in the Epistles of the New. In this latter reference the expression is commonly associated in the popular mind with the second advent, or coming, of Christ. That is the first and principal expectation which the phrase awakens. Our thought goes on to the great Judgment Day, to the reappearance of the Son of Man, in majesty and glory, to the assembled nations of the earth, all gathered at His feet. This is what we commonly understand by "the Day of the Lord;" these are the grand and solemn scenes which are most generally associated with it. But while this expectation is a just and true one, while this interpretation of the expression is the only one that comes up to its entire and ultimate meaning, we must, nevertheless, remember that the phrase is often used in Scripture with a secondary, and what may seem to us an inferior, significance. Any crisis in national or individual experience, any signal visitation of sin, any marked and extraordinary deliverance, is spoken of as a "day of the Lord." God is conceived of as being specially present, immanent, and operative in all such instances. The devout and inspired minds of those holy men of old, "who spake as they were moved by the Holy Ghost," dwelt less upon the natural than upon the supernatural character of the more prominent events in human history. Such crises seemed to them the occasions of the divine revelation—the times and the ways in which God came out, as it were, from the invisible seclusion of His heavens, and made Himself seen and felt and manifest in the affairs of men. Thus our Lord Himself spoke of the fall of Jerusalem, of the overthrow of the Jewish nationality and polity, as a "day of the Lord," as a "coming of the Son of Man." "This generation," He says, "shall not pass away till all" (that is, the predicted destruction) "be fulfilled." And in similar manner the prophets always represent any signal instance of judgment or deliverance in the history of their people as a "day of the Lord." As we read their writings we are impressed by the recurring frequency of the phrase, and by the power and depth of the conviction which it expresses. In their thought every great event took on a most grand and solemn significance. It was a meeting point between God and man. It was a disclosure of the eternal will that shapes and controls all the seeming vicissitudes of fortune. It was a manifestation to human eyes of the unseen power that lies back of all the physical and moral forces of the world. It was a voice speaking from the skies, a face looking down between the parted clouds, an arm stretched forth from out the darkness. It was a "day of the Lord," a day of Revelation, a day in which the supreme and divine Ruler of men made Himself known to their hearts in deliverance or in judgment.

Now it is of just such a "day of the Lord" that we have read this morning in the prophecy of Isaiah. The Book opens with a vision of mingled judgment and deliverance. The time had come, or was coming soon, when God in some signal way should make Himself manifest to His people; when He should punish and save; when men, amid their changing hopes and fears, should be brought back again to the earlier faith of their fathers, and forced once more to believe in and acknowledge the God who judgeth the earth. The age was a sadly degenerate one. Judah had never, perhaps, been more powerful and prosperous, but the true glory of the nation was passing away. The simplicity of early manners, the purity of the primitive faith, the strong fellow-feeling of the tribal times, the respect for morals, the love of truth and righteousness, the reverential consciousness of God—all these were gone or going: and there had come, instead, universal greed and luxury and corruption; a practical disbelief in God, a virtual repudiation of morals, a wide and ever-widening gulf between the self-indulgence of wealth and the sullen discontent of poverty. It seems strange that so many hundreds of years before the final overthrow of the Jewish commonwealth the nation should have presented all these signs of impending dissolution. Yet, as far back as the time of Isaiah, it seemed to him like a man whose " whole head was sick, and his whole heart faint." " From the sole of the foot to the crown of the head," he says, "there is no soundness in it." Such a condition, he knew, however deceitful in outward appearing, was, and could be, only indicative of disaster. There was, there must be, some sure retributive justice to wait upon it. God would not suffer things to go on in this way forever. He felt that a crisis had come, that a "day of the Lord" was nigh at hand; a day in which "the loftiness of man should be bowed down, and the haughtiness of men laid low, and the Lord alone exalted." The future opens in all its dread significance before him. In prophetic vision he sees the avenging nations coming from afar, the uplifted ensigns, the swiftly marching ranks, the bent bows, the sharp arrows, the whirling wheels of the Assyrian conqueror. He sees the " darkness and sorrow " of his own dear land, and the " light darkened in the heavens thereof." This is his " day of the Lord," and it was his sad and solemn mission to speak to deafened ears and hardened hearts of the woe and terror of it.

But why dwell upon this Hebraistic mode of thought and speech? Why linger over this well-nigh forgotten page in a petty nation's history? Why, in these modern days, should we concern ourselves with the prophet or his mission? There is a reason why.

"Whatsoever things were written aforetime," St. Paul says, "were written for our learning." These records that have come down to us are no idle, unmeaning tales. Their interest has not passed away with that earlier world which gave them birth. They are a possession forever, the inheritance of all time. They must have, for each succeeding generation, the very deepest significance as long as the eternal laws which control the conduct of human life shall have any value in the eyes of men. For these Hebrew records are an illustration of universal principles. They set forth and exemplify the conditions of a people's well-being and the causes of their fall. The history of Israel is no isolated or exceptional history. On the contrary, it is the type of all history, the pattern after which it is fashioned, the mould in which it always runs. The story of the world is told over by anticipation in those antique pages. We may vary the names and the localities, we may clothe the principles in philosophic guise, we may put the facts in modern phraseology, but the essential substance of the narrative is invariably the same. Whatever age or country or society we select as our example, we shall find the same law of righteousness controlling its well-being, and the same retributive justice bringing on a decline and fall. And therefore it is that the prophetical writings which deal so largely with the causes of public weal and woe have been so fruitful in instruction to every earnest student of history. Publicists and philosophers and statesmen may sit at the feet of these Hebrew prophets and learn of them lessons which none others can so well teach them. For the prophets were the religious publicists, the religious philosophers, the religious statesmen of their own age. They read the end of things in the character of their beginnings, and poor, indeed, was the vaunted wisdom of the academy and the grove when measured against their moral and spiritual insight. They were, as the wise and scholarly Milton says of them:

> "Men divinely taught, and better teaching
> The solid rules of civil government
> In their majestic, unaffected style,
> Than all the oratory of Greece and Rome."

They have been fitly described as standing on their lofty towers of divine speculation, while ever and anon the question, "Watchman, what of the night? watchman, what of the night?" is asked of them by an anxious world below. For to the simplest, humblest man in every community, no less than to those who may be entrusted with official responsibility and station, is the school of the prophets the school of a world-wide political wisdom. It is a book which even the wayfaring man may read. In its solemn, pictured page we may all discern some prophetic likeness of our own time, and according to its good or ill report we may know whether it is weal or woe, blessing or judgment, which our "day of the Lord," when it comes, shall bring upon us.

Isaiah, in the passage which we are now considering, takes up his prophecy under the form of a parable. He sings, as he says, "A song of his well-beloved, touching his vineyard," and a sad and woful song it is. He tells the story of this vineyard—how it was "fenced," and the stones thereof "gathered out;" how it was planted "with the choicest vine," a tower built "in the midst of it," and "a winepress therein." He recounts in a figure all the various blessings of Judah, all the means and appliances which had been given the people to be a righteous people, and to do a righteous work. He recalls to their remembrance, by a suggestive term of the expression, all the wonderful providences of their eventful history. He asks in the name of their Jehovah: "What more could have been done to my vineyard, that I have not done in it?" Yet this vineyard, whose Lord required that it should "bring forth grapes," had brought forth only "wild grapes." He "looked for judgment, but behold oppression; for righteousness, but behold a cry." And so the prophet, in the same dread Name, takes up the burden of his prophecy: "I will tell you what I will do to my vineyard: I will take away the hedge thereof, and it shall be eaten up; I will break down the wall thereof, and it shall be trodden down: and I will lay it waste: it shall not be pruned, nor digged; but there shall come up briers and thorns: I will also command the clouds that they rain no rain upon it." The desolation of Judah—this was the prophecy which henceforth was to have a growing and ever growing fulfilment—a prophecy finally completed at the Advent in the overthrow and dispersion of the ancient commonwealth of Israel.

And from this parable we may learn two very important lessons. It appears to be grounded upon two broad and comprehensive principles, whose application is not a local but a universal one. And the first of these is this: Every tribe and nation and people and tongue is commissioned with some divine work, and is divinely endowed to do that work. Every community, every society, is in a figure a garden of the Lord; it is, like "the House of Israel," His "vineyard," and, like "the men of Judah," His "pleasant plant." God has called it into being to be a minister and servitor of His will. That is the aim and end for which it exists. That is why there has been given to it an historic life, why its integrity has been fenced in by rights which are inalienable, why the obstacles that might hinder its free and true development are gathered by some mysterious providence out of its way. All these different families of man have one self-same purpose, and, strictly speaking, they have only one, namely, to "bring forth," each "after its kind," that "fruit" of righteousness "whose seed is in itself;" to do the work specially appointed it; to be a witness to the truths so sacredly committed to its care. That is the first lesson of the parable, and the second naturally grows out of the first. For it is a divine decree that when any instrumentality of Providence wholly fails of its purpose, it shall be cast aside as unfit for further use. Against that community which will not be what it was intended to be, which will not do what it was intended to do, the sentence of doom goes forth. The "barren vineyard" sooner or later is "laid waste," its "hedge" is "taken away," its "walls are trodden down." A degenerate and unprofitable people pass eventually from the stage of history. That is the Biblical philosophy of history, and it is verified in the large experience of the world. The prophet, when he predicted the desolation of Judah, only predicted a special instance in the fulfilment of a universal law. He knew that Israel was dead or dying, that it was fast filling up the measure of its iniquity, that the day of recompense was close and ever closer at hand, and he mourned in advance over that retributive judgment which he foresaw to be inevitable.

Isaiah, however, does not confine his denunciation of Israel's degeneracy to the general terms of the parable. He drops the parable as the prophecy proceeds, and pours forth his invective in plain and awful prose. His charges become direct, definite, and specific. His woes follow one upon the other in orderly and logical sequence. He draws up an indictment more awful than anything in Scripture, with the exception of the awful indictment of the Pharisees by Christ. He arraigns the nation before the bar of Heaven, and puts a terrible emphasis upon each successive specification. "Woe unto them that join house to house, that lay field to field, till there be no place, that they may be alone in the midst of the earth!"

This is the first count in the indictment. It is a charge of covetousness, of atheistic mammon-worship. Nothing could be more hateful in the eyes of the prophet than the enormous accumulation of landed property by the nobles, in opposition to the whole spirit of the Jewish commonwealth, which had in view the good of all, rather than the exaltation of any. That condition of things in which wealth is valued for its own sake, in which it is perverted from a means of usefulness into an instrument of self-indulgence or oppression, is a condition of unmitigated evil. And it is always thus perverted whenever it is held in a spirit of covetousness; whenever a man's main purpose is not to use it well, but to increase it more. This charge comes first in the prophet's arraignment, because it lies at the root of all the others. It did so then, it does so now. That society in which the accumulation of wealth has become the absorbing aim and motive is doomed. Political economy may say no; it may prate about stimulated energies and increased development, but none the less that society is doomed. Many a nation's decline has begun just here. For the millionnaire spirit, in whatever form it comes, is a spirit of evil. Great wealth, it is true, in the hands of one or a few, may promote, for a time at least, the well-being of all; but that is due simply to the unity and consequent superior efficiency in its administration. And none the less in the long run, if it be not held, as it were, in trust; if it be not dignified with a noble purpose; if it be not wisely and liberally administered, will it become tyrannical and oppressive. It will make its possessors, consciously or unconsciously, in the strong language of the Scripture, "skin the poor to the quick, pick their bones, and grind them to powder." The spirit of covetousness, of accumulation, in and by itself, is evil, and only evil. No permanent good can come out of it. It may give us millionnaires, but it will not be the millionnaire of just and faithful stewardship, the friend of labor, the benefactor of his kind. It will be, instead, the millionnaire whose fitting type is in the cormorant, ever feeding, and yet never satisfied, adding house to house and field to field, till there be no place left. And then we shall have men of wealth without the duties, without the obligations, without the responsibilities of wealth; men foremost in position and hindmost in good works; men who count a man less precious than the "gold of Ophir;" men who sacrifice, who betray any cause, rather than not accumulate; men who become, and must become, a simple curse to the community in which they live. And when it comes to that, when their numbers grow, when their ranks enlarge and widen, when the rich are richer and the poor poorer, always when the condition of things becomes monstrous and oppressive, then society has only two alternatives—in the history of the world it has never had but two—either to sink into hopeless bondage or to purify itself "so as by fire." Whenever wealth, as a general thing, repudiates its responsibilities; whenever it is given over to and besotted by the greed of gain, you may discern in the horizon, —though the cloud be no bigger than a man's hand —you may discern in the horizon the spectres of anarchy, communism, revolution; and you may be sure the day of reckoning, though delayed, will not always be far off. God's judgments sometimes, nay, often, come in these awful human forms.

The second count in the indictment may seem to be the very antithesis of the first, yet the two always go hand in hand together. For in every community in which the god mammon is set up, there will be not only a covetous class, but also a spendthrift class— an idle, luxurious, self-indulgent aristocracy. There will be the greed of gain on the one hand, and fashionable levity and dissipation on the other. The reverse side of the man of avarice is the man of pleasure. He whose life consists in the abundance of the things which he possesses will have his counterpart in the epicurean liver. And it was a frivolous, dissipated, epicurean life, it seems, that the nobles of Judah were now living. The prophet accordingly proceeds to turn his invective against them : " Woe unto them that rise up early in the morning, that they may follow strong drink; that continue until night, till wine inflame them! and the harp and the viol, the tabret and pipe, and wine, are in their feasts : but they regard not the work of the Lord, neither consider the operation of His hands." The great ladies, too, it seems, were as bad as, if not worse than, the courtiers. "The daughters of Zion," he says, "are haughty, and walk with stretched forth necks and wanton eyes, walking and mincing as they go, and making a tinkling with their feet." He draws the picture of a vain, ostentatious, selfish, immoral aristocracy—an aristocracy for which, in his prophetic vision, " hell had enlarged herself that their glory and their multitude and their pomp might descend into it "—an aristocracy whose doom should be upon lords and ladies both ; humbling " the mighty men," and giving the proud women "sackcloth instead of girdles, and burning instead of beauty."

A fashionable, frivolous, luxurious, spendthrift class! This, then, is another condition of social degeneracy. It is a fatal condition—fatal alike to those who have part in it, and to the general community in which it exists. For there is no greater error than to suppose that the selfish extravagance of one class can be of permanent benefit to any other. Human society is a living body, an organic whole. "If one member suffer," or fail of its true use, "all the other members suffer with it." The wasteful expenditure of the rich never does, never did, never will, in any real sense, help the poor. To think so, to try to find some sort of justification for it in that, is a snare and a delusion. It puts into the production of superfluities time and energy and money which should go, and which otherwise would go, into more natural and necessary industries. All that idle, luxurious self-indulgence can do for the poor is to excite their envy, to deepen their discontent, to make them question why one man should waste in frivolous or wanton dissipation what another man needs for daily bread. And to spendthrifts themselves, whether men or women, the habit of their life is fatal in every way. However refined may be their mind and manners, it degrades them to a mere animal sensualism. Disguise it as they may, they have no nobler creed than to "eat, drink, and be merry." They are "of the earth, earthy;" they "regard not the work of the Lord, neither consider the operation of His hands."

For the prophet goes on to make another charge, which comes naturally enough on the steps of the two that have preceded it. When a people are given over to money getting and money spending, atheism will soon follow. It did follow in Isaiah's time. A scornful, scoffing, mocking infidelity was rampant in the land. "Woe unto them," he says, "that say, Let Him make speed and hasten His work, that we may see it; and let the counsel of the Holy One of Israel draw nigh and come, that we may know it." We have presented here in a single stroke, as it were, the characteristic likeness of that self-sufficient scepticism which comes not from speculative doubt, but from immoral life. These covetous and luxurious men of Judah had not given up their faith in the Holy One of Israel because there were insuperable intellectual difficulties to the further continuance of it, but because the life they led did not want any God, had no place for any, and would not acknowledge any. Wholly given over to a reprobate mind, concerned only with the visible and the temporal, they were disposed to laugh the ancient creed to scorn. "Their eyes were heavy, and their ears deaf," and their hearts "slow of understanding." Their greed and their self-indulgence had made divine Providence nothing more to them than an old myth. And this is the kind of unbelief which is the besetting snare of our modern civilization. The sheer, downright materialism of the world is the cause of nine-tenths of our wide-spread infidelity. Not one man in a thousand ever thinks himself into scepticism. Occasionally, indeed, you may meet with a pure, honest, earnest thinker who is a conscientious unbeliever. But you will not meet with him often, and when you do, the influence will not be altogether evil. He may have, and often does have, a faith which he knows not. But the mass of unbelievers do not believe in God simply because they do not want Him; because this world, and the things of this world, are sufficient for them; because they are determined not to look beyond it; because it would interfere sadly with their gain or their pleasure to acknowledge a Supreme Being and conform their lives to His law. And this is the kind of unbelief which, the Scripture says, "shall be damned." This is the kind of unbelief for which there is only one cure. It is idle to reason, or argue, or persuade. Vain alike will be Moses and the prophets and the Resurrection. The cure must come, and can only come, in a retributive judgment, in a "day of the Lord," which shall strip off from men the things wherein they trusted, and teach them that "man doth not live by bread only," by the work and the might of his own hand, "but by every word that proceedeth out of the mouth of the Lord doth man live."

The final charge with which the prophet brings his arraignment to a close is a befitting conclusion of the whole matter. When the leadership of society is in the hands of millionnaires who are concerned only in adding stock to stock, and house to house, and field to field; when an aristocracy of birth and manners cares only for fashionable, sensational, and wasteful living; when the educated class, the "men wise in their own conceits," can find in the faith of their fathers only an occasion for witticism, jibe, and jest; then there remains only one other condition of degeneracy, namely, that moral distinctions themselves should disappear and pass away. And that condition comes. The perverted heart will not only do evil; it will try to justify the evil. It will convince itself that the immutable distinctions between right and wrong are only illusive, artificial distinctions; that the question of good and evil resolves itself at last into a mere question of expediency. When the life has gone astray, the mind will not be long in proving "the worse to be the better reason." It will juggle with itself, and tamper with its innate convictions. The simplest duties, obligations, moralities, will be all philosophized away. Men will change the name, and fancy that they have got rid of the reality. They will do as it seems they did in the time of Isaiah. They will "call evil good, and good evil; put darkness for light, and light for darkness; bitter for sweet, and sweet for bitter." That is the last step in social degeneracy. When the power of moral discernment is lost, then all is lost. Then comes the era of bribery and corruption. Then "the wicked is justified for reward, and the righteousness of the righteous is taken from him." The society which has come to that is fit only for perdition. Of such a society the prophet said once, and of such a society he is always saying: "As the fire devoureth the stubble, and the flame consumeth the chaff, so their root shall be as rottenness, and their blossom shall go up as dust." For all this the anger of the Lord "is not turned away, but his hand is stretched out still."

We have been looking at a picture which is not a

pleasant picture to look upon. We have been reading a story which sounds like a very doleful tale. But perhaps this indictment of another people may not be without a meaning for us. Would it not be well for each and all to find it, to ponder it, and apply it in our thoughts? It is time misspent to look into the mirror of history, and then be like St. James' forgetful hearer, who, beholding himself " in a glass, straightway goeth his way, and forgetteth what manner of man he was." If " the things written aforetime were written for our learning," it is the part of wisdom to gather their lessons, and lay them to heart. And the one lesson which we should take away with us is this: Every generation, every community, every society, has its own "day of the Lord;" but it is for itself to determine what that day shall be, whether it shall be a day of judgment, or a day of salvation and praise.

XXIII.

THE MURDER OF JOHN THE BAPTIST.

[ALBANY, 1866.]

"And the king was exceeding sorry; yet for his oath's sake, and for their sakes which sat with him, he would not reject her."—ST. MARK vi. 26.

PERHAPS there is no darker chapter of history than that which tells of the murder of John the Baptist. The occasion, the cause, and the manner of that deed all conspire to place it among the very first in the dreary catalogue of crimes. The victim, too, was one of the noblest and loftiest characters of earth. When the executioner's axe fell, it terminated a life than which, in its work and purpose, there had been none worthier and grander since the world began. For it is the witness of One from whom there is no appeal that, "among them that are born of women there hath not arisen a greater than John the Baptist."

Yet this man, whose moral character towered so loftily above his fellows; who brought with him from his long seclusion in the wilderness that intense belief in the invisible which is always so rare and so wonderful a thing; before whose stern denunciations the hypocrisy and infidelity of his age were stricken dumb; whose words of impassioned warning held the multitudes from far and near breathless at his side; who seemed and was the herald, or forerunner, of a mighty revolution in human life and thought—this man with a divine work to do, and divinely endowed to do it, fell a victim to what? Not to the blind fury of the populace; not to the pitiless resentment of the priesthood; not to the inexorable policy of an hierarchy: to neither and none of these, but to a proud, wicked, vindictive woman's hate. One cannot read the brief but graphic narrative of the Evangelist without feeling that there is something strangely sad in the manner and circumstances of his death. It almost seems at first as if his were not only an untimely end, but an unfitting one; as if the bitterness of the abrupt termination of his great career must have been rendered bitter indeed in the consideration of the unworthy and merely individual foe before whom he fell.

We have a certain vague feeling that a great man should have a great death; that if he is to be a victim at all, it should be a power commensurate with his own that deals the blow. It is a kind of shock, a disappointment, when the hero-general of a score of battle-fields dies, not at the head of his troops, amid the thunder of the guns and the shouts of victory, but on the march, or in his tent, by some sharpshooter's bullet. It appears as if there were a lack of dramatic fitness in such an inglorious conclusion. Had the Baptist fallen before the fanaticism of the people, or had his life been the sacrifice demanded by the imperious hierarchy of Judæa as the price of its own stability, then his fate would have been only that which might have been predicted from the first. We see now, as we look back, that his work as the forerunner of the Christ was radical in the extreme; that it was essentially destructive of the existing order of things; that it struck at the very heart of the social and religious falsehoods of the day; that, in his own expression of it, the axe was "laid at the *root* of the trees." Now the reformer, the man who aspires to tear down and to build up, must be prepared, sooner or later, to pay the penalty of his boldness. John inaugurated his work with the most sweeping and unsparing invective. He unveiled and exposed the moral and religious hypocrisy of his age. Against the acknowledged sinner and the reputed saint he proclaimed a wrathful judgment. He denounced Pharisee and Sadducee, the most honored and respected men of the community, as a generation of vipers. It was scarcely to be expected that this should be permitted long. Yet we hear of no efforts made to silence the stern preacher of repentance, no mutterings in the street, no whispers in the council. The men whom he so unsparingly denounced seem to have shown a strange forbearance. We read of no plottings of Pharisee or priest against him; no apprehension, no trial, no judgment. It was another and apparently less fitting and more ignominious fate which was reserved for him. He had incidentally incurred the enmity of a bad, ambitious woman, and *that* brought him to his doom. His death had not even the poor dignity of a judicial murder. He did not fall a victim, like Stephen, to the stately but corrupt and intolerate Judaism which he had assailed. *His* fate was a woman's revenge. It was a capricious tyrant's whim. It was an after-dinner caprice. It was the guerdon of a girl. "The head of John the Baptist in a charger" was the meed, the reward, claimed and given for the light tripping of a dancer's feet.

Is it not pitiable to think of a great man's life bartered away like that? This prophet of the wilderness, in the moral sublimity of his nature, in his rare earnestness of character, in his vivid realization of eternal truth, in the power and influence it was in him to exert over the lives and thoughts of men, was worth more to his generation and to the world than all the scribes, rabbis, and rulers of his day; yet his head was struck off at the bidding of an abandoned woman; it was flung, like a gew-gaw, to a girl after a successful dance. The prophet surely had never contemplated such a fate. Alone in the desert, before he entered upon his work, doubtless he had often thought of the perils which should environ him, of the fierce hostility he should meet with. Most probably he had, as such natures often have, the premonition of an early and violent death. But he could scarcely have predicted a death so sudden and ignominious as this—in a few moments his lifework broken and cut short by an artful blandishment, his death-warrant given amid the jest and revelry of a banquet hall.

And thus it has often been: what is noblest and best sacrificed, not to policy or necessity, or in the hot, fierce conflict of opposing issues, but in a mood of dalliance, and in compliance with what appeals to the baser part of our nature. There is cruelty in the brutal fury of a mob; there is cruelty in the vindictive apprehension of an imperilled order; but there is no cruelty equal to the cruelty of thorough worldliness—the light, careless gayety which sends a prophet to the block because the wine flows, and the jest goes round, and the thrilling mazes of a voluptuous dance have fired the heart of King Herod.

Yet, after all, perhaps there was more of poetic justice, more of dramatic fitness in John's fate, than at first might seem. However he might denounce Phariseeism and the established order of things, it was scarcely apparent to the Judaism of his day how radical his work really was. He had not come into open collision with it yet. The hierarchy was not slow to strike when it recognized an avowed antagonist in Jesus. But as for John, it let him pass unmolested. The world, however, soon found out who and what he was; it found him a stern moralist, an uncompromising rebuker of sin. He struck the world and its worldliness no uncertain blow, and the world, in the person of Herodias, struck back. It found its fitting representative in her. When the prophet fell before the evil hate of that guilty woman, he fell not before that alone, but before the concentrated hate of a world which has no tolerance for a man who dares to put his finger upon her sores, and call her crimes by their right names.

The guilt of the prophet's murder was shared in different degrees by three different persons. When the axe fell, three names were registered in the judgment book to answer for that foul deed.

1. The first of these, and in one sense the most guilty of the three, was Herodias. The crime originated with her. She planned it, and brought it to its pitiless conclusion. It was the revenge of an adulteress. John's rebuke had rankled in her heart. It had not led her to repentance, and had therefore led, as disregarded rebuke always leads, from sin to sin. She was the wife of Herod's brother Philip, who, under the will of his father, had been disinherited, and was consequently only a private individual. But she had left her husband to marry Herod and share his principality. When, therefore, the prophet said to the king in his stern, uncompromising way: "It is not lawful for thee to have thy brother's wife," he not only reproved Herodias for her sin, but he endangered her newly acquired honors. She had no forgiveness for this. She had "a quarrel" against John, and "sought to kill him."

It is very shocking, but is there nothing in our own hearts that can interpret to us this woman's hate? Are we so mild and tractable under rebuke? Has the reproof of some cherished sin never stirred within us a feeling of bitter enmity towards the reprover? Do those words, "It is not lawful," never call out from us a burst of vindictive anger? Doubtless we should shrink back in horror from the mere thought of murder; but, remember, the spirit of hatred, of revenge, whether it lead to murder, or stop short at some lesser vengeance, is essentially the same. "It hath been said, Thou shalt not kill; and whosoever shall kill shall be in danger of the judgment: but I say unto you, That whosoever is angry with his brother without a cause shall be in danger of the judgment."

And look now to what hatred, cherished and brooded over, leads. At first Herodias simply sought to kill John. Probably his death would have satisfied her then. But her evil purpose grew as she brooded on it until at last it became something inhuman and devilish. She not only longed for his death, but she longed to *gloat* upon his death. Her demand now is for the Baptist's head. The executioner brings it to the damsel, and the damsel gives it to her mother. What a sickening picture is this—the revengeful queen feasting her greedy eyes upon the gory head of the prophet! Is not that ghastly spectacle the witness that a cherished hate can obliterate at last everything that is divine in human nature, and transform even a woman into a fiend?

2. The second name in this dark tragedy is Salome. She was the daughter of Herodias and her lawful husband Philip. The very fact of her parentage, one would have thought, would have precluded her from any participation in this crime; but she seems to have been the ready accomplice of her mother. She prostituted her youth and grace and beauty to work out that foul and treacherous deed. It is a picture of human sin more loathsome, as it seems to me, than the other. For this damsel could have had no revengeful hate, no vindictive passion, rankling in her heart. The prophet had not rebuked her. Hers was a cool, deliberate, passionless cruelty

—cruelty at which one shudders when associated with her age and sex; for if not with youth and girlhood, where should pity and compassion dwell? Doubtless Salome had a motive. Perhaps she feared the loss of her position and her pleasures, and fear can be quite as powerful an incentive to crime as revenge or hate. If Herod should at last listen to the remonstrance of John and put away her mother, then she would lose all the fascinations of a court, all the pomp and pride and circumstance which belonged to the adopted daughter of a king. The prophet had unwittingly laid his hand upon this young thing's world, and she turned again and stung him. Ah! believe me; youth, apparently so bright and fresh and winning, if you venture to touch its pleasures, can show a callousness, a steely hardness of the heart, which you would have deemed incredible. It can be as cruel, as pitiless, as unrelenting, in sweeping an obstacle from the path of its enjoyment, as ever manhood in its ambition, or womanhood in its hate. It can disguise, too, as these seldom can. Salome could go into that banquet hall with murder in her heart, and yet wreathe her lips into a smile, and twine her form in all the graceful mazes of the dance. Who, to look upon that panting, flushing, joyous thing, could have suspected the hideous purpose that was lurking there? "I will that thou give me by and by in a charger the head of John the Baptist." What a demand was that to issue from a young girl's lips! Must it not have stricken the spectators dumb? Can you not believe that when youth importunes, though the face be fair and the voice exceeding sweet, sometimes, sometimes it may indeed be Satan himself that stands at thy right hand? And when the damsel's demand was granted, how did she receive her guerdon? When her dainty fingers closed upon that charger on which the noblest head of his generation lay, did she smile her thanks, I wonder, and bow, as dancers do when they accept applause or flowers or jewels? Or did remorse strike her, and a horror of darkness fall upon her there and then? Of her after history we have no certain knowledge. But what a recollection was hers through life—that banquet hall, the prophet's gory head, and her own dance of death!

3. The third murderer was Herod, in one sense the least guilty of the three, for he was *betrayed* into the commission of that crime; and yet in another sense the most guilty of all, for he realized more than the others the enormity of what he was about to do. The king seems not to have been insensible to the influence of the Baptist's character. We read that he "feared John," that is, stood in awe of him, "knowing him to be a just man, and an holy;" that he "observed him," that is, paid him attention; that he did "many things" at his bidding; that he heard him, and "heard him gladly."

We stop a moment here to notice a fact very true to human nature—a fact which has had its repetition many times since the days of Herod. It would seem that this profligate could in a measure understand, appreciate, and admire such a character as John's. There was even a certain fascination for him in the lofty purity, severe simplicity, and stern integrity of the prophet. He appears to have seen and heard him often. It is easy to conjecture what the theme of these discoursings would be; how indignantly John would denounce the shallow unbelief and the religious formalism of the time; how vividly he would paint the terrors of "the wrath to come;" how eloquently he would open up the vision of that "kingdom of God" which was to be. And the king would listen half in incredulity, half in awe, yet always with pleasure. The high enthusiasm and deep earnestness of the speaker would have for this worldling the attraction of such novelty, freshness, and power, as he had never known. Yes, Herod "heard John," and "heard him gladly." As long as the discourse was general, or as long as the invective was launched against others, the king would stand by and cry: "Well done!" But when the prophet's eye pierced into the secrets of the king's own life, when he pointed his finger at the skeleton in *his* closet, and said, "It is not lawful for thee to have her," then "Herod was sore displeased. He laid hold on John, and bound him, and put him in prison." Can we not understand this inconsistency? Are we not willing, eager, glad to hear denunciations of sin as long as they do not touch that private, individual, personal sin which happens to be peculiarly our own? Can we not listen very complacently to the most scathing invective as long as it does not reach ourselves? There is a certain elevation in the enforcement of moral and religious principles, and we can endure it very well if only they be not given too pointed and pertinent an application. We are ready to give a fair field to preacher and moralist, provided they keep their remarks within proper bounds. The rebuke that we can apply to our neighbor we hear gladly, and even second the admonition; but if that rebuke be brought home, aye, unmistakably home, what then? Is it not well for preacher and moralist that every man has not a prison ready?

But although Herod had imprisoned John, it does not seem that he wished to kill him. He stopped short of murder. Herodias could not bring him to that by open means, and had recourse, therefore, to a stratagem. "When a convenient day was come, that Herod on his birthday made a supper to his lords, high captains, and chief estates of Galilee; and when the daughter of the said Herodias came in, and danced, and pleased Herod and them that sat with him, the king said unto the damsel, Ask of me whatsoever thou wilt, and I will give it thee. And he sware unto her, Whatsoever thou shalt ask of me, I will give it thee, unto the half of my kingdom. And she said, I will that thou give me by and by in a charger the head of John the Baptist. And the king was exceeding sorry."

Herod had been betrayed into a promise to do what he had determined not to do; what he knew it would be cruel and wrong to do. The better nature of the man recoiled from the crime. He would willingly have saved John. Perhaps his anger against the prophet had passed away; perhaps he remembered, now, only the rare earnestness, the pure simplicity of character which had so attracted him. At any rate, he shrank from the guilt of the Baptist's blood. But he had "promised," he had "sworn." Under these circumstances what was he to do? What did religion, morality, every consideration of truth and justice bid him do, but revoke his word, repudiate the obligation, and refuse to add sin to sin? But no; "the king was exceeding sorry; yet for his oath's sake and their sakes which sat with him, he would not reject her. And immediately the king sent an executioner and commanded his head to be brought: and he went and beheaded him in the prison, and brought his head in a charger and gave it to the damsel, and the damsel gave it to her mother."

The dilemma of Herod was the dilemma of a man whose conduct was governed not by the principles of an immutable morality, the eternal distinctions of right and wrong, but by a vague superstition and a miserable conventionalism. The petty rules and obligations which he recognized were below the requirements and emergencies of life, and therefore only served to betray him into sin. It is worth while observing the considerations which determined him. "His oath's sake!" Is it not strange to hear this man, face to face with crime, pleading the sanctity of an oath to justify his commission of it? What a moral bewilderment was that! Had Herod been a man of pure life and clear conscience, how long would such a monstrous sophism have entangled him? Is there any child here that does not see that a pledge, an oath, can never bind one to do wrong? If in some wild hour you have passed your word or sworn to do what the laws of God and man forbid, can there be a moment's doubt what you should do? It is only the man whose perceptions are clouded by sin that can hesitate. The guilt of such oaths consists in making and keeping them, not in breaking them. If they are registered at all, they are registered not in heaven but in hell.

And look, too, at this other, still more miserable, plea: "for their sakes which sat with him." Herod seems to have thought that to retract his plighted word, given in the presence of his guests, would have been a kind of slight or affront to them, and, therefore, felt himself constrained to murder John out of deference to the opinions of others, and as a matter of conventional politeness. It is startling to think of a man in view of such an issue speaking and reasoning thus. Yet in trifles we reason and act thus every day. How seldom do we do right because it is right, regardless of what men may say or think of it? Reference to the opinion of the world, and deference to the opinion of the world, and conference with it, and preference of it above all things, above every principle and rule and law, human or divine—is not this a tendency that grows upon us very, very fast? It may be only in trifles, but whenever we do wrong for the sake of others, for "their sakes who sit with us," remember we are acting upon the same principle on which Herod sent John the Baptist to the block.

Yet "the king was exceeding sorry." Is idle sorrow ever availing? It did not save John. Will it save Herod in that day when all shall give account for the deeds that they have done? Before that bar to which we all are going, I think the plea will scarcely be accepted that one was a reluctant accomplice in crime; that another, by the force of circumstances, was constrained to be dishonest; and a third, very much against his will, had yielded to the temptation of impurity. We are "exceeding sorry" to sin, yet we sin nevertheless. We had much rather not if it were only an even choice, if the path of truth, virtue, duty were only more easy and less rugged. But being what it is, we turn aside, as it were, under protest. Perhaps that protest may be the heaviest accusation recorded against us. For in Scripture the burden of woe is proclaimed against him who knew the good and did it not. And when these three guilty ones come to stand before the bar of heaven, which, think you, will be guiltiest in the sight of God: the passionate hate of the woman, the light cruelty of the girl, or the stifled conscience of the king?

XXIV.

THE JOY OF HEAVEN OVER EARTH'S REPENTANCE.

[ALBANY, 1865.]

"I say unto you, there is joy in the presence of the angels of God over one sinner that repenteth."—ST. LUKE xv. 10.

THERE is nothing more distinctively characteristic of Christianity than the value it has put upon human life. The religion whose reign on earth was inaugurated with the sacrifice of life, has yet become, more than any other power in the world, the guardian of it. All its teaching has tended, both directly and indirectly, to this end. Wherever the Cross has been lifted, there human life has been invested with a new sacredness. We need only contrast the times before and since the Christian era, or compare Christendom with what we know of heathen lands, to realize the humane influences of the Gospel. Milder laws and wider charities have always marked the progress of Christianity among men.

But in this, as in other respects, the Gospel has worked from within outwards. All its humanities proceed from its assertion of the worth of the human soul. It has declared that, over and over again, with fullest and strongest emphasis. It never wearies in its reiteration of the value that attaches to each individual. It asserts that there is something divine in every man—something priceless, inestimable, of more value in the sight of God than all the material universe. It is, indeed, a religion for the race; it embraces in its scope the whole family of man; its redemption is for all mankind; but while its aim is thus universal, it is none the less careful of the individual. It is not concerned merely with the mass of men, the great body of mankind, and comparatively indifferent to this or that member of it. It has given to every separate human soul a worth and dignity as great as if it were the only one, as if no other soul had been created in the image of its Maker. The sacrifice of Christ was made for me as truly as if it had been made for me alone. Our Lord has taught us that with God there is nothing small or insignificant; that the very hairs of our head are all numbered. He declares of Himself that He knows His sheep, and calleth them by *name*. He has contrasted a single human soul with all created things, and given the preëminence to it: "What shall it profit a man, if he shall gain the whole world and lose his own soul? Or what shall a man give in exchange for his soul?"

But perhaps the strongest assertion of the worth of the individual soul is to be found in the connection of our text; for the scene was one which demanded that assertion. We read that "all the publicans and sinners" drew near to Jesus "for to hear Him; and the Pharisees and scribes murmured, saying: This man receiveth sinners, and eateth with them." Our Lord replied to that in the three parables of the lost sheep, the lost coin, and the lost son. It will open up our theme if we pause a moment here to examine this objection, and the master's answer to it.

Why did the Pharisees murmur against Christ? Evidently, not because He preached to sinners. They had no objection to that. It could scarcely have been in accordance with the mission of a religious teacher to neglect the class which stood confessedly in greatest need of his ministrations. The scribes themselves were accustomed to preach, to warn, to exhort, to denounce; and if Christ had done that, and only that, they would have applauded, and not have censured Him. If, standing apart, as they did, in the isolation of self-righteousness, He had been content to proclaim against the reprobate all the terrors of the law, both scribe and Pharisee would have been eager to commend Him. In all ages human nature is much the same; and then, as now, the sermons that pleased moral and religious people best were those that were filled with denunciations of other men's sins. But our Lord did not confine himself to that. In point of fact, His discourses had very little of denunciation in them, except when they were addressed to the professedly moral and religious themselves. To sinners His words had more of invitation than of warning, more of entreaty than of invective. Yet even against that, had He stopped there, perhaps the scribes would not have ventured to murmur very loudly. But He did not stop there. The scandal of His ministry, that which outraged scribe and

Pharisee, was this: "This man receiveth sinners, and eateth with them." He refused to hold Himself proudly aloof from the outcasts of society. He showed toward the vile and degraded a human compassion and sympathy. He treated them as His fellow-creatures. He made His appeal to their hearts. He strove in every way to lead them to a new and divine life. He entered into the house of the despised Zaccheus, and supped with him. He suffered "the woman who was a sinner" to follow Him, even to the rich man's table; He called a publican from the hated "receipt of customs," and made him His disciple. Nothing could have provoked greater indignation in the Pharisee, or outraged more his conventional propriety. But to his murmurings the substance of our Lord's answer, as given in these parables, was this: No conventional propriety is to be weighed against the salvation of a single human soul. That is priceless in the sight of God. Nothing can compensate for it or replace it. As the shepherd rejoices over his lost sheep, and the woman over her recovered treasure, so there is joy with God over a prodigal's return. The vindication of His own conduct was in His intense personal concern. Scribe and Pharisee might stand carelessly apart, might hedge themselves round with formal decencies, might pride themselves upon being separative and exclusive, but He who came "to seek and to save that which was lost" could leave no way or means untried "to seek and to save" it. To their indifference the recovery of a lost soul might seem a trifle, a very little thing, but it was something that made the heavens glad:

"I say unto you, there is joy in the presence of the angels of God over one sinner that repenteth."

This is the point, brethren, to which I wish now to call your attention. We can never sufficiently realize the fact that our salvation—yours and mine—is not exclusively our own personal concern; it is not something which is of interest only to you and me. Our eternal happiness or unhappiness is never simply our own affair, an individual matter, an issue which does not reach beyond ourselves. Such a thought would be a depressing one, and could have nothing helpful in it. It would throw us back upon ourselves in utter loneliness, drearier than any desert solitude. The sense of individual insignificance, the consciousness of earth's and heaven's indifference, would fill our hearts with despair, and tempt us in turn to be careless of our fate. We all know the value of sympathy, and the mysterious aid which comes from that. He who has friends interested in his eternal welfare is partly saved already. Their aid and counsel and support, their appreciation and their sympathy, their joy in his repentance and their sorrow for his sin, are helps which no words can overstate. Many a wanderer has been called back by a mother's unwearying love, and many a sinner has learned the value of his own soul from one whose prayers and tears were with him in the midst of all his degradation.

But there are some, alas! who have no friends; all whose associates are evil; whose very sin has shut them off from the companionship of the good, and who seem to know nothing of purity and holiness except that they are banished from its presence. And, to such a one, the temptation is to say, bitterly: "No man cares for my soul;" to value it at the estimate which the world has put upon it; to think that its salvation or perdition is of no consequence to any but himself. What wonder, then, if the man becomes reckless of his fate, and sees in the indifference of earth only a reflection of the indifference of heaven? He is only one among myriads of the human race. What matter, then, whether he be lost or saved? Must not the difference with God be inappreciable? But that dark doubt has its contradiction in every assertion of the Gospel! Heaven is not indifferent, though earth may be. However friendless, lonely, and forlorn the sinner's life here may seem, yet he is *not* alone. He has friends and visitants whom he cannot see, whose sympathy is always with him, who follow him with anxious eyes through all his weary ways. Let him once realize that, and all despairing bitterness is gone. There comes, instead, a consolation unknown before. Alone, and yet not alone! How can I be indifferent to my own fate, when the very heavens are not indifferent to it? How can I think lightly of my own soul, when my repentance can send a thrill of joy up even to the throne of God?

If we were always mindful of the sympathy that comes to us from the unseen world, how much more hopeful should we be, how much more self-reverent! Yet this is the reiterated assertion of the Scriptures. They tell us that we are the object of human, angelic, and divine solicitude. What stronger assurance of the infinite worth of the human soul can there be than this? It is a thought to startle one, to overwhelm a man with astonishment, when he begins to realize that the whole universe of God is concerned in his own fate. And is it not?

1. The Bible is the witness to us, first, of unseen human sympathy, the sympathy of those who have "gone before." It nowhere leads us to suppose that there is any absolute separation between the living and the dead, that those whom we have loved and lost are unmindful of us now that they have been translated to the skies. It speaks, instead, of "the family of earth and heaven," and teaches us to believe in the reality of a communion which we cannot see. And what unspeakable comfort is there in that! What consolation to the man who has lost, perhaps, his only earthly friend, the only one who ever seemed to care for his soul, the only one who ever strove to win him to the paths of righteousness and peace! What consolation, I say, to believe that that love is solicitous and watchful still; waiting and expectant of the hour when it shall herald His return with anthems of celestial joy! Be sure the affection so faithful and true on earth has not changed in its passage to the other world. It has only grown and deepened there. No life can be utterly alone and desolate, utterly bereft of human sympathy, which can claim kindred with one pure spirit in the Father's house.

But our assurance of human sympathy is not limited to those whom we have known and lost. The sainted dead of whatever age or clime are with us—that "multitude which no man can number." The writer of the Epistle to the Hebrews, after his grand enumeration of great names, prophets and martyrs and confessors of the faith, men of whom " the world was not worthy," proceeds to make the fact of their sympathy and presence a ground of stirring, urgent appeal: " Wherefore," he says, " seeing we are compassed about with so great a cloud of witnesses, let us run with patience the race that is set before us." Thus each man, the highest and the least, is attended by an unseen company. They are watching him while he runs the race which they ran, and fights the battle which they fought. When hardest pressed and most out of heart, their sympathies are with him. He is never friendless or alone. His weal or woe never passes into his own exclusive individual concern. The solicitude of innumerable witnesses follows him through all his struggle and warfare here below. There is no indifference to his fate in the host of the redeemed, the great company of heaven. His sin, we may believe, can stir in them the sense of unutterable loss, as his repentance can bring to them an added joy, even in the height of their divine beatitude.

2. Nor does the far-reaching influence of a sinner's repentance stop here. It passes beyond the human race, and extends even to the angels of God. After all, perhaps, it may not seem to us a thing incredible, that those who share our nature, the good and holy of all ages past, who in their time were tempted as we are, and know by sad experience all the trials that beset our way, should follow us with their solicitude, even in the regions of their rest. It requires no

great effort of our faith to believe that the sainted dead, the "cloud of witnesses" that doth encompass us, should look with pity upon an erring brother's sin, and welcome his return with joy. But we are assured of even more than this. Our Lord has declared to us the fact of angelic sympathy. Those bright, celestial spirits, those pure intelligences of God, those flaming ministers of His will—they, too, are not indifferent to the issue that is set before us; they, too, sorrow over a sinner's fall, and are made glad by his repentance. Thus our weal or woe reaches on to an order of beings of a nature other than our own. In the wide universe of God, in the range of all created things, there is neither man nor angel unconcerned in our salvation.

The Bible is filled with assertions of angelic sympathy. We read that in the beginning, when the foundations of the earth were laid, "the morning stars sang together and all the sons of God shouted for joy." And again in that new creation, when the Prince of peace was born, and the great work of redemption had begun, we hear of a heavenly choir praising God and saying: "Glory to God in the highest, and on earth peace, good will toward men." And still, again, in that revelation of the things which shall be, we are told that in the final harvest "the reapers are the angels" of God. Let us not lose the comfort of this thought in its vastness. It may not console us very much; it may not be a source of much personal strength or encouragement to know that these celestial beings wait with wonderment and adoration and praise upon all the manifestations of divine omnipotence and grace; that they celebrated with exultant songs the creation and redemption of the world. There may be nothing helpful to us individually in that. What we need is to bring the assurance of their sympathy home to ourselves, home to you and me. And this too we may do. We may believe that, though unseen, they minister to us as truly as they did to the patriarch Jacob while he slept, and to our Lord when tempted in the desert; that they wait now to receive the departing soul, even as they carried the beggar, when he died, to Abraham's bosom; that they are set to watch and guard us, the lowliest and the least. For has not the Master said even of the humblest, the very little ones, that "their angels do always behold the face of my Father"? And is there no strength or encouragement in the thought that in all the seeming loneliness of our earthly way we have the sympathy of all the heavenly angels, they that "excel in strength," who "fulfil His commandment and hearken unto the voice of His word"? Does it not bring to us a deeper conviction of the worth of the human soul to know that our repentance can add even to their untroubled joy? We are not told that any mere greatness of human achievement can do that. At all our boasted science, at all the fruit of our best intellect, at all the long triumphs of the race, we may believe that these high intelligences of Heaven can well afford to smile. But that at which they cannot afford to smile is a single contrite, humble, broken heart. "I say unto you, there is joy in the presence of the angels of God over one sinner that repenteth."

3. And, above and beyond this, there is joy with God Himself. This is the final fact, which, if we only seriously consider it, cannot fail to astound and overwhelm us. The issue of our trial here below passes beyond all creatures, and reaches up even to the Creator. That is the representation of our Gospel. The God whom we worship does not sit indifferently apart, unaffected by the weal or woe of the souls whom He has made. He feels a deep and intense concern in the salvation of every single one—concern intense and deep, just in proportion to the intensity and depth of His nature. He is not the God of philosophy, cold and impassive, a mere bundle of laws and forces, with no feeling and no heart; a kind of no-person, a being whom we can neither conceive of nor reverence, but "the Father of our spirits," who is pained by our sin, and who delights in our obedience. Even from the earliest revelation of Him, we can gather that. The Old Testament is filled with expressions of the yearning solicitude of God. He loves the tears of repentance. "He pitieth them that fear Him." "All day long He stretcheth forth His arms to a disobedient and gainsaying people." He calls after them "as a woman forsaken and grieved in spirit." He is affected with "joy" over their return, "even to singing." In these expressions the Scriptures speak of God, indeed, after the manner of men; but they, nevertheless, contain a truth concerning Him. They witness to the fact that He cares, that He is anxious, that He is concerned for our souls. How, indeed, should we ever doubt that, when we know that He has made a measureless sac-

rifice in our behalf? How should we ever think our fate a matter of indifference to Him, when " He gave up His only-begotten Son " to die for you and me? In these three parables our Lord has reiterated the assurance of the Father's solicitude. He has emphasized that with a marvellous wealth of illustration. He has represented God as a shepherd seeking his lost sheep ; as a woman searching diligently for a lost treasure ; as a father going forth with compassion and tears and gladness to meet his returning son. And therefore, O sinner, whosoever thou art, however contemptuous of thyself, however much despised by others, in all the wide world however desolate and alone, be sure of this : that thy contrition, although no earthly eye may see it, is yet a spectacle to angels and to men ; that thy repentance, although no human voice may welcome it, can yet stir the heart of God Himself with an infinite joy!

From the consideration of our subject, brethren, we may come away with two great lessons. And, first, let us learn from it to have a deeper concern in the spiritual welfare of others; let us learn from it the unspeakable worth of a human soul. Perhaps we have never fully realized that; perhaps we, too, might be convicted of Pharisaic indifference ; perhaps we, too, have been tempted to think that it mattered little, among so many, whether one more or less were lost. Let us remember, then, that what we think lightly of is, in the sight of God, of great price. All indifference is a fearful, dreadful, inhuman thing. Shall the heavens break forth into singing over the contrition of some forlorn man or woman, and shall we stand coldly by with unresponsive hearts, and let our lips be dumb? Nay! Shall we sneer and doubt and taunt and mock until the "bruised reed" is broken and the "smoking flax" is quenched? It is often in our power to exert an influence for good—to snatch, it may be, a brand from the burning. No sacrifice that we can make is too costly for that. It may be given us to save a brother.

"There is joy in the presence of the angels of God over one sinner that repenteth." But in this world of ours we need most the encouragement of human sympathy; and there are times when a human hand in ours is more to us than any angel could be. Let nothing tempt us, then, to withhold our aid and sympathy from any whom aid and sympathy may reach; and if we need the inspiration of reward we may remember that "he that converteth a sinner from the error of his way shall save a soul from death, and shall hide a multitude of sins;" and "they that turn many to righteousness shall shine as the stars for ever and ever."

And again, brethren, let us strive to realize for ourselves the wondrous depth of God's love, and so reach at last a real and true contrition. "The goodness of God," says the Apostle, "leadeth thee to repentance." I do not know that aught else can do it. Fears and penalties have ever failed to accomplish that. One often suffers even here the retribution of his sin; the anguish of his soul may be sharp and bitter; he may be very sorry, very remorseful, full of pity for himself; but *that* is not repentance. And although our sin may not as yet have found us out, still we cannot escape "a certain fearful looking for of judgment;" we cannot always shut out the terrors of the last day; and sometimes the dread as of coming night dismays and clouds the spirit; yet neither is *that* repentance. The essence of all true repentance is in the conviction that we have sinned against God; that we have wronged Him; that we have grieved and outraged His affection. And when that thought comes it absorbs all others. It was so with David when he said: "Against thee, thee only, have I sinned and done this evil in thy sight;" and with the prodigal in that confession: "Father, I have sinned against heaven and before thee!" And then the one petition of the soul is for renewed nearness to God: "Restore unto me the joy of thy salvation, and uphold me with thy free spirit;" "Deliver me, and my tongue shall sing aloud of thy righteousness; O Lord, open thou my lips, and my mouth shall show forth thy praise." One can really and truly repent in this high sense only when he begins to realize how deeply he is the object of divine solicitude, how loving and merciful and good God is. And then, I had almost said, he cannot but repent. For love shall quicken love, and we needs must love the highest when we see it. The truest and the deepest experience is that of him who knelt upon the Idumean plains, and, after long doubt and darkness and misgiving, said: "I have heard of thee by the hearing of the ear, but now mine eye seeth thee; wherefore I repent in sackcloth and ashes."

www.ingramcontent.com/pod-product-compliance
Lightning Source LLC
Chambersburg PA
CBHW030406230426
43664CB00007BB/773